A PAGEANT OF PATTERN FOR NEEDLEPOINT CANVAS

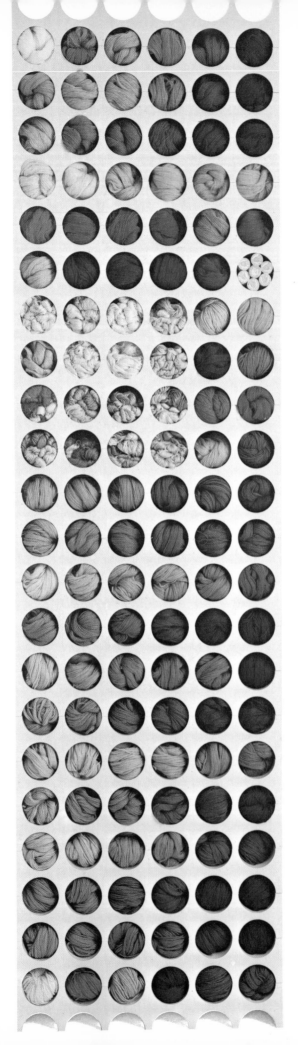

A PAGEANT OF PATTERN FOR NEEDLEPOINT CANVAS

Centuries of Design, Textures, Stitches
A New Exploration

by

SHERLEE LANTZ

with diagrams by

MAGGIE LANE

GROSSET & DUNLAP
Publishers · New York

FRONTISPIECE *Wine racks transformed into a floor-to-ceiling yarn cabinet. Residence S. Lantz*

To the Artisan, past-master, present mentor
S. L.

For my Mother and Father
M. L.

ACKNOWLEDGMENTS

For permission to examine their libraries, photographic files, fragile collections of textiles and embroideries, and for most graciously finding room for me to study in their often limited space, I very much want to thank:

JEAN MAILEY, Associate Curator, Textile Study Room, Metropolitan Museum of Art, New York.

ELSIE MCGARVEY, Curator, DORIS ASHLEY and CHRISTINE JACKSON, Philadelphia Museum of Art, Pennsylvania. I am especially obligated to Mrs. Ashley and her nephew who responded so quickly to my request for photographs.

AUDREY KOENIG, Registrar, Newark Museum of Art, New Jersey.

ALICE BEER, Textile Consultant, and ELIANE ZUESSE, Librarian, Cooper-Hewitt Museum, New York.

In addition, I am indebted to:

SYLVIA HILTON, Librarian, and HELEN RUSKELL, Assistant Librarian, New York Society Library, New York. They have accorded me so much help, many favors, a few mild and deserved scoldings for overdue books; much of this book evolved from my many happy hours of research in that serene and patrician building—one of New York's rare treasures.

DEBORAH DENNIS, Weyhe Book Store, New York, for unfailing good humor when she so frequently stumbled over the clutter of books (hers), legs and arms (mine), obstructing her aisles while I searched out an elusive, but often discovered, volume.

KATE and JOEL KOPP, ED CLINE, America, Hurrah!, New York. Particularly Kate, a blue-jeaned dervish whirling about in a kaleidoscope of American patchwork, for inexhaustibly unstacking, unfolding, outspreading, refolding her extensive collection of quilts. Much of my education in patchwork design was acquired on these premises.

JANE JORDAN, Hallmark Gallery, New York, for her kindness and cooperation in making available material from past exhibits applicable to this book.

LEO LERMAN and GRAY FOY, who generously allowed me to borrow and photograph their fine samplers.

TILLIE DAVIS, whose skilled carpentry and warm friendship lent such welcomed and needed support, both literal and otherwise.

CANDIDA DONADIO for her enthusiasm and steadying counsel.

JULES FEIFFER for reading the manuscript. His affectionate and wise comments were invaluable.

GIDEON LEWIN of the Richard Avedon Studio, whose photographic work enhances this book and whose exceptional kindness enhanced the time we worked together. I must also thank many others of the Avedon staff for their time-consuming and most generous labors on my behalf.

HELEN LINCOLN, whose systematic care and meticulous work made the burden of preparing captions, index, photographic permissions, etc., so much lighter.

DOROTHY PARKER of Atheneum for her much needed and appreciated assistance.

DAVID ROGERS, Production Editor Extraordinary, whose painstaking devotion and organizational expertise (unstintingly given and gratefully received) dissolved the many discouraging hurdles and complicated difficulties inherent in the preparation of a work of this nature.

RICHARD AVEDON. There must be words to express the extent of my indebtedness and gratitude but the ones I know are insufficient.

ROBBY and TONY, who are my family, my best friends, and who, with forebearance and generosity, permitted me to impose on both relationships.

I gratefully acknowledge the permission to reproduce the following illustrations:

Altar frontal of Henry IV of Castile and two photographs of the altar frontal, Mass vestments of the Order of the Golden Fleece from *A Pictorial History of Embroidery* by Marie Schuette and Sigrid Müller-Christensen. Reproduced by permission of Verlag Ernst Wasmuth.

Plaster panel from Nishapur from *The World of Islam* by Ernst J. Grube, Landmarks of the World's Art Series. Reproduced by permission of the Metropolitan Museum of Art, New York.

Donatello's tomb of the Bishop John Pecci from *The Cathedral of Siena* by Aldo Lusini. Reproduced by permission of the author.

Photograph of a living-room floor from *Styles Regionaux: Architecture, Mobilier, Decoration*, Collection Plaisir de France Series. Reproduced by permission of Baschet & Cie, Editeur.

Swiss needlework, 1533, and 17th-century Anatolian carpet from *Europa und der Orientteppich* by Kurt Erdmann. Copyright © 1962 by Florian Kupferberg Verlag, Mainz. Reproduced by permission of Florian Kupferberg Verlag, Mainz.

English samplers, 16th or 17th century; Scottish sampler, 18th century; English pulled work, 16th century; Japanese sampler, early 20th century. Reproduced by courtesy of the Cooper-Hewitt Museum of Decorative Arts and Design, Smithsonian Institution.

ACKNOWLEDGMENTS

Mid-17th-century sampler from *Samplers: Yesterday and Today* by Averil Colby. Copyright © 1964 by Averil Colby. Reproduced by permission of B. T. Batsford Ltd.

Silk chasuble; Windmill quilt, c. 1890; Pineapple quilt, 1920, from *Patchwork* by Averil Colby. Copyright © 1958 by Averil Colby. Reproduced by permission of B. T. Batsford Ltd.

Shrine of Zayn al-din courtyard, A.D. 1007, and minaret, c. 12th century, from *Islamic Architecture and Its Decoration: A.D. 800–1500* by Derek Hill and Oleg Grabar. Copyright © 1964 by Derek Hill and Oleg Grabar. Reproduced by permission of The University of Chicago Press.

Mid-17th-century English sampler and mid-19th-century English sampler from *Samplers* by Donald King. © Crown Copyright 1960. Reproduced by permission of the Victoria and Albert Museum.

Steeple Chase quilt and Tide Mill quilt from *Old Patchwork Quilts and the Women Who Made Them* by Ruth E. Finley. Copyright 1929 by Ruth E. Finley; renewal copyright 1957 Manufacturers Trust Co., Bruce R. Tuttle and William E. Dague, Executors. Reproduced by permission of the publishers, Charles T. Branford Company, Newton Centre, Massachusetts.

Detail from 1841 English sampler. Reproduced by permission of the Philadelphia Museum of Art: The Whitman Sampler Collection: given by Pet Incorporated, '69-288-394.

"Cardinal Bandinello Sauli, his secretary and two geographers," Sebastiano del Piombo. Reproduced by permission of the National Gallery of Art, Washington, D.C., Samuel H. Kress Collection.

"St. Martin brings to life a dead man" and "St. Martin offering the wine cup to the priest" from *The St. Martin Embroideries: A fifteenth-century series illustrating the life and legend of St. Martin of Tours* by Margaret B. Freeman. Copyright © 1968 by the Metropolitan Museum of Art. Reproduced by permission of The Robert Lehman Collection, New York.

Detail from late-12th- early-13th-century Persian cup from *Islamic Pottery, 800–1400 AD*, the catalogue of an exhibition arranged by the Islamic Art Circle and held at the Victoria and Albert Museum 1 October to 30 November 1969. Reproduced by permission of Edmund de Unger, president of the Islamic Art Circle, publisher.

Seljuk carpet from the mosque of Ala al-din, Konya, 13th century, from *Turkish Art and Architecture* by Oktay Aslanapa. Copyright © 1971 in London, England, by Oktay Aslanapa. Reproduced by permission of Faber and Faber Ltd. and the Museum of Turkish Art in Istanbul.

Death chamber from an Italian "Arte del Bene Morire," Florence, c. 1495, from *Devils, Demons, Death and Damnation* by Ernst and Johanna Lehner, Dover Pictorial Archive Series. Copyright © 1971 by Dover Publications, Inc. Reproduced by permission of Dover Publications, Inc.

Mosaic pavement, Collegiate Church crypt, Saint-Quentin, and niche, 2nd-century A.D., Rome, from *The Carolingian Renaissance* by J. Hubert, J. Porcher and W. F. Volbach. Reproduced by permission of Editions Gallimard.

ACKNOWLEDGMENTS

Nineveh, Assurbanipal dispatching a lion, 7th century B.C. (British Museum), from *The Arts of Assyria* by André Parrot. Reproduced by permission of Editions Gallimard.

Indiana Puzzle quilt, 1920, from *The Romance of the Patchwork Quilt in America* by Carrie A. Hall and Rose G. Kretsinger. Copyright 1935 by The Caxton Printers, Ltd., Caldwell, Idaho. Reproduced by permission of The Caxton Printers, Ltd.

Detail of mosaic tilework in the Sirçali Madrassa, Konya, 1243, from *Islamic Art* by David Talbot Rice. Copyright © Thames and Hudson 1965. Reproduced by permission of Mrs. Talbot Rice.

Clay palace pillars from the ruins of Uruk, Babylonia, c. 4000 B.C.; Indonesian braided bag; knitted bag, Rio Pilcomayo, South America; antique gold buckle, from *Das elementare Ornament und seine Gesetzlichkeit* by Wolfgang von Wersin and Walter Müller-Grah. Copyright 1940 by Otto Maier Verlag, Ravensburg. Reproduced by permission of Otto Maier Verlag.

Detail from the main portal, Chartres Cathedral. Reproduced by permission of Alinari/Mansell.

18th-century drawing room (photo by R. Guillemot—TOP) and Bakhtiari-type Persian carpet in a Louis XIII period bedroom (photo by Millet-Connaissance des Arts) from *La Decoration*, edited by Pierre Levallois. Copyright © by Librairie Hachette 1963. Reproduced by permission of Agence TOP.

Boucicaut Workshop, "Female votaries dance before a goddess," from *French Painting in the Time of Jean de Berry: The Boucicaut Master* by Millard Meiss. Published by Phaidon Press Limited, London, and distributed by Praeger Publishers, New York. Reproduced by permission of Phaidon Press Limited.

Detail from tomb at Sangbast from *Design and Color in Islamic Architecture* by Sonia P. Seherr-Thoss and Hans C. Seherr-Thoss. Smithsonian Publication 4741, 1968. A portion of Plate 3 was reproduced by permission of Smithsonian Institution Press.

All other photography by the Richard Avedon Studio, New York.

CONTENTS

PART I

PART II

PART III

CONTENTS

COLOR PLATES

Wine racks transformed into a floor-to-ceiling yarn cabinet.

BALADE.

CONSIDERANT le vouloir des humains
Au temps préſent, du tout atalenté,
A bien comprendre & ſçauoir des artz maintz
Par vn bon zéle & curioſité.
Ce preuoyant ie me ſuis incité,
A compoſer ce liure treſ-vtile,
Pour profiter, comme il eſt recité,
A toutes gens, qui œuurent de l'eſguille·
   Au temps iadis du regne des Romains,
Les gens eſtoyent de grande auctorité,
Pour les façons qu'ils faiſoyent de leurs mains,
Et les labeurs de bonne antiquité:
Telle ſcience & grand' ſubtilité
Plaiſt à chaſcun, tant des champs que de ville,
Pour profiter, comme il eſt recité,
A toutes gens, qui œuurent de l'eſguille.
   Les tapiſſiers ne ſont pas inhumains,
Contrefaiſant ceſte noualité,
Et les Brodeurs quaſi ne plus ne moins,
Dames auſſi en bonne equalité:
Pour euiter du tout oyſiueté,
Ce liure icy eſt à elles fertile,
Pour profiter, comme il eſt recité,
A toutes gens, qui œuurent de l'eſguille.
   Prince, ie dy, ſelon la verité,
Qu'il eſt parfaict en façon très-ſubtile,
Pour profiter, comme il eſt recité,
A toutes gens, qui œuurent de l'eſguille.

Mieux que iamais.

BALLAD

In consideration of the eagerness of the people,
So strongly inclined at present,
To understand and learn the diverse arts of the hand
With true interest and careful attention.
Foreseeing this, I bestirred myself
To put together this practical book
"For the benefit" as we have heard recited,
"Of all" who work with the needle.

When Romans ruled in days of yore
People toiled with utmost skill
To fashion the works of the hand
And the products of distant antiquity:
Such knowledge and distinction,
Pleasing to all, in country and town, are
"For the benefit" as we have heard recited,
"Of all" who work with the needle.

Tapestry weavers are not supernatural beings
Magically forging these creations
Nor the embroiderers, are they more or less.
Noblewomen too, equally
Wishing to be useful,
To these this book is fruitful,
"For the benefit" as we have heard recited,
"Of all" who work with the needle.

Prince, I declare in good faith
That my task was accomplished with minute care
"For the benefit" as we have heard recited,
"Of all" who work with the needle.

Better than ever.

TRANSLATED BY SHERLEE LANTZ

THIS BALLAD was printed in Paris in 1584 as an introduction to *Le Livre De Lingerie*, a compendium of intricate lace patterns compiled by Maistre Dominique de Sera, Italien, and augmented by Jean Cousin, Peintre à Paris, whose work is still exhibited in the Louvre and other French museums. The book carries the Imprimatur of the King of France with the customary interdictory warning against reprinting and selling, but it fails to mention that all but a few of the plates are facsimile duplications from the great Venetian Esemplario books published decades earlier.

I recall reading some years ago, in an old study of Venetian history, about a Venetian lace worker who made off with the secrets of his trade and sold them to France. The stolen patterns and techniques supposedly became the foundation of the French lace industry and made France a formidable and unwelcome competitor. The textile manufactories of the day may be likened to the automobile companies of our own time; their products were vital to the economy and of major concern to the countries controlling them. Outraged by this blow to its commercial dignity and monopoly, the legendary long arm of Venetian justice reached out to pluck the hapless rogue from his new and profitable home and return him to the Serenissima. The reproach was severe; the council sentenced him to be put to death.

Of course, Venice herself had taken nearly all her geometric designs from the supreme masters of this form of ornamentation, the Seljuk Turks. These remarkable tribes, who dominated Central and Western Asia for a few hundred years, are the true begetters of geometric decoration as we know it in the West. If we look at the architecture, miniature paintings, carpets and tiles produced during their reign in Turkey, Persia and Syria we cannot doubt this. This book owes much to their genius and you will find that I have made frequent reference to their work. Their origins have faded with time, but whoever they were—they deserve our respect, our applause and our acknowledgment.

PART I

1) *Working* History

THE REPERTORY OF abstract geometric pattern is endless. And it is limited. It is at once playful and solemn, archaic and modern, mysterious and straightforward, intricate and simple, restless and serene, whirling and static, an optical paradox. The effect of paradox is itself paradoxical for it either stops us short and immobilizes thought or provokes and activates it. Throughout history, man has responded to the peculiar challenge of its unsettling power, tension, and magnetism. An example of the delight he found in these contradictions may be seen in his lavish, inventive, and consistent use of the divisions and subdivisions of geometric forms and patterns and his joyous employment of their visual conundrums and amusing labyrinths and these are, with some personal views on their historic travels and significance, the main concern of this book.

Variations of geometric motifs and diaper* patterns (and stitches as

---

* Diaper is the medieval word for a repeating textile pattern, usually diamond- or lozenge-shaped. This scheme of weaving warp and woof, causing reflections of light to dance on its surface, gave it subtle visual mystery. Subsequently, the term was applied to

well, for they properly belong in this architectural family) were created, tooled, and treasured by many peoples from many lands and centuries; the majority are constructed on the pure, clean angles of the squared graph and they may be logically, appropriately, and accurately transferred to the threaded, interwoven squared graph we know as needlepoint canvas. I have been adventuring on this much traveled, historic, and beguiling ground, a sleuth searching out angles, so to speak, and I have recorded my finding in yarn on the canvas. If the book shows some traits of the thriller, as is my hope, it will quite correctly convey my approach to the exploration of this lively heritage and to the invitation I feel its puzzles hold out for present-day work. Ancestor worship has its partisans but I think it better to pay respect to the past by attempting to put it to fresh use. The most magnificent achievements can lose dignity and become merely ornamental when they do not contribute to our immediate spiritual, physical, or intellectual lives, thereby reacquiring their initial force. I do *not* think that artisan or hand work is, as some would have it, a mild opiate for our relaxation, nor is it a puritanical method for avoiding indolence, nor a harmless diversion made anachronistic by industrial progress. Surely, it is vital to our natures as it is to that of all living species, to realize personal, seeable, tangible, functional accomplishment. In the modern Western world, surrounded by machinery, mass production, and mechanical devices, we have really denied ourselves the satisfaction of saying "I made this." Our remedy for this lack of essential nourishment, or social ill, is substitute action: the frenetic pursuit of fiercely competitive or arduous sports; restive, constant travel; or the elitist exaltation of mental capacities and products. But I think many of us do feel our loss even if we are unaware of its cause or the extent of our deprivation.

My research yielded many pleasures and puzzles, odd trails of human endeavor that led from four-thousand B.C. Babylonian masons to nineteenth-century American quiltmakers, from thirteenth-century Islamic architects and carpet designers to sixteenth-century Venetian and French

---

heraldic ornamental sectioning, later still to all small-scale geometric repeat pattern that, irrespective of material, related to the diamond and square. Often interspersed by parallel lines, the fields left by these diagonal, horizontal, and vertical divisors may be further decorated by varied motifs. Diaper is Greek-based, usually thought to mean "white at intervals."

4

lace manuals, from Pompeian and medieval mosaic pavement artists to English Victorian samplers. These discoveries, kinships, and enigmas are to be seen in the sampler squares I adapted, designed, and worked for your use. I tried to include all the stitches and small-scale geometric patterns that, in my judgment, could enter into legitimate, handsome, and organic partnership with the needlepoint canvas. You will notice that they have been gathered from many disciplines other than needlepoint. If I thought them appropriate, I borrowed them. I arranged them all as sampler squares to illustrate how they look when worked and to form a biography of geometric diaper pattern in yarn. They are not intended to be formal designs but springboards for readers.

Maggie Lane has rendered these patterns and stitches into the fine graphic arrangements we call diagrams. These are, in themselves, an homage from a contemporary artist to the great masters of other ages; a salute to those anonymous and unknown artisans whose own labors enrich our past and, if we wish, our future. It is my hope that our reconstructions in yarn and diagram will faithfully convey the distinction and diversity of their work so that you will be prompted to recycle it for use. I have accompanied many of the sampler squares with historical notes that should enable you to learn about and enjoy their previous lives at the moment you are reincarnating them. My aim was to give you a *working* history, not one embalmed in descriptive eulogy for the benefit of passive spectators.

Although this is an unusually extensive study, I have intentionally avoided the words "dictionary" and "encyclopedia" because they imply objective, universal, and final knowledge. I cannot claim objectivity, nor do I admire it, and I know the book carries the stamp of personal selectivity. As for universality and finality, I would find it presumptuous to think that further search along parallel or tangential lines would prove unprofitable or unnecessary.

To assist me in bringing some order to the vast territory we will cover, and for the ease of the reader looking for specific information, I have divided our many subjects under different headings so that you may find what you need with rapidity. What may seem, in fact is, discursive as we travel through the centuries, cultures, and continents on a geometric journey is unavoidable. We have a multiplicity of purposes and a little hopscotch in time and space is an exercise that can do us no real harm.

Although we aim to restore for modern use the distinguished work of our forebears, I am not suggesting that you put your hand to pseudo-archaic or imitative design. The squares and diagrams offer a basic vocabulary to advanced workers who require texture and pattern to realize their concepts, and a clear guide to the beginner who can proceed step by step as his curiosity and ambition dictate. I have taken great pains to preserve the mathematical and tonal relationships of the patterns so that they may serve as reference for those more interested in history or for those who wish to use the historic designs for work unrelated to embroidery.

2) The Hand

Words that apply to the work of the hand like "artisan," "craft," "art" are unsettling because they are amorphous. Like patients who won't disrobe or lie still to oblige the doctor, they do not cooperate with our need to examine them. Human beings have a natural desire to illuminate, to give form to shadows. The inscrutable or undefined makes us uneasy and disorients our sense of placement; we may resort to false or arbitrary conclusions to give ourselves security. We are disconcerted when our subjects are not amenable to our efforts to define them, so we simply prepare niches for them and assign them their places; if their contours don't quite fit, we shove them in to make them behave themselves. We are then content even if we have warped them beyond reason. By tradition, we have used exactly this procedure to slot "craft" into that which is functional, made primarily for use, and "art" into that which is nonfunctional, made primarily for beauty. Aside from the moral implications of exalting our ephemeral notions of beauty over direct utility, can we rest on the soundness of this distinction or will it wobble under scrutiny?

How shall we classify a magnificent piece of sculpture, created specifically and exclusively for use (function) in religious worship? Have we to remove it from its temple, deprive it of its employment, pretend the creator was governed solely by aesthetics before we permit it to join the club of fine arts? How shall we classify a magnificent, luminous prayer rug, created specifically and exclusively for use in religious worship by the tribal nomad, whose travels required a portable area of sanctified ground? It may be a masterpiece of color and composition, but it is called craft. Is the difference between these two articles of faith entirely clear to you? It certainly seems to be to those who declare the first "art" and the second "artifact," but, as for me, I definitely see wobbling. Shall we say that art and craft are separate but equal? No? Separate and unequal? Identical twins? Distant cousins? Sibling rivals? Are the great "artists" of geometric mosaic distinctly and solely "craftsmen"? Is the celebrated and precise geometric "craft" of a Vasarely or a Mondrian distinctly "fine art"? When the patchwork quilt quits the bed for the wall, do we reclassify it and call it graphic art because it has lost its job? Is a beautiful scroll art only when it is unintelligible and therefore nonfunctional? Only then? I know arguments have been made before and will be made again for the superiority of work that is both utilitarian and beautiful over that which is merely the last, and vice versa. This particular arena has been trampled by too many antagonists to make further contention worth your while or mine. The ground will remain hazy anyway, and individual bias or, if you prefer, "viewpoint," will shape your decision if you cannot live with ambiguity. I will therefore obey custom and keep "craft" and "artisan" in their usual places and, high above, the "fine arts" in theirs . . . except when an occasional fit of logic makes me do otherwise.

I think I am on less hazardous ground when I say that all artisan work finds its most dignified expression when it is engendered by human need. Add skill and we may be sure of works of honest utility and even "aesthetic" merit. We can really rejoice when tenacity, obsession, and the rage to explore join as propellants. The results may be among the best man can achieve. That they may also appeal to the current standard of beauty is incidental. This sort of ferocious intensity is contagious. If it were malignant, we would call it a plague. When it is not, we often call it art.

The Middle Ages of Europe blazed with this dynamic fire. Western man could no longer contain his fierce craving to transform his world with his genius. We may see the fury of his energy, like a captive whirlwind, in the names Chartres, Giotto, Siena, Dante, Limbourg, Westminster, Chaucer, Duccio, Cluny, Villon; we can sense the magnitude of his ambition in his cathedrals, stained glass, woodcuts, illuminated manuscripts, floors, walls, bricks, altar cloths, and tapestries. Medieval man called God the Great Geometer, possibly to make the world of His manufacture, tormented as it was by pestilence, harsh privation, and inexplicable tragedy, seem more planned, logical, and consequently more endurable. I think much of the work of this era reflects this need to see reason rather than chance as the chief mover and arranger of lives. In this sense, medieval geometric design has certain aspects of the talisman. Its angles and divisions seem to speak of man's hope of containing and understanding a complex and capricious world.

The Catholic Church heeded this need to remake earth into heaven; the patronage of the nobility and the great merchants, smitten by religious or egotistical fervor, made an ordered and perfected world seem possible. In France, England, Germany, Spain, Italy, Flanders, armies of architects, masons, painters, sculptors, weavers, glass and mosaic workers, enamelers, goldsmiths, and embroiderers were recruited to glorify the houses of God; the great cathedrals rose to confident heights from this collaboration of faith, worldly ambition, and creative need.

Celebrated artists were hired to design the embroidery schemes of altar cloths, vestments, and hangings. These were worked by nuns in convents, often patrician ladies discarded by their families for being female and thus commercial liabilities and, more surprisingly, by men in monasteries whose names and occupation as embroiderers are listed in the records of their orders. These remarkable technicians mastered the diverse stitches and patterns with such accomplished dexterity and exquisite refinement of form and texture that their works stand unchallenged in the Western world.

The medieval artisan fell under the spell of Unplumbed Possibilities and applied himself to his tasks with the exuberant inquisitiveness and intense preoccupation of a child with an unfamiliar object. His works are fresh and frisky today because they still shimmer with inquiry, and

Detail from the Altenberg altar cloth, 14th-century, in German geometric whitework. The workers stitched their names in the border: "Sophia, Hadewiges and Lucardis made me." The linen ground and the yarn are white. It was probably photographed against the light to show detail. Metropolitan Museum of Art, New York.

we will turn to him constantly throughout the pages of this book because he is the Western sire of most of our patterns and stitches. Inspired by those magicians of geometric ornament, his Islamic neighbors, he too juggled with the square and its offspring, and these feats of decorative prestidigitation are still dazzling to see in his pavements, walls, bricks, and the other crafts I have mentioned. Art and craft alike give us a great privilege when they permit us to share in the uncertainty, danger, and challenge of the search. Stalking the answers is far better for the creator than predetermination or omniscience; too much beforehand assuredness, like too much behindhand wisdom, can be boring. People who feel as I do may find the perfection of Greek vase painting to be learned lectures in red and black; they may respond strongly to Monet, Proust, Buster Keaton and be more indifferent to Van Dyck, Ibsen, Orson Welles. I know I will always believe that the art that is most satisfying is the art that asks us to roll up our sleeves to join both the hard labor and the joy of discovery. We are asked to participate as well as applaud, our involvement is required as well as our appreciation. Needlework, when it lacks this spirited, questing approach, becomes inert embellishment.

We don't know what sparks it, but it is obvious that some generations of man seem to be ignited by this exploratory demon while others suppress it. Handcraft invariably harks back to these most functionally urgent and fertile periods for guidance and inspiration. Techniques of structure and design are relayed down to successive generations. Unfortunately, through no particular fault of the transmitter or receiver, they tend to become more and more dilute and inexact. This conservative predilection to looking backward as embroidery techniques passed to younger nun from older, to daughter from mother, to apprentice from instructor explains its failure to thrive or evolve more interestingly. Imitation without intelligent modification or invention is a static and enervating process. It is an oddity, but handwork does resist absolute imitation. Copied motif for motif, tone for tone, knot for knot, a fine old Oriental carpet will show life and character in the original that it lacks in the copy. The imperceptible changes that bring this about can be ascribed to this hand-me-down, reverse progression. In the twentieth century we are at a far remove from needlework's best and most inventive moment—

perhaps far enough to look at it with the spontaneous delight necessary for a bright and healthy rebirth rather than a plodding reversion or revival.

Technological advances hurried the decline of artisan work by appropriating the tasks for which the hand was so expertly trained and suited. As the machine "learned" more, the hand "forgot" more. Conversely, this very triumph of the industrial machine has now produced a craft resurgence so fervent its intensity might be thought eccentric if it were not understandable. The sovereignty of the machine is forcing the hand to fight to stay alive or, at least, vital. If we do not become indignant and check this imposition of idleness or expendability on our capable bodies we may one day witness a Lear-like tragic war between the once-proud human brain and its powerful child, the computer.

Although there may be no strictly utilitarian demand today for hand-made objects, it seems that the ominous specter of our own obsolescence has created a new functional need. This imperative assertion of the hand's right to work has brought a rush of activity that can be nourishing and valuable if we will take time to learn skill and to respect our materials. If we do not, if we are lazy and incurious, overly susceptible to trendiness, too careless to observe or care about the fundamentals of proportions, fitness, restraint, and taste, then this beehive of frenzied activity is no more than a forlorn hope. If we don't call up our best efforts, we may as well say our good-byes, give the hand a decent burial, and let the machine take over. It will do the job better.

In addition, I am very nearly convinced that our national "religion," Galloping Consumption, is now grinding down to a balk. The American consumer seems less willing to develop, on order, an appetite for things he never hungered for. Madison Avenue may think of assessment reappraisal, skepticism, and divestment as subversive activities, but they seem to be burgeoning steadily and healthily. As they say, one can't depend on anything these days, not even acquisitiveness. This wish to be more than obliging receptacles for goods encourages our participation in the manufacturing process and gives us more intimate knowledge of the objects we use, the satisfaction of contributing to their creation, and the comforting certainty that we retain some conrol over quality and workmanship.

12

This recent attention to handwork has attracted many men and women to needle and yarn. Can it be denied that most of our work is mechanical or torpid at best? At worst, it is unruly and unskilled, often in the name of "creativity." Those people who have had the advantage of working with fine designs, such as Maggie Lane's, will have no doubt that dignity, good taste, and schematic soundness can be made to serve needlepoint work. Her loyalty to the integrity of her materials and her meticulous artistry have had, directly and indirectly, a salutory and wide influence on a field that was ailing from meretricious composition, intemperate coloring, and devoted commercialism. There are fine examples of traditional eighteenth-century Aubusson-type designs still available in painted canvas form in one or two distinguished shops, but this book is meant to be an aid to those who wish to create their own patterns, textures, and compositions.

The ornamental explosion of the Middle Ages took many forms but our attention will be given exclusively to the geometric work of this period, its antecedents and its offspring. I have not attempted a complete textual survey because this has been adequately covered before; I was reluctant to omit for want of space practical guidance that was heretofore unavailable, or difficult of access, in order to replace it with information that may easily be found elsewhere. I consider both stitched squares and diagrams to be language in that they convey, in concrete and technical vocabulary, the results of study.

The geography of my research was limited, in the main, to my areas of interest and, I believe, competence, and to those places and times that proved pertinent and fruitful. We will examine, in the West, the works of England, Germany, France, Flanders, Spain, Austria, Italy, and the United States through these reconstructions; also those of their parents in the Near and Middle East and of their grandparents in antiquity. I have included some photographs to show you the striking, continual, and visible link connecting the artisan work of these countries (*see* Chapter 5). I think the survival of identical motif in these varied cultures is intriguing and provocative. They avoided decadence by modifying designs to fit their materials, times, and needs. Whether this mysterious and puzzling durability of pattern from antiquity to nineteenth-century America is irrefutable proof of a true chain of human recollection

The relationship between this deeply cut plaster work and Pulled
Yarn and Drawn Thread work is obvious. The panel is from
Nishapur, Khurassan, Iran, 10th century. Metropolitan Museum of
Art, New York.

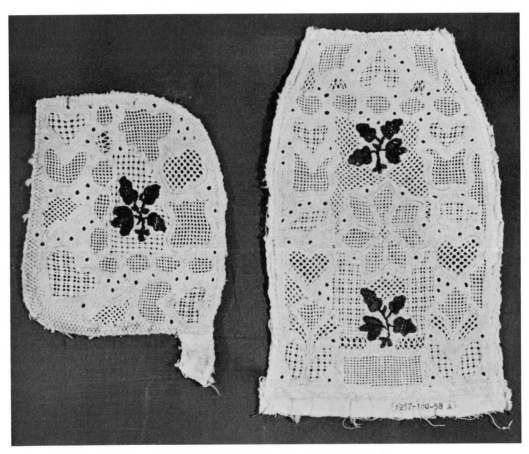

A very early example of English Pulled work (16th century).
The ornamental concept is not unlike that governing the plaster
panel; the structural ornamentation may be considered kindred
although the materials differ. Cooper-Hewitt Museum, New York.

Enlarged sections of the *Master Sampler*.

PLATE 1

The *Master Sampler*.

PLATE 2

or the inevitable consequence when the square is employed for geometric ornamentation can be only conjectured. Certainly, if we play about with combinations of triangles, diamonds, squares, octagons, we are all bound to arrange some duplicate patterns. However, I find it not only reasonable but probable that conscious borrowing is evident in much of the work, including our American mosaic, the patchwork quilt. European emigrants often left behind youths spent in impoverished and mean circumstances. They had had little visual nourishment except that to be found in the lavish splendors of their cathedrals and churches. The memory of the ecclesiastical appointments and vestments, paintings, mosaic walls and pavements, and tapestries, many of them medieval or Renaissance, must have been indelible and thus at hand when they pieced together their colorful fragments of cloth in noticeable duplication of those old patterns. Geometric forms are, of course, easier to transfer and adapt than other styles of ornamentation and these are what they used. The patterns were of their own devising or that of the professional patternmaker, who had recourse to the same sources. And this may be why we see Roman, Islamic, and medieval European designs in homespun quilting. There are some people who might ascribe this to Jungian collective-unconscious theory, but this attribution requires a more mystical viewpoint than my own. The survival of pattern and motif, in the Bethlehem Stars, Jockey Cap counterchanges, Irish Chains, Boxes, Pineapples, Log Cabins, and other geometric arrangements familiar to the quilt, whether by coincidental or conscious transference, attests to an arresting, beguiling, and curiously reassuring connection between modern inhabitants of the earth and those who preceded them.

As you look through this book, you may reasonably ask why an inquiry into needlework makes so many way-stops in other fields. This was not far-fetching to force unrelated or unjustifiable analogies. The designers of brickwork, mosaics, carpets, architecture, painting, tiles, basketry, and counted embroidery employed interchangeable motifs; their structural schemes are almost identical although conditioned by the demands of their different materials. They all put the square and its angles to work for them, designing in close cooperation and watching each other's labors. Their adage was "borrowers and lenders be" and the passage of devices from one medium to another was so swift in medieval Europe

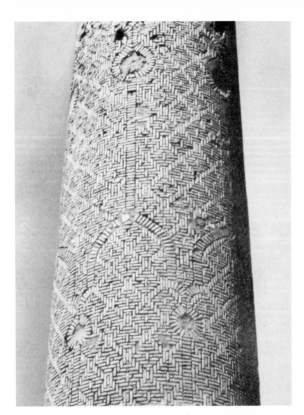

The kinship of embroidery pattern structure with that of Seljuk brickwork is clearly visible here. Minaret, early 12th century, Gulpaygan, Iran.

Altar frontal of Henry IV of Castile, Spain, 15th-century embroidery. El Monasterio de Guadaloupe, Madrid. *See* Diagram 42 for background pattern.

The celebrated Assyrian sculptured reliefs are unusually detailed and rich in embroidery motif. They invariably depicted ferocious hunting scenes; hunters and victims were elegantly embroidered (in stone) for the ceremonies of death. Assurbanipal Dispatching a Lion, 7th century B.C., Nineveh, Assyria. British Museum, London.

Cardinal Bandinelli Saulli, his secretary and two geographers painted by Sebastiano del Piombo, c. 1510, National Gallery, Washington, D.C. An example of carpet pattern and its Kufic interlaced border as preserved by the painters of the Middle Ages and the Renaissance. *See* Color Plates 7 and 8.

that it is not possible to arrive at a chronological sequence or to guess at the original source.

An exception to this persistent intermingling of geometric ornamentation is the equilateral hexagon which, much to my sorrow, does not accommodate to the square; the square is erected on a ninety-degree angle while the hexagon is fixed at sixty. I cannot look at Persian miniature painting, tiles, and architecture without mourning the loss of this exceptionally versatile and curiously active geometric form. Even snowflakes upset me in their obstinate hexagonal purity; strewn on a dark background, they would make a magnificent carpet! No hexagonal ground is manufactured for the needle except for frail netting. Alarmed one day by my grieving, Mrs. Lane suggested I try chicken wire, and perhaps I will. The equilateral hexagon is generally not used in simple or primitive weave; the warp and woof of textile and knotted carpet also lend themselves more easily to the square. When you do find the hexagon in handwork, it often signals a more sophisticated culture. I have simulated the six-sided structure a few times but it really is an artifice that goes counter to the natural construction of the canvas. However, the square is the procreator of so varied and talented a progeny, we need not feel very deprived.

It is interesting to see how one type of handwork is frequently the unexpected and inadvertent recorder of another. Assyrian stone relief sculpture and Byzantine mosaics and icons preserve extinct embroidery and cloth patterns. Embroidery performs the same service for long-forgotten or lost details of costume, church artifacts, and household objects. This secondary and unintentional feature of manual work will be familiar to those who have looked with attention at the patchwork quilt. Its makers occupied themselves with its display of fine stitchery, its robust and colorful pieced design, and its warmth. That they have also provided us with a fine record of fabrics is lucky accident; these motley scraps give us a reliable and splendid textile history, one that would have been lost to us had the quilt not acted as custodian.

Because many of the stitches and patterns were adapted from photographs, affording me no opportunity to inspect or analyze underside structure, I have had to infer or invent systems to arrive at the same surface effects. Some of my solutions are probably unconventional, but I believe them to be sound in principle and practice.

I think I should point out that the term "embroidery," as used by our forebears, presupposes the existence of a ground cloth or canvas onto which the needle applies its yarn. In this respect, it differs from tapestry, lace, woven stuffs, and knotted carpets, which construct ground and design concurrently. I think I should also point out a personal bias: I do not really like the word "embroidery." I am attracted to design that, in some sense, is *of* the canvas square, not *on* it. Embroidery has come to mean superfluous embellishment; when we embroider a story, we add the unnecessary. Poor word, it's not responsible for what we have done to it, but I prefer "needlework." Whatever we call them, oblivion is no fit place for these worthy stitches and patterns.

CHRONOLOGICAL NOTE

Arranging our cultural past by decades, centuries, eras is the scholar's diversion and the historian's convenience. It allows the extraction of an isolated component from an unwieldy whole, making the infinite more finite and, thus, more amenable to analysis and theory. The line of demarcation between the Late Middle Ages and the Early Renaissance is often shifted to the biased compass of the individual writer and theme. It is, however, generally conceded that the Middle Ages fade away and expire some time before the start of the sixteenth century. But the date may vary by a hundred years or more.

IN THIS BOOK, the Late Middle Ages will mean the thirteenth through the fifteenth centuries. Artisans tend to rely on tried techniques and much of their work retains characteristics of earlier times. This may be seen in needlework; the embroiderers of the fifteenth century were guided by those of the fourteenth, the fourteenth by the thirteenth etc.; work of the sixteenth and seventeenth centuries reveals strong ties to the past too. It appears that the compelling need for breakthrough innovation, resulting in personal recognition and identification, is more common to the artist than artisan.

There are profound sociological and political conclusions to be drawn from the difference in attitude. Toiling within the security of group en-

19

deavor (the craft collective or guild), the artisan was denied world acknowledgment; he is Anonymous to following generations. In his own time, he was known mainly to his colleagues and employers, as is any worker, and his labors served society. The artist, on the other hand, must view society as the adversary. He must simultaneously disturb it by seeking to destroy its customary modes of thinking, seeing, and hearing even while he is asking its recognition. Because he is the assassin of habit, he must overcome resistance, even fury. When he does, an overwhelming and lonely accomplishment, he receives universal appreciation and acclaim, which offer him a unique, alluring, and terrifying position. For within the sweet melody of applause there always lurks the threatening refrain of the *mene tekel* and, still alone, he can be, and often is, destroyed when it emerges.

Essentially, the artisan was content to make modifications or alterations required by the new materials, attitudes, or needs of his fellows; he was a community creature and shattering the past would have been alien to him; the metamorphoses in his craft, therefore, are gentle and undisturbing and this enables us to trace some of his ideas through the articles that have lived on after him.

3) The Square

IN A SENSE, this book is a celebration of limitation and its marvels. Within defined borders, the dedicated and inquisitive searcher can find unending and challenging variety. Think of the sonnet, the egg, the fugue, the spectrum, the alphabet, the apartment, one beloved friend. How interesting if we could remove the façade of high-rise buildings, for a moment, to see how the identical, mathematically determined space was used by human beings to convert cubes into dwellings.

I have focused my attention on the steadfast square, its subdivisions and extensions. Its presence is an invariable; it lies behind every stitch, and all the patterns and designs are predicated on it. When designing them, I tried always to honor the integrity of the square by not concealing its presence. I admire it because it is invincible, resistant to disguise, and the magnanimous nurturer of countless fascinating ornamental off-shoots for the artist who respects it.

There are some people who react to an invariable as to personal malevo-lent attack. Boundaries affront their creativity, structure suffocates inspiration, reality itself is unendurable because it exists independently of our dreams and is oblivious to our fantasies. These people, often unconsciously, determine to force reality to submit to their own design. Although they cannot really escape reality or change it, they imagine they do by altering their own perception of it. This effort to re-create and dominate reality is essentially romantic; romantic because the metamorphosis is illusionary and subjective. Finding actuality repellent, boring, or threatening, the romantic camouflages and refashions it. This defense is not at all reprehensible, but it sometimes seems to imply contempt for the "real" by a refusal to acknowledge it.

The antithetical approach to the romantic is the sensuous. Sensuous? Well, yes, because those who lean in this direction are not disposed to deny or disguise what their uninhibited senses apprehend. Instead, they are intrigued by reality just because it is not and cannot ever be entirely of their own manufacture. The mysterious entity of the "other," its firm inviolability, arouses appreciation and curiosity. They try to recognize and explore it rather than re-create it. This recognition is a first step, and a hard one, because it requires unblinkered receptiveness and unlearning of the romantic education that begins in the nursery.

Few people fit exclusively into any one of the categories we confidently devise for them, thank goodness, but I do think we show leanings. Some of us actually list rather noticeably. We may easily detect a romantic or sensuous bent if we take note of our attitudes toward food, animals, lovers, children, our bodies and clothing, films, music, painting, and even needlework.

Let us imagine that you have by now reached the point of really seeing your canvas. It is a field of squares formed by interwoven warp and woof threads. This will not change. Now, do you desperately wish to make these squares and the steps of warp and woof disappear? Do you favor needle painting, elaborate curves, third-dimensional relief shading, landscape in perspective arrangements, *trompe l'oeil* optical illusions? Do you want your finished canvas to look like an oil painting, a sculptured form, a real slice of malachite, tortoise shell, a representative portrait of an animal? Do you hope your stitches look like brushwork? Then you are a romantic and you are going to try to make your substructure and its irritating squares vanish beneath your own imposed composition. Great masters in all the fine arts have found stimulus in this sort of challenge;

22

some of our most celebrated works of art are the direct result of it. Nevertheless, even though there are splendid embroidery examples in this style from Flanders, Germany, Spain, China, France, and England, it can be a hazardous route for us. This absolute freedom to impose concepts and break down barriers is usually best handled by genius and, talented though they be, I don't think this is a common characteristic among those plying the needle. Museums and libraries will be helpful guides to those who wish to work all unfettered by the innate characteristics of their materials, and the world around will be beckoning from all directions with inspiration. The stitches and patterns in this book can be used very well to contribute to this work but they will not be dominant.

Because this approach allows you so much liberty with respect to composition, yarn, coloring, subject matter, there is a temptation to run wild with the possibilities. Have a care or you may find you have worked absurd distortions. Garishly shaded Victorian cabbage roses may be received in some circles as high-camp lovelies, but I sense a strong element of derision in their welcome. Aside from the expense, needlepoint demands too much labor, thought, and time to be served up for a giggle. One of its strongest virtues is durability, and if it is meant for a laugh, it will linger on in your home, too stale and too familiar to be funny. A worse misuse and disregard of substructure may be seen in the embroidered malapropism known as stumpwork. Here, artifice parading as naturalism requires that the yarn be understuffed with wadding so as to produce "real life" protuberances and declivities. Buxom cheeks, bosoms, and thighs are plumped out like pincushions; lace, satin, and pearls are applied in "appropriate" places, and the figures are so stiff and overdecorated they look like the work of a dotty undertaker. Ground should be worked, not garnished.

If, however, you wish to venture into a more sensuous appreciation of your materials, you will want to acknowledge their unique properties and come to partnership terms with them. You will be working with and featuring the squares of your canvas, your yarns, and your needle. These are your tools and colleagues and with them you may create wonders. Think of the child performing within the rigid constriction (and reality) of his ten fingers and an ordinary length of string. In the confinement, or game, we call Cat's Cradle, with the aid of mind and question, he encounters the magical world of geometric, perpetual-change design. He is fashioning simple diaper patterns in the air. This child may become the adult, accomplished poet or composer, painter or mathematician, chess player, surgeon or chef, who also works within strict form and finds limitation may offer limitless rewards and stimulation. In a way, then, Cat's Cradler's all. The painter of the Italian Renaissance, for instance. Inhibited by the commission system upon which he was financially dependent, held to strict iconographic concepts for his Madonna, Child, St. Sebastian, St. Jerome, St. Anthony, their clothing and environments dictated by long custom, he used this artistic "jail" to probe the worlds of light, matter, composition, pigment, etc. with such extraordinary power, depth, and wonder that we can only be grateful to his prison. We live in a more liberated world now, where artists claim and cherish freedom. But this usually means a freedom to work within limitation of their own choosing. If the boundaries are not superimposed from without, they frequently erect them themselves. The true meaning of "license," although we may misuse it, connotes fixed limits.

When you are in the stage of planning a large piece of work, a carpet or hanging, which you are going to adapt from another culture, country, or century, let your mind and spirit stay within its pale for a time. You will find the sampler an invaluable aid in this respect. If you confine and thoroughly steep yourself in one specific period by working out various themes on a sampler, you will find that the intimate understanding this brings will guide your decisions with regard to color, form, etc., as you work your larger piece. What we call unerring instinct or taste usually is knowledge we have absorbed so well we can call upon it without the ceremony of conscious recollection.

Maggie Lane was born in China. It is not happenstance that her oriental hangings, photographed for this volume, seem uncanny in their perfection of color, form, and arrangement. This is profound inner knowledge given form and substance—which is what all work should aspire to. The serenity, mysterious order, and beauty of these pieces are the result of artistry, yes, but they are also the result of the deepest awareness of the Eastern culture and spirit, and the keenest perception of the intrinsic qualities and limitations of her materials. Not all of us are fortunate enough to have spent our youths in the areas that intrigue us. But if you wish, you may travel there with the aid of yarn, needle, and canvas and have an adventurous and rewarding stay right on your sampler.

24

4) The Sampler

YESTERDAY

Most samplers still enjoying fairly good health have been well documented and illustrated in previously published books and museum catalogues—please see Bibliography. What follows, therefore, is a personal and idiosyncratic evaluation, which may be—probably is—at variance with that of other admirers.

The word "sampler" reaches us from the Old French *essemplaire*, derived from the Latin *exemplarium–exemplum:* "example." The *e* is later dropped and we arrive at "sample" and its residence, the sampler.

Few specimens remain from sixteenth-century Europe and, I believe, none at all from the fifteenth. In the Middle Ages, most painters worked from pattern books that illustrated techniques, iconographic or symbolic format, and the most popular themes—a religious Hit Parade. The painter, or artisan, as he was then considered, was commissioned to paint, for instance, a St. Sebastian or St. Nicholas. The pattern books would show him the dramatic biographical highlights, the animals or other associated symbolic appurtenances, the appropriate robes and colors, and the environmental format. Embroiderers, at that time considered equal masters, also had need of assistance in techniques and composition. The painted page was not the most practical way to illustrate stitches and textures, so these were worked on pieces of cloth that came to be known as samplers. I shouldn't be at all surprised to find that the painter's pattern books were known by this name as well, because they depicted religious and artistic *examples*. If we look carefully at the painting and embroidery of this period, I think we can deduce what these samplers or pattern books consisted of.

In the seventeenth century, embroidery skill was still remarkable, if past its zenith, and curiosity had not yet dimmed. During this time, the sampler was not yet burdened with the "good works" aura that later became glued to it like a pious barnacle. Rather, it was an altogether necessary and temptingly rich library of stitches, pattern, design, and an instructive handbook of the methods of coordinating them all for their mutual enhancement. It was also a rehearsal hall for the needleworker because he could try out new combinations or perfect his dexterity on its accommodating ground. Samplers were extremely valuable to their owners and they bequeathed them in their wills to their heirs. I would assume, if there were no family, that they were sold to other embroiderers. All the artisans' guilds of the period referred to their technical knowledge as the "mysteries" of their crafts and, as such, they were scrupulously guarded. The workers were, in fact, attempting a copyright procedure because their incomes were dependent on their maintaining strict vigilance over the knowledge that gave them sustenance.

The tactile pleasure of these sampler workers, whether male or female, professional or leisure class, in their fine silks, wools, linens (flax), gold, and silver is evident to the viewer, as is their buoyant response to the joys of texture and geometric structure. Many of them were German or English and they shared with their medieval ancestors a keen appetite for inquiry and controlled experiment. They also shared a marked interest in geometric ornament and a sizable debt to Islam. Virtually every geometric motif in the samplers of this time can be traced directly to its medieval Islamic ancestry. It is generally accepted that the Islamic religion proscribed the ornamental use of lifelike human images or representational flora and fauna figures as an affront to the true Creator. This taboo was taken very seriously by the Turkish people (less so by the Islamic Per-

26

sians), and thus they converted all creatures and plants to geometric forms, with occasional clandestine exceptions. We see here another example of the extraordinary versatility and variety to be found within rigid restriction. It is not surprising that the European made use of the rich mathematical patterns even though "graven" images were not forbidden by Christian dogma. The seventeenth century shows sampler work at its best. Its repertory of pattern, stitch, and texture obviously served its makers very well and enthralled them too. It has provided us with an exhilarating record of the human desire to employ the hand for works of accomplishment and beauty.

This eagerness diminishes somewhat in the eighteenth century. The sampler begins to show more sobriety than inquiry; it becomes exemplary rather than exploratory. Stitch vocabulary narrows, borders and composition are formally planned, the work becomes exhibitionistic rather than self-satisfying, designed to impress the viewer with its display of cautious virtuosity. Then we see the re-emergence of ambitious pictorial designs—of houses, interiors, landscapes—and in its high but generally unrealized pretensions, high craft descends to inferior art. The sampler is now in staid adulthood and, for me at least, the thrill is gone. Many samplers show the hand of the professional and were undoubtedly used to instruct apprentices or to entice clients who wished to place orders for embroidered linens and cloths. They are skilled and handsome but not really engaging.

Sometime between the eighteenth and nineteenth centuries a novel and ignoble purpose was foisted on the sampler. It was put to use as a torture chamber concocted by their elders for female children. We see in it all the faults of punitive education. Curiosity was stifled and these youngsters, many of them eight to twelve years old, were forced to stitch exact copies of alphabets, numerals, homilies, biblical texts, dire self-warnings of death-in-idleness, and fulsome praise of their parents. Even the amusement of stitch variety is denied them and the full or half cross stitch reigns supreme. This brutal and crushing effort to uplift the spirit may be seen within many American and English frames; I hope one day to find a secret rebellious message stitched in by one irrepressible, unsubmissive child.

Some relief to these exercises in tedium came with the invention of chemical dying agents in the nineteenth century. Whether promoted by

27

Two 17th-century English samplers showing the prevalence of geometric Islamic-type patterns. Cooper-Hewitt Museum, New York.

Scottish sampler, 18th century, mainly Pulled work. Cooper-Hewitt Museum, New York.

manufacturers or natural hunger, the emergence of these new tones brought fresh impetus to geometric needlework. Oddly, the geometric motifs in these unusually long and narrow strip samplers are quite unrelated to those of the seventeenth century. They show little Islamic influence. Many are, in fact, distinct and unmistakable duplications of the three-dimensional mosaics of an earlier time. Suddenly, in Victorian yarn and canvas, the pavement work of Rome and Pompeii stands before our eyes, reflecting the current fascination with the archeological excavations of the period. You will see many illustrations of this curious throwback in my stitched sampler squares and accompanying notes on provenance. The relief modeling, so favored by antiquity, was made possible by the marketing of the new yarns with graduated color tones. The motifs traveled swiftly; identical patterns are worked in the samplers of Germany, Austria, and England. Perhaps the patterns were made available by the yarn manufacturers as promotional lures for their products. The new hues, some as fugitive as they were wild, were a spur to activity, and samplers get quite bouncy again. In Germany and Austria particularly, the use of these colors was, let us say, injudicious, but the patterns have vitality, and more tempered shading is easily substituted. Some of the experiments on these samplers are artless or inappropriate to their materials, but the fact that the workers enjoyed their labors is happily visible.

One peculiarity to be seen in Victorian samplers is the insistence on covering over the decorative holes left by the needle. Medieval and Renaissance artisans featured the perforation of ground as a respected and important design element, but the Victorians seem to me quite comical in their frenzied efforts to conceal it. Marked perforation is almost always made to hide its shame under superimposed transverse stitches that delicately cover it from the tender public eye. They also issued stern admonitions against the sin of leaving any part of the canvas ground visible (unworked). Can they have viewed even nonhuman structural components as unseemly? In any case, this stricture against nudity was applied to all canvas ground irrespective of function. Of course, articles meant for use on the floor or as upholstery must be completely stitched to insure durability. Other work may not require this treatment and the ground has, in the past, made its own unique contribution to the design of needlework. If, indeed, the Victorians were concerned with strength,

Mid-19th-century English sampler, Victoria and
Albert Museum, London. This is a superlative example
of Victorian geometric work. The skill of the worker
is superior to all others (in this particular strip style)
I have seen from this period.

Japanese sampler, 20th century.
Cooper-Hewitt Museum,
New York.

they were not consistent, because they executed some of their carpets in a variety of stitches and textures. It is obvious and logical that a raised stitch will suffer greater assault from the foot than one that is recessed. This makes the wearing process less uniform because the tread brings most injury to the higher texture. An even surface is obligatory for carpets, and it is usually advisable to confine yourself to one stitch, or to two that produce matching textures.

In the years following, there was a gradual diminution of interest in the sampler. The word itself became synonymous with patience, tidiness, decorum, and Cross Stitch. These banal, sanctimonious, and wearying exercises undoubtedly discouraged the youngsters who slaved over them; those who viewed them in their frames were surely not tempted to embark on similar pursuits.

By the beginning of the twentieth century the sampler had fallen into another decline, and the middle of the century finds it entombed, its epitaph engraved, no doubt neatly, in Cross Stitch.

It would be hypocritical for me to try to summon even the most meager regret for the passing of the torture-chamber sampler and its kinfolk, the embroidered country house, the bead-eyed lap dog on a cushion, and the shrieking, bulging flower. But what of that enchanter, the kaleidoscopic pattern book in yarn? Does it hold any allure or function for us today?

TODAY

Is the sampler only a dear fossil? A charming memento of the past best left undisturbed? Back sliding nostalgia? We have at our disposal printed records of design, instruction books within lazy reach, prepared painted canvases in an explosion of art needlework shops. Why dust off this quaint form just now, and what are samplers anyway?

Technically, a sampler starts as a piece of ground cloth or canvas that may be cut to convenient, suitable size. You may divide its surface any number of ways (large and small squares, oblongs, octagons, tiers, crazy quilt, among others). If you think of its foundation as an interwoven graph, it will be unfailingly hospitable to almost all the geometric structures and patterns you may care to ply onto its threads—except the hexagon and its offshoots.

31

I myself think of the sampler as a scholarly playground, a patchwork of exploratory handwork, a lighthearted mosaic of serious curiosity that is given permanent life by needle and stitch. You may use it as a notebook, in which case you will be left with handsome and lasting evidence of your studies instead of fading pages of notation. You will find it an invaluable aid in developing techniques. It is generous and tolerant because errors often turn out to be revelations rather than catastrophes. It is a practical guide for future work when you wish to incorporate texture or pattern, and it is never, never boring because each of its units offers a unique problem to be solved. If you have a "horror vacuui" and feel oppressed by row upon row of unbroken background, the sampler's multiform and multipurpose versatility will lift your spirits and claim your friendship and gratitude.

Unplanned at first I came to realize that each of my samplers was based on a specific theme and search, frequently not specifically related to embroidery. In other words, I provided both goal and limitation. The needle was my shovel and the canvas my site for an archeological dig. My interest is usually directed to medieval, pre-perspective composition, which, fortunately, transfers very satisfactorily to threaded canvas. I have never completed a sampler (I call many of my pillows and carpets samplers too because I brought similar attitudes to their work) without gaining significant and useful insight into other forms—woodcut, stained glass, early playing cards, strap or plait work, antique Islamic carpets, mosaic pavements, brick and tile structure, icons, stitch architecture, Venetian lace patterns, Byzantine textiles. It is an entertaining method of study. But the sampler will be equally welcoming and helpful to more personal creation, innovative ideas, and artistic experiment.

If your primary interest is pattern, you may play with counterchange, investigate primary color limitation or graduated toning, discover yarn peculiarities, rejoice in textural oddities, uncover cultural traditions and influences. Your knowledge will be personal, your analysis original, your sense of accomplishment rewarding; your perceptive ability will improve and this will alter your accustomed habits of thinking and seeing. This is much, much better than hand-me-down academic theory. No two people ever see things in exactly the same manner and no one can have experienced your particular adventure before you; if you feel and act like the first explorer, then you are.

5) Geometric Pattern Through the Ages

GEOMETRIC DIAPER PATTERN can be considered a magnetic field exerting an irresistible, possibly eternal, hold on man's optical imagination. This thralldom has kept a dynamic geometric highway running from Babylon to the 19th-century patchwork quilt. On the following pages are a few patterns from my sampler, shown with photographic biography, to demonstrate this continuity.

In Part III I have accompanied many other squares with notes on provenance so that you can follow the historic trail and consult original sources or illustrated books for additional information.

33

13th-century Seljuk carpet from the Mosque of Alā al-Din, Konya. Museum of Turkish and Islamic Art, Istanbul. Note border. I have discovered no earlier use of this Seljuk pattern than in the extraordinary border of this carpet.

Early 15th-century shrine, Zayn-al-Din, courtyard building, on the Persian-Afghan border. Seljuk design. One arm of the pattern is reversed and it is joined differently.

Brussels, 15th-century altar frontal. Mass vestments of the Order of the Golden Fleece. Seljuk design in left background. Schatzkammer, Vienna.

Lace pattern, Seljuk design, Esemplario book, Zoppino, Venice, 1530.

Swiss needleworked carpet, 1533, Anatolian pattern. Landesmuseum, Zurich, Switzerland. Note Seljuk border design.

English sampler, mid-17th century, Victoria and Albert Museum, London. Seljuk design. Most of the geometric patterns in this sampler, and others within the same period, are Seljuk (Turkish, Syrian, Persian), probably via the Venetian lace pattern books.

Sampler Square, Diagram 31.
See also Diagram 26.
Triangles are based on the
60 or 90 degree angle.

Clay palace pillars, Babylon, 4000 B.C. Staatliche Museen, Berlin. These geometric motifs are to be found in many medieval embroideries throughout Germany, England, France, and Spain.

Niche, Ostia, Rome,
2nd century A.D.

St. Martin Offering the Wine Cup, embroidery, note mosaic pavement, 15th century. Lehman Collection, Metropolitan Museum of Art, New York.

Detail from *Female Votaries Dance Before a Goddess*, a painting from the Boucicaut Workshop, c. 1413, Bibliothéque Nationale, Paris.

Arte del Bene Morire ("The Art of Dying Well"), Florence, 1495. Block book (illustration and text were cut on the same wood block). The death chamber is dominated by the geometric motif on ceiling and floor.

Knitted bag, Rio Pilcomayo, South America. Linden Museum, Stuttgart.

Pennsylvania patchwork quilt, c. 1870, cotton, called Triangles. Collection Jonathan Holstein, New York.

37

Sampler Square, Diagram 101.

Islamic plate, in underglaze colors and enamels with gilding. See costume, right horseman. Persia, late 12th century. Victoria and Albert Museum catalogue.

Sculptural detail, pedestal, Kings and Queens, Chartres Cathedral, 12th-century France.

Antique gold buckle. Cologne Museum, Germany.

Silk chasuble, date and country
unknown, pieced work.

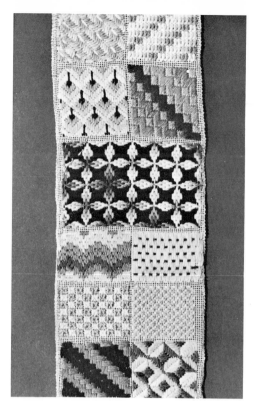

A few geometric motifs from an
English strip sampler, 1841,
Philadelphia Museum of Art.
Note "Pineapple" pattern.

American patchwork quilt,
Pineapple pattern, 1920,
red and white calico.

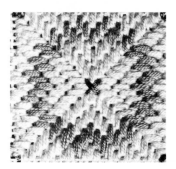

Sampler Square, Diagram 30.

Sampler Square, Variation, page 472.

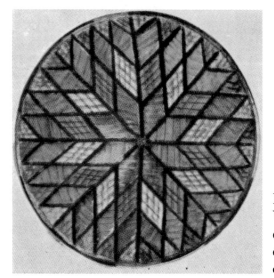

Hat ornament, Malaya, Museum für Völkerkunde, Berlin. This design, in a different color arrangement, is one of the 12th-century window patterns in the Cathedral of St. Denis, France.

Pennsylvania pieced quilt, c. 1880, Star of Bethlehem. Collection Jonathan Holstein, New York.

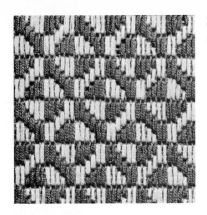

Sampler Square, *see* Diagram 39 and following pages.

14th-century inlaid marble design, Italian, Victoria and Albert Museum, London. 'Jockey Cap' and Baptistery motif.

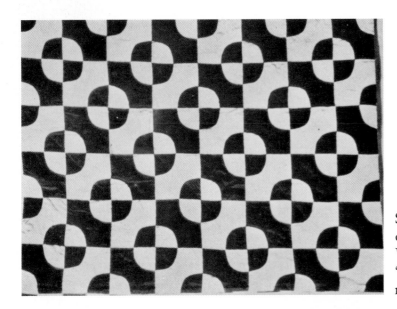

Section of an American pieced quilt, Steeplechase Pattern. White and Turkey red cotton. "Jockey Cap" and Baptistery motif.

A variation of the Steeplechase pattern, 19th century American patchwork quilt, blue and white homespun, collection Kate and Joel Kopp. *See* Diagram 39 and following pages for further variations from the Baptistery, Florence.

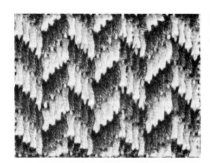

Sampler Square, Diagram 33
See also Diagrams 34 and 35

8th-century mosaic pavement,
Carolingian period. Collegiate
Church, crypt, St. Quentin,
France.

Seljuk geometric tile work, 13th
century, in the Sirçali Madrassa,
Konya.

St. Martin Brings to Life a Dead
Man, medieval embroidery, Lehman
Collection, Metropolitan Museum of
Art, New York.

A lace pattern published in
Venice, 1530. Esemplario book,
Zoppino.

Mid-17th-century English sampler on
linen ground.

Samoan coverlet, Museum
für Völkerkunde, Hamburg.

18th-century American pieced
quilt. The design is known as "Tide
Mill." Note "Windmill" corners, see
following pattern.

Sampler Square, Diagram 18.

Patchwork quilt, 1890, "Windmill." This highly effective counterchange may be seen in countless medieval mosaics, paintings, tiles, embroideries, windows, etc. The "pinwheel" pattern, even when not activated by the wind, has surprising motion.

Sampler Square, Diagram 25.

Mosaic pavement, Mass Vestments of the Order of the Golden Fleece, Brussels, 15th century. Another simple, oddly powerful, lasting geometric pattern. It too may be found in 18th- and 19th-century pieced quilts.

Sampler Square, Diagram 169.

Indonesian woven bag, National Museum, Munich. Hound's Tooth pattern.

A very old patchwork quilt pattern called Indiana Puzzle. It is what we call Hound's Tooth in fabric. The design is a medieval Islamic counterchange. This quilt was made in 1920.

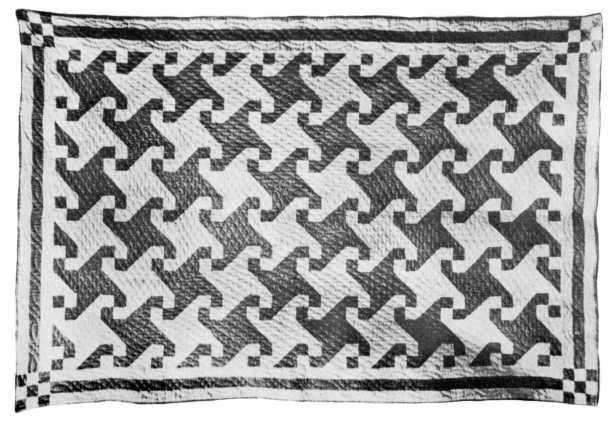

Floor of an ancient fishing cottage near the Gironde, France. Hexagonal boxes used, uncomfortably and inconsiderately, as a *trompe l'oeil* under-foot pattern.

Pennsylvania patchwork quilt, c. 1880, cotton, hexagonal pattern called Baby Blocks. Collection Jonathan Holstein, New York. When hexagonal patterns are shaded they almost always result in optical illusions of depth or motion.

The tomb of Bishop John Pecci, Donatello. Mosaic hexagonal boxes, c. 15th-century. The hexagonal background may predate the sculpture.

Hexagonal boxes. Its similarity to the Baby Blocks quilt and other hexagonal designs is readily apparent although the toning is dissimilar. This is from an Esemplario Venetian lace pattern book, 16th century.

46

6) Hungarian Point

A MYSTERY STORY

DEPENDING ON MOOD OR TOLERANCE, we may view the legends surrounding this style of needlework as mystery, comedy of errors, or as an example of historymaking at its most frivolous. What is factually established is sufficiently limited, intriguing, and perplexing to earn it some future scholarly attention. Until then, we can try to penetrate its romantic gauze and appreciate it for what it really is. I will try to separate what is known from what is unknown, what may be fairly conjectured from what is fantasy with some degree of accuracy. Hungarian Point needs no fictional cloak to engage our attention or merit our respect. It is a method of using straight stitches in varying ratios of long and short, together with shading (usually but not always ombré), to create its own peculiar texture and pattern. These patterns may take many forms but the most familiar is the sharply delineated peak-and-valley line known to many as Flame Stitch. The juxtaposition of these long and short lengths of yarn accounts for its individual and unmistakable character. Its architecture is unique to itself but it is often confused with Florentine Stitch,

47

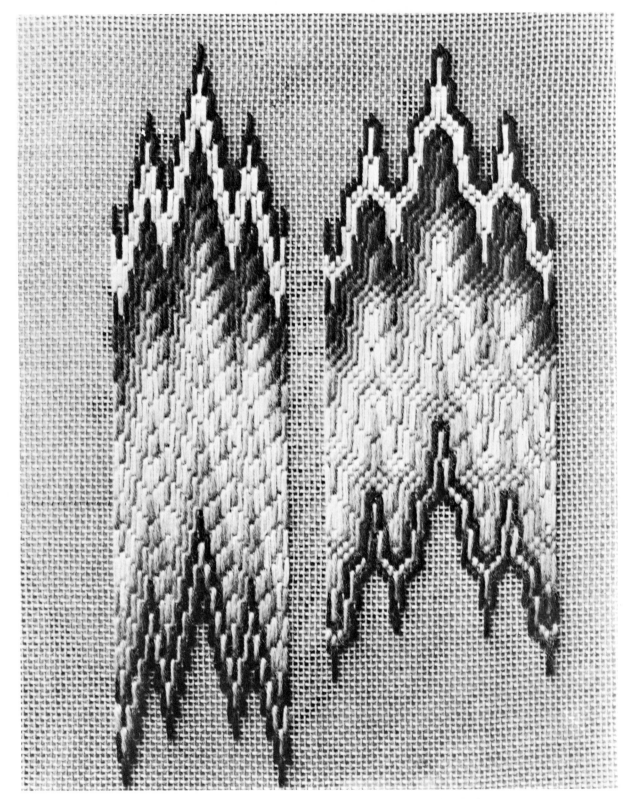

Florentine Stitch   Hungarian Point

which uses a similar design but dissimilar structure. Please refer to the two simple examples of Florentine and Hungarian Point stitching I worked in similar three-spire structures, and in the identical tone arrangement, to emphasize their similarities and marked differences. You will see that repeat lines follow through in kind in Florentine Stitch, whereas in Hungarian Point they do not. Within the peaks of Hungarian Point, the stitches fit inside one another like a series of Chinese boxes. The textural surface of Hungarian Point, caused by its special configuration, distinguishes it from any other stitch form. Once you have recognized it or, better still, worked it, you will never again muddle it with Florentine or other styles. For comprehensive technical instruction or for design elaboration see Barbara Snook's commendable book *Florentine Embroidery*.

ALIASES

I will take up birthday questions further on, but I have seen no evidence of this textile or embroidery pattern before the eighteenth century. At this time, Hungarian Point became fashionable for such things as wall hangings, bed hangings, ecclesiastical furnishings and chasubles, and small boxlids and purses in England, France, and Italy. For reasons unknown (we will deal with this further on, too), it acquired the name of Hungarian Point (England), *Point d'Hongrie* (France), and *Punto Unghario* (Italy). The name may have been current before, but the first references I have seen occur in the eighteenth century. Within the last decade or so, the American penchant for coining superfluous words has given us the additional names of Bargello, Flame Stitch, and Florentine Stitch. At the same time, Florentine stitching has been rechristened Hungarian Point, Bargello, and Flame Stitch. This tangle of titles is confusing. We can readily understand how the sharp descents and climbs and the similar method of shading brought about this imbroglio of names —especially to those not particularly sensitive to structural, textural, and technical distinctions. Flame Stitch is merely one way of describing one design effect, in either form of work. As other effects are frequently employed (lozenge, carnation, etc.), it should be demoted from a name to a simple adjective, if only for clarity.

As for Bargello: The Bargello is a Florentine building, started in the

Late Middle Ages. It has been used for various purposes including that of fortress and jail, and it has its own fascinating history, but one that does not concern us here. It is now a splendid museum, very rich in medieval and early Renaissance artifacts. More important, it houses a most glorious collection of Donatello's sculpture, making it an imperative stop for art lovers from all over the world. Scattered about the rooms of this aged fortress are a number of unremarkable chairs that were upholstered in Hungarian Point embroidered cloth in the middle or late eighteenth century. Some visitors assume that they are part of the original furnishings of the building and mistakenly associate both chairs and embroidery with medieval Florence. Because the name of the building, the Bargello, antedates that of Hungarian Point, they apply it to the embroidered work itself. This is like calling all High Renaissance paintings Louvres simply because that ancient fortress holds the Mona Lisa. The embroidery of these chairs shows no extraordinary skill in work or design, and its bilious green and yellow hues are not very pleasing. Needleworkers in many countries, including Italy, have done far better by Hungarian Point. I find it demeaning to place all their beautiful work under the umbrella of a few unexceptional chairs. But at least these chairs are actually executed in Hungarian Point, so the exchange of names can be given some justification. When Bargello is used (as it always is at present) to mean Florentine Stitching, we are confronting inaccuracy. Florentine Stitching has its own individual properties, as does Hungarian Point. We do them no service to muddle them and deny their uniqueness; we merely denigrate both.

NAME

As noted, the terms Hungarian Point, *Punto Unghario*, and *Point d'Hongrie* probably surfaced sometime in the eighteenth century. I have seen some exceptionally beautiful French hangings, not embroidered by needle but woven in one of France's great eighteenth-century weaving centers (Elbeuf), that bear labels of date and the name *Point d'Hongrie*, but we can't be certain when these labels were affixed. Although it proves nothing, therefore, about the birth of the name, it does present us with an interesting tangent. It is possible that this mode of design may have

18th-century wall hangings,
Parham Park, England. Worked
in a style resembling Hungarian
Point.

Hungarian Point work, 18th-
century European burse. A
particularly interesting linear
arrangement. Cooper-Hewitt
Museum, New York.

begun in the manufactories of textiles and tapestries and that it was copied thereafter by the embroiderers.

In medieval embroidery there was a stitch method that shows a distant relationship to Hungarian Point. It too employed long and short stitches, but it was always worked in monotone to devise small-scale diaper patterns. Two of these (popular in England, France, Germany, and Italy) have come down to us in exact duplication. We know them as Hungarian Ground and Hungarian Stitch (*see* Diagrams 274 and 276). Perhaps they were the precursors of Hungarian Point. These patterns then traveled to lacework and later had a riotous revival in the new yarn tones of nineteenth-century England, German, Austria, and the United States. Although I have searched diligently and stubbornly, a country where I find no evidence of this work, in medieval or Hungarian Point form, or any form whatever, is Hungary. I have studied its history and consulted books devoted to Hungarian ecclesiastical and folk embroidery and other crafts and arts, including *Studien Nationale Sticherein aus Bohmen und der Ungar* (Professor Josef Sima, Slovakei, 1909) and *Ornament der Hausindustrie Ungarns* (Fishbach-Polsky, Budapest National Museum, 1878), to no avail. There are charming legends about newly married countesses bringing their native arts to Italy, but these Hungarian "Catherine de Médicis" have no historical authentication. I must doubt that this work originated in Hungary—any and all of the other embroidery-prone countries mentioned above appear to have a more substantial claim. Perhaps it was a misheard or misapplied or misunderstood word that gained respectability by popular usage.

Hungarian Point is what it has been called by its finest practitioners for about two hundred years and there would seem to be no reason for the United States to impose a gratuitous new misnomer on an accepted old one.

DESIGN

We know the shaded, sharply peaked lines of stitching in Hungarian Point can be documented back to the eighteenth century. But where does this strange design come from, by what route and when? I refer now not to the structure of the stitches but to the craggy pyramid line we

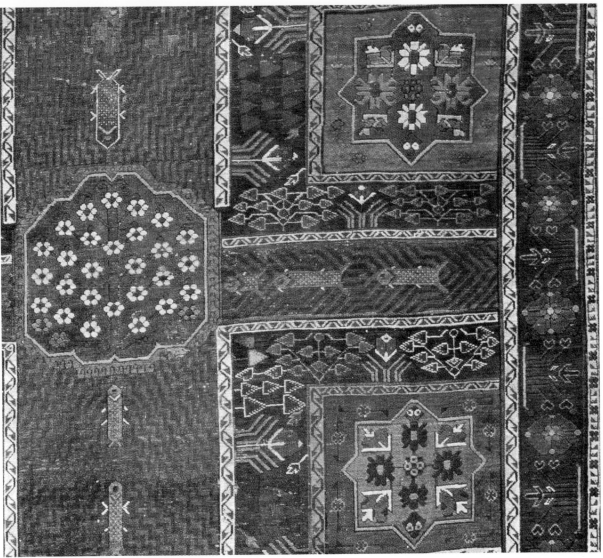

18th-century Persian Garden carpet. Irrigation canals show a Hungarian Point-type linear formation.

Seljuk-Persian tomb, 997–1028 A.D., Sangbast. Early architectural "Hungarian Point" in incised plaster. The linear design may be compared to the water symbol in the Persian Garden carpet and with Hungarian Point structure.

know as "flame" or "lightning." Many have ascribed it to the late medie-val period, but if it had indeed existed then, I cannot believe it would have escaped the attention of contemporary painters or those who fol-lowed shortly thereafter. These artists, Ghirlandaio, Lotto, Crivelli, Memling, Van Eyck, Holbein, etc., the earlier anonymous miniatur-ists, enamelers, and the painters of Siena, took great pains to depict all man-ner of textiles, carpets, and wall decoration. Surely they would not have overlooked this visual thunderbolt, had it existed. I have a special interest in the arts of the fourteenth, fifteenth, and sixteenth centuries and I feel certain that I would have come across it in museums or in the many well-illustrated art books devoted to these years.

There is no question that this design, with its perpendicular thrust and Gothic-like spires, looks better suited to the iron and oak of an earlier age. Yet it seems to have flourished with intricate ormolu em-bellishment, delicate Sèvres porcelain, tender Aubusson carpets, and frail Louis Quinze furniture. It is this visual incongruity, plus the fact that Hungarian Point is such a fit accompaniment to a more severe style of furnishing, that is so misleading.

Hungarian Point must be worked with multigraded tones. We know these dyes were manufactured and made generally available after the start of the eighteenth century. If you look closely at the great Flemish and French tapestries of the Middle Ages and the Renaissance you will see how limited yarn shades were. This limitation, of course, does not militate against artistic achievement. These are the greatest tapestry works in his-tory. The emergence of elaborately shaded yarn provides us with another clue to the probable beginnings of Hungarian Point work.

Having determined, more or less satisfactorily, that this lightninglike design appeared later than the seventeenth century, I must ask the next question. Where did this peaked design come from that suddenly enrap-tured Paris, Florence, and London? I have seen only two designs that resemble the particular structure of Hungarian Point. Both are Islamic. One is a detail of Seljuk architectural ornamentation from eleventh-century Persia; the second also came from Persia—but seven hundred years later. By the eighteenth century, the famed and glorious Persian Garden carpets had become known to Europe. These carpets show a bird's eye view of flourishing plots of land interspersed by canals. These

54

17th-century Islamic carpet,
Bergama, private collection,
Berlin.

Fabric design by Leonard, Paris,
1971, based on 17th-century style
carpet. *See also* Color Plate 7.
Courtesy Bergdorf Goodman.

canals, or irrigation symbols, are almost always constructed in a linear sequence we see in Hungarian Point. The carpets were widely admired in Italy, France, and England. It is not unreasonable to conjecture that the designers in the weaving and embroidery centers adapted this design soon after they saw it. Virtually all European geometric composition up until the eighteenth century was borrowed from Islamic carpets, tiles, textiles, architecture, and miniatures. This would simply continue the process and extend the debt. When considered in time context, this ornamental appropriation during the Middle Ages and the Renaissance represents only a fraction of the whole. While referring to their neighbors to the East as Moslem or Saracen pigs and crusading to bring about the destruction of these "pagan barbarians," European man was also grabbing the Arabic principles and systems pertaining to numerals, algebra, medicine, optical lenses and mirrors, windmills, physics, anatomy and biology, as well as the techniques and designs of architecture, mosaic, and textiles.

The oriental carpet has been a fertile and frequently used source for designers in all fields in all countries. To aid me in my study of early Anatolian-Turkish carpets, I adapted and started to work one of my own, using motifs from the fifteenth, sixteenth, and seventeenth centuries, some of which I had already explored in my samplers (*see* Color Plate 7). When I was half finished I was interested to find that a contemporary French fabric and dress designer named Leonard had made use of the same or similar seventeenth-century carpet and the same dominant central motif (*see* page 55). This designer and I had looked back more than three hundred years for our inspiration. The designer of Hungarian Point had only to look round the corner. I have used photographs of the Persian Garden carpet and Seljuk brickwork so that you may compare their structures with Hungarian Point.

I know I have presented more puzzles than solutions. Hungarian Point is very significant in the development of needlework design. You have only to glance at the displays of the large New York, London, and Paris textile houses to know how many designers are imitating it today. I am not sorry that there remain so many unanswered questions; a continuing mystery is more entertaining than one that has been solved. Future studies will undoubtedly bring us more information and I shall be pleased if my hypotheses, wrong or right, acted as a spur.

PART II

7) Geometric Patterns–
Techniques

CONSIDERATIONS OF TIME AND SPACE prevented my working the Mosaic, Brick, and other Diaper Patterns on large enough areas to reveal their character. Their visual fascination increases proportionately with every repeat. Do give them the advantage of providing a ground that permits them to develop their special geometric rhythm and unique optical interplay. A good number are, by themselves, sufficiently interesting to stand on their own if your field requires one pattern only.

You will see that some of my squares are not centered in plan. When I arranged them, I was more mindful of providing a guide for stitch and pattern than of the requisites of formal composition. If you wish to balance the pattern, find the central axis point of your work area by counting, select the dominant motif of your pattern, place its center on the axis point, and work outward. If you are working a stitch that must be started in an outer corner rather than the center, count the number of squares in your work area, divide by the number of squares needed for your stitch, and plan accordingly.

At their best, samplers are dashing, sportive creatures reflecting the alert inquiry, fortuitous accidents, and enthusiastic learning of their makers. The most engaging, to worker and viewer, are never solemn displays of diligence or grim labor. After you have acquired a basic and reliable technique, there are many variations that offer themselves for your amusement and further knowledge.

I stitched the Master Sampler squares in neutral tones of medium browns, pale beiges, and white to avoid imprinting a color concept on the viewer. I imagine it would be quite tedious always to duplicate color by color, stitch by stitch, pattern by pattern, the format shaped by another mind. You will want to do some searching out on your own after you get on familiar terms with the basic principles of structure and stitchmaking. Slide-rule conformity and copybook slavishness will eventually dull your enthusiasm, limit your learning, and depersonalize your work. As I have said before, the square of the canvas and the geometric nature of our patterns are invariables but within these boundaries you will find much opportunity to exercise ingenuity, imagination, and individuality. If you are inexperienced, you will want to rest heavily on the diagrams and sampler squares, and you may need a friendly hand to encourage you when you embark on your own ventures. The following suggestions are made with this in mind, to help you find interesting variations while retaining structural integrity.

Some colors recede, others advance, some are hot, others cold. Use your sampler to find out which are domineering, which subservient. Subject one pattern to different color treatments. This will reveal more to you about spectrum analysis than theory. You will almost automatically learn how to "parse" a pattern when you re-arrange tonal values. This will often completely alter the appearance of the design because you will be depriving some areas of power while invigorating others. If you are using shades of one family, as I did, replace the darker yarn with lighter and vice versa. If you find one stitch or a composite particularly interesting, celebrate its pattern and architecture in monotone. Try yarns of different composition in one design and observe how they interact and transform one another by subduing and highlighting. This last applies to color as well. Do *not* blend unrelated fibers or varied color tones in the needle. They never merge and your work will have a poor complexion. The canvas square does lend itself to the technique of Pointillism or Impressionism and you can use adjacent color units to modify and influence each other.

For a simple variation, simply turn stitches around from vertical to horizontal or horizontal to vertical. They often look new this way because the light is reflected quite differently on their surfaces. *CAUTION:* Do not turn your canvas while you work if you can avoid it. When necessary, make a *complete* turn from top to bottom. Do not, under any circumstances, turn it sideways unless specifically indicated, as in some some Pulled Yarn stitching.

I have stitched some of the squares in different scales. This enlargement or diminution frequently and unexpectedly alters the entire appearance of the pattern. Rescaling may be most easily accomplished by reproportioning the pattern rather than the stitches within it. Stitches, except flat, are best left in their original sizes—especially by beginners. This may require some clarification: let us say you are looking at an octagon I have worked in Single Leviathan Stitch (Smyrna). You wish to make this octagon larger. Do not change the stitch itself: use additional stitches, or fewer, to suit your needs. If my first row was composed of six stitches, my second eight stitches, you may increase this to eight for the first row, ten for the second, and so on—or decrease to four for the first row, six for the second. You will be changing the number of *units*, not the size of the stitches.

If you wish, you may interchange and substitute many of the stitches within the patterns—especially when the stitches are similar in contour. Naturally, if your new stitches are larger or smaller than mine, your pattern will alter accordingly. I make suggestions for substitutions on many of the diagram pages. Look for examples. (*see* page 171, Seljuk motif in various stitches.)

It is not necessary, or even preferable, to divide the field of your sampler into equal or unequal squares or rectangles. The ground may also be sectioned into octagons, triangles, diamonds, stepped oblongs, controlled variety, or into free-form crazy-quilt improvisation. You may outline these shapes with a dark, pale, or patterned border, or allow them to touch each other without interruption. If you use the last method, be sure that adjacent patterns are significantly differentiated in tone or scale or texture. Otherwise they will merge and blend into one another. This is difficult to do in Pulled Yarn work, which is usually carried out in monotone and in closely related pattern. I think it advisable to use barrier frames around the individual squares (or other shapes) to distinguish them from one another. These stitched frames will also provide a firm hitching post for your yarn. This is an important consideration because of the tension required by Pulled needlework. You may also wish to use pastel tones in this work and I suggest that you lightly paint or dye your canvas to match your yarn, or dye both together.

Some of the stitches and patterns have lain fallow so long, they can be newly met as strangers and we may discover values in them that overfamiliarity would have obscured. This kind of familiarity acts as an obstacle rather than an aid to composition and has to be unlearned if we are to be inventive. Ignorance is not always disadvantageous.

Mrs. Lane designed her diagrams in bold and large architecture so that visual guidance, which is best suited to our subject and most easily absorbed, could replace verbal instructions. These last (in the form of notes below the diagrams), I provided only when absolutely essential.

The diagrams have been constructed to show you first steps and, when advisable, sequential moves. My sampler squares give you enough pattern to enable you to make repeats with ease. The diagrams are numbered to assist you in working the stitches and patterns. Follow the numerical order carefully.

The sampler squares in the photographs on the diagrams pages have been enlarged considerably over their actual proportions in order to offer the clearest possible guidance. This rescaling, which acts as an aid to the eye when learning, can be unkind to design and yarn; minor twists of the silk are exaggerated and the pores of yarn and canvas are unduly stressed. The colored squares (Color Plate 2) while smaller than life-size, will give a more accurate idea of final appearance. The playing cards (Color Plates 12 and 13) use the sampler patterns and show how these squares may be incorporated into more formal composition. Do make allowances for the occasional wayward strand of yarn or rare skipped stitch in the blown-up squares; they were reproduced from my working samplers and these minor imperfections will not effect their usefulness.

62

Although you will probably want to use tones of your own choice, the shades of French silk I used in the Master Sampler (Color Plate 1) are as follows: Blanc, Mode, 4531, 4532, 4533, 4534, 4535, 4536, F 13, 3831, 3832, 3811, 3812, 7311, and 7312.

A word of encouragement: I cannot sew. I stitched my first needle-point design (painted, and bought from a shop) in Tent Stitch a few years ago; to be most charitable, it might be called Error Encanvassed. I still own it and am very fond of it. I later became interested in investigating multiform stitches and patterns. This required long and always gratifying hours of exploration, travel, magnifying-glass research. There may be a few hurdles to be negotiated, but you will find yourself on intimate terms with these stitches and patterns in very short order because you will be acquiring method, analytic enlightenment, and architectural discipline as you work.

Eventually, your own samplers will serve you as *aide-mémoires*, and I think you will find them as useful as they are decorative. *Stitch* (texture) samplers make exceptionally handsome pillows and hangings. *Pattern* (design) samplers are also superbly suited to the wall and, when worked in Tent or other hardy stitches, they can be used as carpets.

8) Notes on Needlework

To THE UNINITIATED, there is much in the world that seems strange, magical, and arcane. When exposed to clear light and viewed plain, the incomprehensible enigma often turns surprisingly intelligible and workable. The cobweb is, after all, no mystery to the spider. So we will try to strip stitchery of its mystic veils. The complex texture and pattern produced by diverse stitches is not the work of sorcerers, but of artisans who allow themselves to be governed by simple mathematical rules. If you are willing to use them, you will find that your technique develops with ease and rapidity.

When you work with Mrs. Lane's diagrams, you will notice that they are composed of cut-out forms (stitches) imposed on a grid (canvas threads). Each time you work out a diagram and master a stitch, you will learn something about structure. This will assist you in your next try. The more stitches you learn in this way, the more accomplished you become. Each succeeding effort will be easier because you will have entered a methodical procedure. Because the sturdy canvas square works as your assistant, lending architectural support to your formation, you will find that you do not need extraordinary dexterity. The canvas is your partner and will aid you in regularity. Rely on it and respect it. I think you will see that stitching is nothing more than a fairly simple method of passing a threaded needle over and under the juncture points of the canvas.

Stitches are yarn architecture. When you accept this, you will understand why the direction of the understitching is equal in importance to that on the surface. A building must stand on its invisible foundation. That which is executed on the reverse, invisible side of the canvas is the foundation of your stitch. The direction in which you have carried your yarn underneath determines the pull and form on the front. If you are careless or think the mode of formation is inconsequential, you will find that distortions, initially imperceptible, will eventually become all too apparent. Remember, stitches are simple geometry; they require logical moves to maintain harmony. In a mistaken attempt at frugality, some needleworkers "square hop" to save yarn. This is like neglecting essential steps in the preparation of food; you will save time, but you may not enjoy your meal. Structure is all. Every care must be given it. Your small saving will not compensate for a discordant texture.

I think instructions carried in solid paragraphs look intimidating and sinister. The numbered suggestions below can be used for a general guide to stitchmaking.

Immediately preceding the appropriate diagrams and sampler squares, we will consider the requirements of the separate stitch groups, loosely classified in structural kinship. When you are working on the diagrams, you may wish to turn to the pertinent paragraphs for suggestions.

1. Keep uniform tension while working. Some stitches require more vigorous pulling than others. Whether gentle or firm handling is necessary, maintain consistency.

2. Stitches that slant in one direction only may distort the canvas. If the slant is strong, the pull is increased and so is the distortion. When working the sampler patterns, I tried whenever possible to use a compensating stitch in the reverse direction in order to restore balance.

The diagram pages that contain these squares will point this out to you. It is a good method to use. If no counterbalance is workable, use these stitches sparingly. Some of the names of these culprits are Milanese, Oriental, Diagonal. They are all exceptionally handsome.

3. Try to avoid combining stitches with very disparate styles or structures. Tent Stitch is often called upon to perform make-do service with stitches that do not partner well with it—for example, straight stitches such as Brick. The Tent Stitch is there for want of a better, more integrated solution and looks it. Stitches should be compatible or they shouldn't get married.

4. I start my first stitch with a length of knotted yarn. This knot should remain on the *right* side of the canvas about one inch distant from the starting stitch. When the inch on the underside has been covered over by subsequent stitching, the knot is carefully cut off. After the launching, when a new piece of yarn is started, you simply thread the yarn in and out of solidly worked areas on the underside of the canvas. For extra security, reverse the direction of the interweaving for a half inch or so. This method of weaving in and out applies to fastening off, too.

5. When trying out a complicated new stitch, concentrate on its construction. Unless it is a simple procedure, do not attempt to make a reverse journey back after doing one line; let professional embroiderers jeer, but return on the underside to the starting margin and begin your new stitch again. You will need time to acquire confidence. After you have mastered the structure of the stitch, you can plan the return trip. If you are working a very long line, fasten down your yarn on the back when you reach the end, cut it off, and return to the starting base. Don't try to absorb too many ideas simultaneously. It can be discouraging and it is unnecessary.

6. Some stitches require lighter or heavier yarn, which means more or fewer strands in the needle. You will have to determine this by seeing how well you are covering your canvas. Keep a piece of identically gauged canvas handy for tryout when you have doubts. Advice here would be impractical because you will be using differ-

ent canvases, yarns, and stitches. The thickness of yarn needed is not always in proportion to the length of the stitch. Some of the short vertical and horizontal stitches, like Brick, do not cover well and may require thicker yarn or more strands than the longer stitches do. Slanted stitches, on the other hand, can be worked in fewer strands.

7. I have adapted a great number of stitches from work other than conventional needlepoint. Many of these stitches seemed illogically glued to other categories by traditional usage. If I thought a stitch from "lace filling" work or darning work or pulled work would serve the canvas well, I tried it. If it performed well, I designed a square to be diagramed. Many stitches were simply not arranged for a counted ground, and I adapted them.

8. Prolonged concentration on geometric construction led to some stitch inventions of my own, which I have so designated for the traditionalist who wishes to remain within historic boundaries. Some of these may have led good healthy lives before. If so, they have been reincarnated. Experiment in embroidery and stitching is considered by many to be heresy. But we are dealing with yarn structure, not religion. If you are inclined to speculative curiosity, by all means have a go.

9. Certain stitches are conventionally designated for only penelope (double-thread) canvas (*see* page 73). It is quite simple to adapt them to mono canvas and I have done so. Other stitches, Web, for example, were too minute, and painstaking to work in their usual presentation, therefore I adapted them by rescaling.

10. All stitches demand your concentrated attention. There can be no Mme. Defarges in needlepoint, so do leave your canvas at home when you attend your next guillotining or other social events.

11. Don't get gluttonous or delirious about stitches. It is very satisfying to work out one good design in one absolutely appropriate stitch. Be especially careful when planning a large, important piece. Decide which elements should dominate, do not allow color, texture, and design to battle for preeminence. That is *your* decision to

make, not theirs, and you must make it in the planning. Make certain that the texture produced by your selected stitch is suited to its job. Use restraint or your stitch vocabulary will produce a babble.

12. Stitches have unashamedly grabbed each other's names over the centuries. Some must have checkered pasts, for they have many mysterious aliases. I have always selected the one closest to the construction when this was possible. Example: Crossed Corners instead of Rice, Detached Chain instead of Lazy Daisy.

13. Handcraft responds best to respectful treatment. Esteem your materials, make orderly housing for your yarn, whenever possible keep colors numbered for reordering. Keep hands and needle clean, yarn untwisted.

14. If you blunder in work or color, rip. It's not a waste of time, you can learn from it. A tweezers and a pair of sharp small scissors help. Don't let a poorly worked area spoil a piece of good work. And don't fret. It's happened to the best.

15. Never use ripped yarn over again. Never.

16. If, by mischance, you cut a canvas thread, don't panic. The situation is crucial but not fatal. Restructure your canvas as near to its original form as you can by re-interlacing its threads; hold these together with fine sewing thread. Then cut a piece of canvas, identical gauge, slightly larger in size than that of the disturbed area; place it *under* the canvas, matching thread to thread, hole to hole exactly. Bind together by sewing with fine sewing cotton. Then stitch as usual. The extra piece of canvas will not disturb the surface of your work, because it lies beneath the ground you are working. Therefore, you will have no bump. Needless to say, make every effort to avoid the mishap and resultant doctoring by using your scissors most cautiously.

17. There are certain stitches, like Chain, that can be used to follow a curved or angled outline exactly. This is the embroidery method. The stitch, in other words, is worked in parallel conformation to the outline. Or you may prefer, as I do, to use stitches in the manner

of weaving, which disregards the outline, maintains its own structure, and is, in fact, intercepted by the outline. The two are very different in approach and it is usually advisable to be consistent.

18. Be sparing with color if you wish to feature stitches and texture strongly. If you want to turn them into absolute stars, work in monotone. Pale tones show texture most clearly.

19. I have made a few changes in stitch construction, which you will come upon in the diagrams. The alterations are based on logic and, in my opinion, increase facility. In the case of Rococo Stitch, my method is entirely unconventional. I suspect that I may actually be reviving a lost technique. Rococo, used beautifully by seventeenth-century English and French embroiderers for complex geometric patterns, is a simple development of a form of up-and-down Buttonhole as I have structured it; this system preserves intact the form of the stitch but increases tension and stabilizes the pulled thread. This enlarges the perforation, an essential element, and makes the hole easier to achieve and maintain. Mrs. Lane and I shared the responsibility of numbering the diagrams. Some of my sequential arrangements, especially for those patterns stressing perforation, may seem peculiar (Diagram 292 for example), but their order protects the architectural and textural schemes of the designs.

20. If you wish to save on yarn, don't cut corners with stitch formation. Relinquish silk, gold, and silver. They are the most costly and are rarely vital to the scheme of needlepoint composition. Wool sufficed for the most beautiful Flemish tapestries; it is the hardiest of the yarns and, I think, the most dignified. All yarns make their valuable contributions owing to their particular and distinctive properties, but wool alone is indispensable.

21. In one form of stitching, you must use economy in yarn placement. It would be folly to work laid stitches by extravagantly (and needlessly) duplicating the surface yarn on the underside. The Diagram will show you how to be sparing of yarn without injuring form.

22. When working a very large piece, a rug or a hanging, the un-

wieldiness of the large area of canvas sometimes makes it necessary to use the two-move, two-hand system of stitching. Usually the left hand stays above the canvas, to make the downward thrust, and the right hand below to propel the needle up. It is a relay method, right hand receiving from the left and vice versa. It is also the frame method, because one-move stitching is made impossible by tautly held material. I have been told that the Royal School of Needlework in London holds that this is the preferred method for all needle-work, framed or not, because it produces a more evenly textured surface. Should you find yourself resorting to this system, you will notice that harsh new canvas is abrasive and that the knuckles of the hand underneath the canvas will begin to smart after a while. To avoid this injury, which makes work unpleasurable, wear an old, soft cotton glove from which you have cut the fingers. Your freedom of movement will not be impaired and you will have a protective shield. The canvas will become pliable with more handling and you will be able to dispense with the glove.

23. I do not like to see metal or wooden frames superimposed upon needleworked hangings. These frames introduce extraneous and alien elements that run counter to the suppleness of the material they surround. Hangings are part of the textile family and, even when small, they should be suspended on the wall in the manner used for carpets and tapestries. If you wish to have a decorative frame around your work, plan for it when composing your design and stitch it on your canvas. Should a pronounced contrast between field and frame be required, a careful selection of stitches or tones will give satisfactory results. Articles in the textile families should be allowed to live and breathe, and to receive the warmth of human touch, so try to avoid putting them behind glass—unless you must offer this protection to ancient specimens that would otherwise disintegrate.

24. I have called stitches simple geometry in yarn. This may put off women who regard mathematics as male territory. In actuality, and throughout history, women have been responsible for much if not most of the geometric textilework so highly regarded today. We

associate this sex with quilting, pieced patchwork, lacemaking, and complex knitting. We do not realize that tribal women in Turkestan, the Caucausus, Turkey, and Persia are the creators of the truly extraordinary carpets, saddle bags, tent furnishings, and camel rugs of the Middle East and that the hands of Navajo Indian women fashioned and manufactured their distinguished blankets and rugs. All of these present geometric pattern in its most elegant and useful form. Men may appreciate these articles, bid them up at auction, pay dearly in high-priced shops and galleries, become proud collectors and dealers, but women designed and made them. When the disorderliness of war, plague, or privation brought terror and uncertainty, it is possible that women sought a measure of comfort in the serene logic of geometric formality. It stands in opposition to chaos and it is indisputable that women have used it magnificently. Even today, I find that many women respond to geometric design more readily than men. Some do this unconsciously, just as many people cook without realizing that they are dealing with basic chemistry. That the kitchen is a laboratory or the canvas a mathematically structured ground should in no way discourage their being used with inventiveness, taste, and joy.

9) Tools and Materials

CANVAS

CANVAS IS THE NAME we give to the woven material used for needlepoint work. It is rectilinear, composed of warp and weft (horizontal and vertical threads). The lines of these warp and weft threads form open squares, whose sizes vary with the spacing of the threads. This variation in alignment is called gauge. The gauge of the canvas I have used for the sampler squares worked in the book is fourteen threads (stitches, when they are covered singly) to the inch. Canvas can be bought by the yard and is available in a large range of gauges. The higher the thread count to the inch, the finer the canvas. The finer the canvas, the smaller the stitch. The fourteen-gauge canvas is suited to stitch sampler work for a variety of reasons. A lower count, ten or twelve threads to the inch, produces a coarser canvas and a concomitant coarseness in pattern and stitch. I find the time saved by using the larger-gauge canvas negligible and I think some stitches look unrefined on this scale. Sixteen- or eighteen-thread-to-the-inch canvas can be found in some shops and will produce a fine, elegant patterned surface. It will also allow for an increased number of repeats in diapering when you work within a limited area. They require more time but give good value for extra labor. Some workers find that ground material this fine strains the eyes. There is no need to make your work unpleasant with eye strain or headache. Fourteen-gauge will do very nicely for any small-scale pattern arrangement.

Buy the best quality you can find, as the canvas will be your partner in many long hours of toil. For durability, regularity, and reliability of thread count, I have found that French canvas is the most dependable. The dignity and strength of flax or linen threads are no longer available to us, but we can expect manufacturers to supply adequate materials. Some canvas is unsatisfactory because it is heavily coated with sizing, and when manipulated, the sizing relaxes, the material turns thin and limp, the hands sticky. Sizing should be used judiciously to keep the warp and weft threads stable and not to disguise deficiencies.

Inspect your canvas and refuse material with knotted breaks. The knots may give with the stress of work or blocking. They also produce an untidy surface, because they distort the stitches worked over them and remain stubbornly visible no matter how hard you try to conceal them.

French canvas is made in double-thread or single-thread structure. Double is called penelope and single is called mono. Penelope allows you to split the threads for smaller-scale stitching. Ten-to-the-inch penelope becomes twenty when it is split. Some people like to work their canvases in both scales—we usually call this *gros* and *petit* point. Mono is easier and cooperates extremely well with almost all stitches. All the stitches diagramed in this book were worked on mono canvas. You usually have a choice of white or ecru. This is a matter of taste. Some people find the white ground glaring and tiring to the eye. Others find the presence of an ecru ground disturbing to yarn colors. If you are working with white yarn, you will see it more clearly on the ecru background. Beige yarn patterns will be given clearer definition by a white ground. Remember that the color of the canvas will become part of your design if you use stitches that leave some of the ground exposed, as in Darning or Pulled Yarn. In this case, the tone will be an important consideration.

Before starting to stitch, you will have to deal with the cut edges of the canvas or they will ravel. Sew them down or bind them with masking tape. Do this carefully so that there are no loose canvas threads. They are harsh and will be magnetic traps for your yarn if you let them stay unconfined.

If you are planning an extra-large piece, like a carpet or hanging, you may find the conventional width—approximately thirty-six inches—is too narrow for your design. To avoid the difficult and arduous chore of sewing two pieces together, try to use French canvas in the sixty-inch (approximately) width. It is manufactured in ecru penelope and is to be had in eight and nine threads to the inch, a good gauge for most carpet designs and appropriate stitches; it is firm and hardy.

Canvas is a dignified material because it is well manufactured, tough, durable, and, to my eye, handsome.

FRAMES

Embroidery frames are manufactured in graded sizes. Their stretchers hold your working material taut. This makes for easier blocking because your now-rigid canvas will resist the pull of your stitch, and distortion is kept minimal. Frames are not in general use today and I see no particular need to revive them. Correct blocking will counterbalance warpage more than adequately.

If you do wish to try a frame after having learned without, you will have to adjust your working method; the firm tension of the framed canvas will not cooperate with the conventional one-hand, one-move technique of stitching. You will be relinquishing old habits for new, so allow time for a little practice. One hand must ply the needle from above the canvas while the other remains underneath for reciprocal moves.

I do own one floor-standing, inexpensive, assemble-at-home model, which occasionally serves as a support for a really heavy piece. When working on a large carpet, I have too often found that my left arm and shoulder become strained and cramped from the strong, gravitational pull of the worked canvas. When this occurs, I toss the carpet on top of the frame, keeping the immediate work area free and near my lap. It's more useful than a table because it is open, except for stretchers and bars, and it is adjustable in height and tilt. I do not, however, make the intended use of the stretchers at all. The frame really replaces my aching arm as a support.

THE NEEDLE

You will be using what is called a tapestry needle by its manufacturers. It has a long eye, which houses your yarn without undue compression, and a blunt point, which prevents the splitting of canvas thread and injury to yarn and fingers. No substitute will serve so, if you're a misplacer, keep a supply on hand.

The numbers on the packet describe the needle's thickness and the size of the eyes. Your choice depends on your yarn, not your canvas; make certain that your needle accommodates the yarn. Oversize needles allow too much yarn slippage, and will push canvas threads out of place. Undersize needles will felt your yarn, fray it, and be difficult to thread. When stitching, move the position of the yarn within the eye so that the pressure point changes: otherwise, the yarn may break off with steady pulling.

Keep your needle clean and smooth by stabbing it into a pincushion containing emery or another abrasive, or wash it with fine steel wool and soap. Or, if you are lazy, take a new one when you notice that the old has become resistant to smooth manipulation or that it has darkened. A needle in poor condition will slow down your work and soil it too. Clean tools, clean hands, clean materials: a basic rule. I know it sounds like kindergarten but many have ignored it and damaged their work.

I rarely use any but a size eighteen or twenty needle. I have often read that a bigger needle will proportionately enlarge the perforations in Pulled Yarn work. This theory is better in principle than in practice. When the eye size is increased, the yarn slides about too easily, traction is reduced, and so is the size of the perforation. Your puncture points can be made as large as you wish with the ordinary needle. All you need is a strong tug and, most important, thin yarn.

Needlemakers seem to be manufacturing a fairly uniform product. At least I have not encountered much variation in standards. I was once given a fourteen-carat-gold needle by a friend. It must have led a very privileged life. After a few Tent Stitches, it lay broken in my palm, proving, I suppose, that a tool when it's gold is soon parted. So stay with steel.

YARN

The most widely accepted and easily available yarn for needleworked canvas is made of wool. Wool is indispensable because of its versatility, strength, and utility. It responds beautifully to dye and handles well. Its qualities are such that there is no reason to feel unhappy if this service-able and fine yarn is the only one your shop stocks. For stitch variety, which depends so much on the clear delineation of architecture, I suggest that you try to find wool that is fairly smooth—unfuzzy and untextured. Different stitches will demand thicker or thinner yarn, so you must use yarn that has either fine strands that can be threaded together (Crewel or Médicis) or a thicker yarn (Persian or Worsted) that is divisible into thinner strands. Below, I list the woolen yarns I have used happily:

MÉDICIS FRENCH WOOL

Very desirable for sampler work, this wool is exceptionally fine, smooth, and agreeable to work with. It lends itself to geometric small-scale pattern. A very distinguished product. However, it is not yet available in all stores, delivery dates are not always honored in Paris, its fine colors are limited to tones that conform to those in medieval Flemish tapes-tries (which is as close to vegetable dye as you are likely to get un-less you produce your own), and, because of its delicacy, you may ex-perience an occasional break—it sometimes does not withstand the friction of the canvas thread. Used in relatively short lengths, it does not fray. It must not be exposed to exceptionally hard wear, so it is not a sensible choice for carpets, although I say this with regret, for its tones would be perfect. I am partial to it, as is Mrs. Lane. We have both used it, along with silk, for the large hangings in the photographs. Most of my samplers were worked in this yarn or in silk, or both.

APPLETON CREWEL WOOL

Slightly thicker than Médicis, made in England. The color range is wonderful, many of its dyes being based on those in antique English embroidery and carpets. It is stronger than Médicis but has a slight twist.

76

FOR NEEDLEPOINT CANVAS

I have used it for samplers and, in multistrands, for carpets when I could not find the right shade in stronger yarn. It is very reliable in quality and wear. But it is not easy to obtain in the United States. There are some shops that carry it in small skeins. You may order hanks from London stores. They have supplied many people in the United States and will not find an American order a novelty.

PATERNAYAN PERSIAN (AMERICAN) WOOL

The best wearing of the wools. It is three ply and you may add or subtract strands as need dictates. It has a good sheen and is without doubt the yarn of choice for all carpet work. It has a slightly hairy texture but if you do not mind this, it works very well for samplers or stitches. The color range is wide, if a little vibrant, and you will find it readily available in almost all art needlework shops. It has many virtues and, if you are willing to order in sufficient quantity, you may avail yourself of custom dying. This may be necessary if you need tones of subtlety or mellow restraint. Persian yarn produces a lively, interesting, prismatic surface.

FRENCH AND ENGLISH TAPESTRY WOOL

Both are of high quality in the Bon Pasteur and Appleton lines. They are manufactured in an exceptionally wide color range. Tapestry wool cannot be divided and is too thick to be doubled for most stitches. Therefore, it is best suited to Tent or Brick Stitch.

SILK YARN

Expensive, rather more difficult to work with, it makes a delicate and supple textile when employed for Tent Stitch. It is very handsome in sampler stitch work. All the squares in the samplers I prepared for diagraming are worked in Au Vers à Soie silk. This French silk is seven-stranded and sufficiently hardy for canvas work. The color range is wide and beautiful. It works well into stitches. It is costly but goes further in stitching than one might think. Most stitches on fourteen-gauge canvas require only four strands; Pulled Yarn work requires two, three, or four strands, depending on stitch design and desired effect. However, the brightest, deepest, and darkest tones often bleed when subjected to wetting down for conventional blocking. Unless you block by pinning and steaming, stay away from these shades. When in doubt, test by immersing a strand in water and rubbing on a white handkerchief. If you see color, beware. This silk seems to lose a little luster after exposure to air, but I know of no other silk yarn so well suited to canvas needlework. The dye lots are particularly stable and there are some American shops obliging enough to place orders for you. These special orders are filled from Paris with rare courtesy and dispatch. When using these small skeins of silk, it is a good idea not to remove the label (wrapper). This way, you will keep your silk tidy and you will always have the number when you need to reorder. To do this, carefully cut the knot tying the skein, then pull one end through the wrapper, return to the knotted end of the skein and cut through. You may then extract, from the remaining uncut end, individual strands as you need them.

I have tried English silk floss but its tendency to adhere to the fingers makes for difficulties when working large areas. It has a beautiful glow, which it retains, and is especially good for highlights.

Although one must not combine different fibers to form one strand, you may use silk and wool or silk and embroidery cotton on separate areas of the same piece.

COTTON AND LINEN

They are most suitable for Pulled Yarn work and monotone diaper pattern. Crochet yarn, such as marketed by DMC and Cartier Bresson, is very handsome but not always obtainable. It is made in various thicknesses, which are numbered. I am sorry I have not had time to explore the possibilities of cotton and linen more fully; I do find them very tempting. DMC embroidery cotton may be used with silk as it has a similar sheen. Ordinary string is excellent for Pulled work.

FRENCH GOLD AND SILVER METALLIC YARNS

These are packaged in spools and they are costly and difficult to handle.

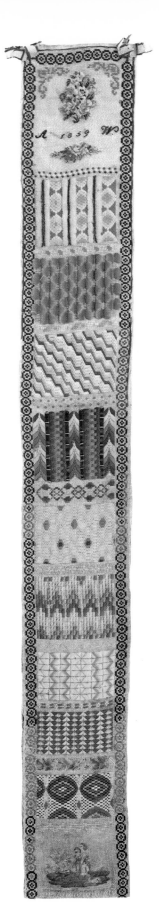

Victorian geometric motif "strip" sampler.

Heraldic field pillow

PLATE 3

Patchwork pillow.

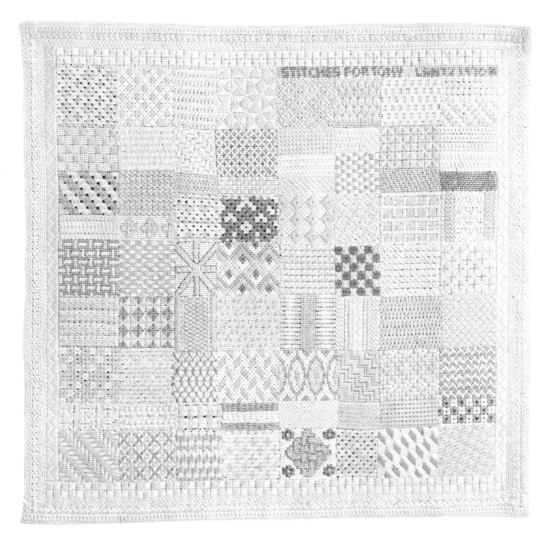

Pastel stitch-and-pattern sampler.

PLATE 4

FOR NEEDLEPOINT CANVAS

They fray, tear, and twist too easily. It is imperative to double over the yarn so that *both* ends may be lodged securely in previous stitches on the reverse side. Metallic yarn is an incorrigible mischief maker and will give you trouble if you do not follow this procedure. If you find that you must use a single strand (not doubled over), I have found that a delicate single knot tied at the very end of the free end (not the end you weave into the underside) is essential if you wish to prevent raveling. You will find that the tiny knot on the thread will not impede the flow of movement through the canvas. It is always advisable to use a wider eye than normal for these yarns, to allow for a free, frictionless glide. Some workers suggest that candle or beeswax be applied to the yarn before use, but I have never done this.

SYNTHETICS

Avoid nylon and rayon yarns. I dislike the phrase "plastic age" because I think it is too frequently applied by those who are unreasoning in their fealty to the past. Technology has brought us both marvels and monsters and we really should discriminate between them. When artificial substances significantly ease life, lend comfort or a measure of repose to those who are overburdened, and permit simplified maintenance without loss of quality, they are utile, fitting and, to me, beautiful. But nylon and rayon simply do not function well for needlepoint canvas. They are too slithery in the hand, look inanimate on the canvas, and do not have a natural spring. Your foundation will probably be made of linen or cotton and the blending of old and new, so intelligent in household furnishing, looks incongruous in needlework. Needlepoint articles do not require frequent cleaning and they are not created by the harried worker with five minutes to spare. They require time, thought, and energy. When we give so much of ourselves, we may as well have the pleasure of using the best and most appropriate materials available to us.

PART III

10) Stitches by Structure

WE WILL NOW BE CONCERNED with the requirements of various stitch groups. Groups are formed by joining individual stitches that share certain basic architectural similarities. It may be considered a tenuous classification because many stitches have overlapping characteristics that could justifiably offer them a place in a number of groups. I have tried to settle them under the heading that seems to describe their most prominent structural feature.

The ideal arrangement for the diagram and sampler plates would have allowed each stitch to be shown first worked in monotone (for learning), then in vari-tone (for patterning), and last in conjunction with other stitches (for more complex texture and design). This would have trebled the size of the book. Therefore, many of the sampler squares are worked in the first, second, or third ways only. After you have learned a stitch, it is a simple matter to transpose it from vari-tone to monotone, whereas the opposite would prove much more difficult. Bear in mind that all stitches look beautiful in monotone samplers because one color emphasizes both their kinship and their distinction from one another.

Stitches have been lovingly manufactured by the hand for countless centuries. Archaeological finds may still bring us many happy surprises. Perhaps you will unearth an unknown stitch through your own exploration and thereby add to a growing repertoire. If I have overlooked any, the slight was unintentional. I have made every effort to be thorough but an inadvertent oversight is unavoidable.

Before concentrating on the architectural families, there are two odd groups and some omissions I would like to give attention to. These are:

COMPOSITE STITCHES

"Composite" is the term used for stitches used in partnership to form other stitches (really, a pattern). At times, the contours of a stitch are not contiguous. Because they do not mesh, another stitch may be added to complete the ground. They may be properly thought of as composites. There are also stitches meant to be used as single ornamental lines or motifs, and these too require the addition of another stitch to cover the remaining ground.

After some experience, you may wish to make composites of your own. I think you will find diversion and education in this. Do combine stitches with some plan or purpose. You may wish to use some that have a strong kinship or you may prefer to stress contrast (high and low textures, smooth and pebbly, delicate and robust). Guard against using too many in one design. Try to avoid slants that do not compensate, but war with each other. Take a piece of scrap canvas and work Tent with Brick, or Mosaic with Upright Cross, to see what is meant by incompatible structures. You may not always arrive at a perfect solution, but you should strive for architectural unity.

There are some stitches with individual names that have become composites. The traditional coupling of these stitches has led to their acquiring a new identity and name, for example, Chequer, Double Cross, Triple Leviathan, and Scottish. I have placed them within the families that adopted them in the past.

84

CREATED STITCHES

I have invented some stitches or treated others with unconventional variations. I was understandably loath to give them too much importance by attaching names to them and have not done so except where their constructions lent themselves to logical labeling. I have marked the invented ones with an asterisk (*) and the adapted ones with a dagger (†) on the diagram pages. When you see this, you will know that it represents a deviation from tradition. The dagger also indicates adaptation from other media (painting, architecture, etc.).

OMISSIONS

Although I have included many stitches not ordinarily suggested for the counted canvas, there are some that resist adaptation. They are either unsuited to geometric patterning or would have too limited an application to warrant inclusion and diagraming. But you may be interested in knowing their names and my reasons for excluding them.

LOOP AND CUT PILE STITCHES

This work is characterized by the formation of long loops that are either retained or scissored into a tufted surface. The pile and loops obscure the outline of stitch and pattern and they have an unpleasing fustian appearance. I find the simulation of velvet pile and carpet loop both unnatural and unappealing. The Victorians loved this style and used it for many designs that are barely discernible because of the fuzziness of the texture. They were addicted to bright, varied coloring, and the motifs worked in this manner look like flattened out mops-in-motley. Many examples are to be found in German, Austrian, English, and American nineteenth-century strip samplers and cushion work.

BEADWORK

Beadwork or sequin work entails the use of an extraneous material. It also demands a different technique. Our book is concerned with results that stem from the use of yarn, canvas, and needle. However, this method

85

of ground ornamentation need not be disdained. Beads and sequins have lent their luster and hard glow to much outstanding embroidery of the past, particularly in Elizabethan England. The National Portrait Gallery in London displays many paintings that reveal the artists' delight in beadwork at its most intricate and refined stage. We can marvel at the complexity and sumptuousness of these details but I doubt that we would wish to reproduce them today. The American Indian tribes, on the other hand, made beads an integral component of their less complicated patterns and it would be hard to envision their garments without the adamantine, luminous geometric surface produced in this manner. Many of our museums own substantial collections of these articles. Their sunny, robust designs have a great deal to teach us. Last, and least, is the extravagant vulgarity of the overencrusted gargantuan flowers and arch landscapes that appear in Victorian times. Again we see their makers being wayward in color, texture, and composition. Well, perhaps one can admire their vigorous and prolific labors. There is something disarming about such intense devotion and industriousness.

I have no experience with bead work. To give you some idea of its look, I have photographed two pillows in my possession. One is American, the other East Indian; both were made in the nineteenth century. Beads and sequins (used in the mosaic opaque glass tesseral technique) would be marvelously exciting materials for the diaper-pavement designs from the sampler.

NEEDLE PAINTING

Needle painting was known in the past as *Opus Plumarium*, for its resemblance to plumage. This method, exquisitely employed by Chinese, English, and French embroiderers, uses delicate satin (Flat Stitch) shading, usually in radiant silk, and imitates brush painting with its feathery, multidirected strokes. It demands the greatest manual dexterity and delicacy. Perhaps it should be left to the professional. In any case, it is outside our terrain because the square has no place at all in its composition. It adheres to a naturalistic line and the stitches follow the arrangement of representational art. A soft ground cloth is essential because it must succumb to the needle wherever the worker directs it.

19th-century beadwork, U.S. Collection S. Lantz.

19th-century beadwork, India. Collection S. Lantz.

BLACK WORK

This work can be distinguished only by its use of color. As the name suggests, it is carried out by embroidering black thread onto a white ground. It needs no special technique or stitching. Black yarn outlines form a pattern and the white ground represents the rest of the design. If the idea attracts you, you may use simple flat and cross stitches. They should not be ornate or complicated because stitches are subordinate to the black yarn and white ground. It lends itself very well to geometric forms.

DOUBLE RUNNING OR HOLBEIN STITCH

Running stitches, dark on light or light on dark, are applied for geometric or free patterning. They are not well suited to the canvas because they leave so much ground uncovered. English embroiderers of the sixteenth and seventeenth centuries made deft and striking use of this style, particularly for garment detail and textile borders.

STUMPWORK

I have described this padded, hyper-adorned work in another area of the book and may already have injured the feelings of those who are devoted to it. So I will say no more except that the techniques required are special and specific, and instructions on the subject may be found under the above name in many embroidery books. There may be some books given exclusively to this form of work, but I have not seen them. *See* page 23.

THE SAMPLER SQUARES AND
THE DIAGRAMS

The design and execution of the needlework squares, the technical and historical notes are by Sherlee Lantz. Those stitches and patterns invented by Mrs. Lantz are so designated by an asterisk (*); those that she adapted from other media or re-interpreted from photographed needlework are marked with a dagger (†).

The design and execution of the diagrams are by Maggie Lane.

The numbers (or letters) on the diagram indicate the entry (up) point for the needle. There are a few instances where it was necessary to indicate the exit point (down) also, this was done by adding an a to the number (1a).

Whenever possible, white starting dots have been provided so that your eye will be immediately directed to the initial stitch (1) or (A). The dot is not meant to represent an entry point for the needle; it is a convenience for fast orientation. If the first stitch must be started amongst many surrounding stitches, which allows no neighboring square to serve as ground, the dot has been omitted.

Some stitches, especially those in the Interlaced-Herringbone and Woven groups, require a weaving action; that is, the needle and yarn move under, or under and over, previously worked stitches without penetrating the canvas itself. This action is indicated by the presence of arrows placed just before and after the weaving points.

89

11) Patterns

MOSAICS

The historical patterns have been placed first to keep them close to the history that preceded them, and because many may be made with simple Flat Stitches that do not require extensive knowledge or experience. These designs (Mosaics, Medieval Grounds, Islamic Brick, Historical Samplers) are followed by the stitches themselves, which I have worked in monotone or pattern toning. If you find a difficult or unfamiliar stitch in the historical groups (the stitches employed are named), consult the index where the stitch diagrams best suited for learning are listed.

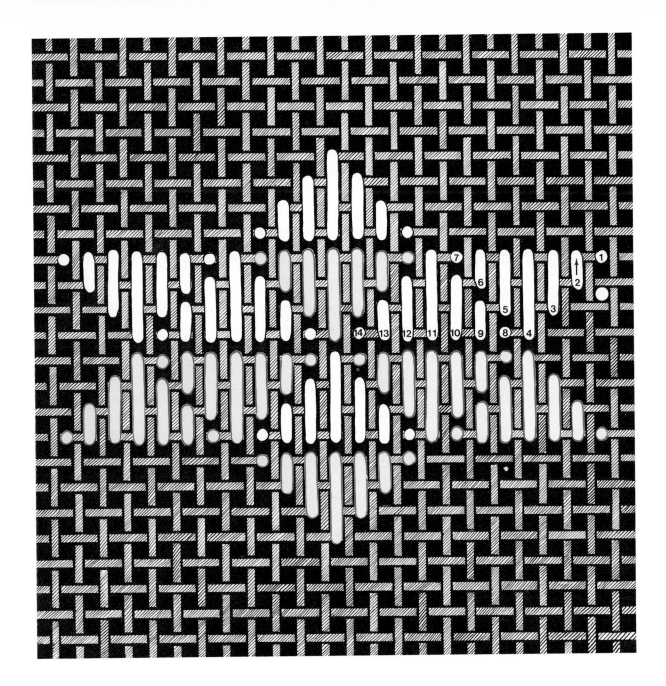

STITCH: FLAT *(Flat)*

DESIGN:[†] Mosaic pavement, 13th century, the Baptistery, Florence.

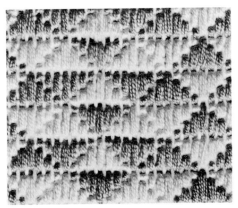

DIAGRAM 1

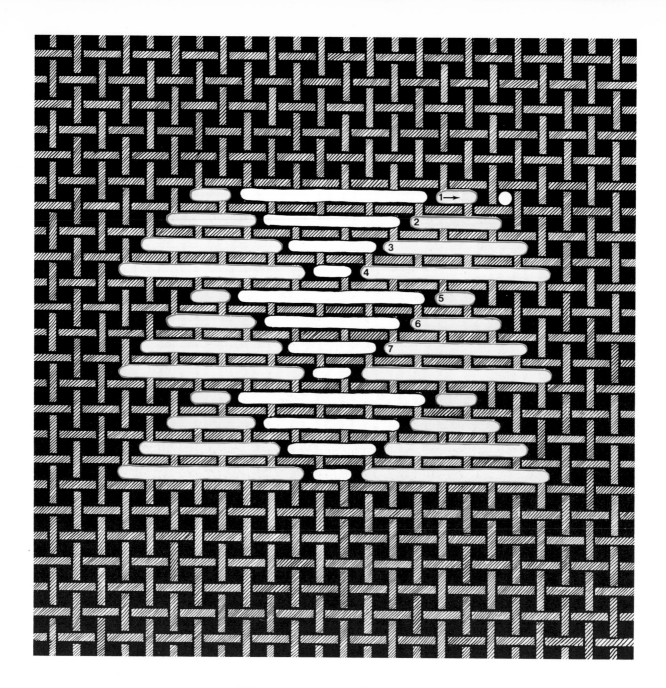

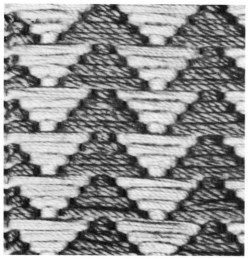

STITCH: FLAT *(Flat)*

DESIGN:[†] 1. 13th-century mosaic pavement, the Baptistery, Florence; 2. Franco-Flemish medieval embroidery, pavement design; 3. This pattern is called Wild Goose Chase in American patchwork quilting.

STITCH: FLAT *(Flat)*

DESIGN:† Medieval Mosaic, San Marco Cathedral, Venice. Many of the San Marco mosaics make use of three-dimensional *trompe l'oeil* effects. Three tones of brown (light to dark) and white were used, *see* Color Plate 2, upper left area.

DIAGRAM 3

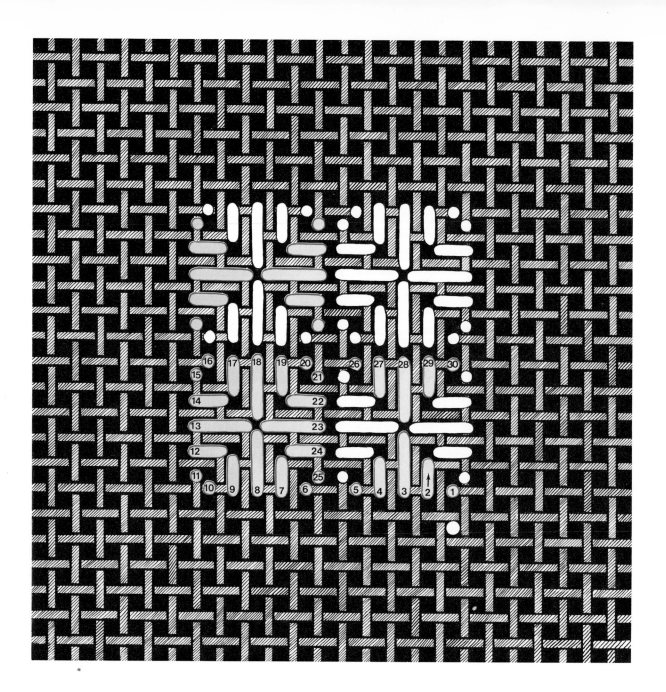

STITCH: FLAT *(Flat)*

DESIGN:[†] 1. Star pattern from 14th-century Sienese painting, Madonna of Humility, mosaic detail (dark and light toning reversed), Philadelphia Museum of Art; 2. Roman mosaic pavement, Museo Antichita, Trieste; 3. Marble panel, 13th century, Santa Maria Church, Rome; 4. Called Ohio Star (and sometimes Shoo Fly) in American patchwork quilting.

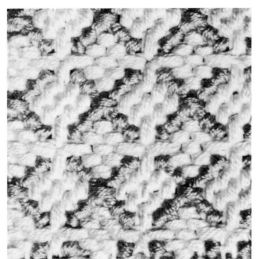

STITCH: FLAT *(Flat)*. FILLER: UPRIGHT CROSS *(Cross)*

DESIGN:[+] 1. Wall design from the Wilton Diptych, 1380, The National Gallery, London; 2. Hugo van der Goes painting, 15th century, in reverse shading, Kaiser Friedrich Museum, Berlin.

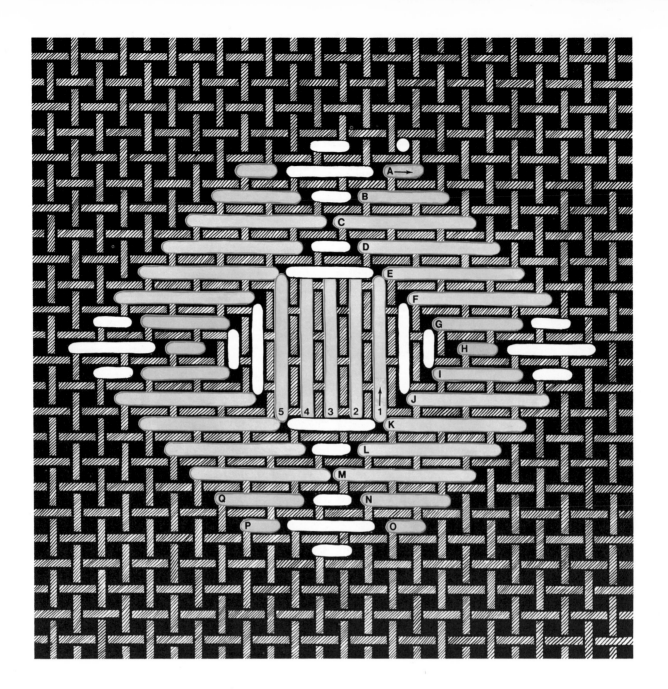

STITCH: FLAT *(Flat)*

DESIGN:[†] Medieval mosaic, Siena Cathedral. In the
original, the diagonal bars are slightly narrower;
otherwise the sampler square duplicates the pattern.

DIAGRAM 6

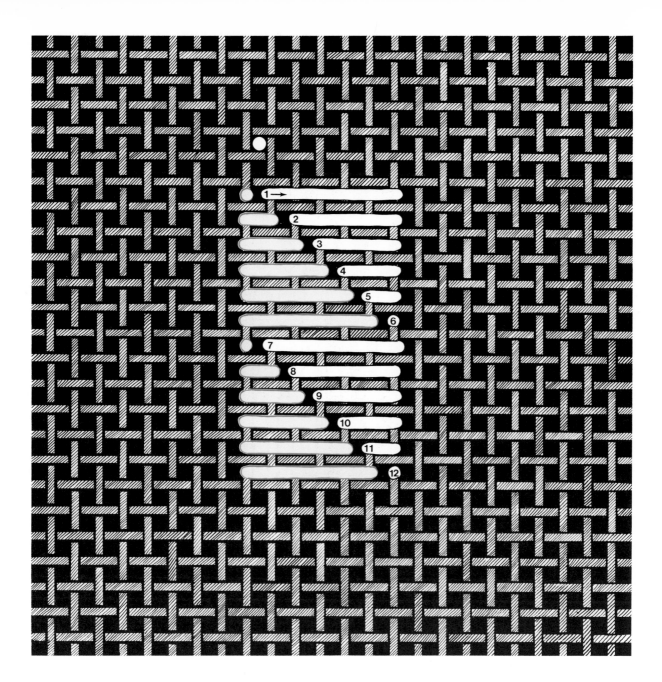

STITCH: Flat (*Flat*)

DESIGN:[†] One of the most frequently used medieval pavement motifs. 1. St. Martin and St. Hilaire, medieval Franco-Flemish embroidery, Lehman Collection, New York; 2. Bedford Trend, mosaic motif, medieval miniature painting; 3. Tobacco pouch, Northwest Cameroon; 4. In American patchwork quilt patterning this is sometimes called Birds in the Air. It is also one of the designs formed in Log Cabin quilting, called Straight Furrow by some collectors.

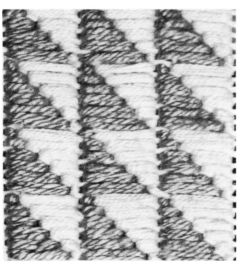

DIAGRAM 7

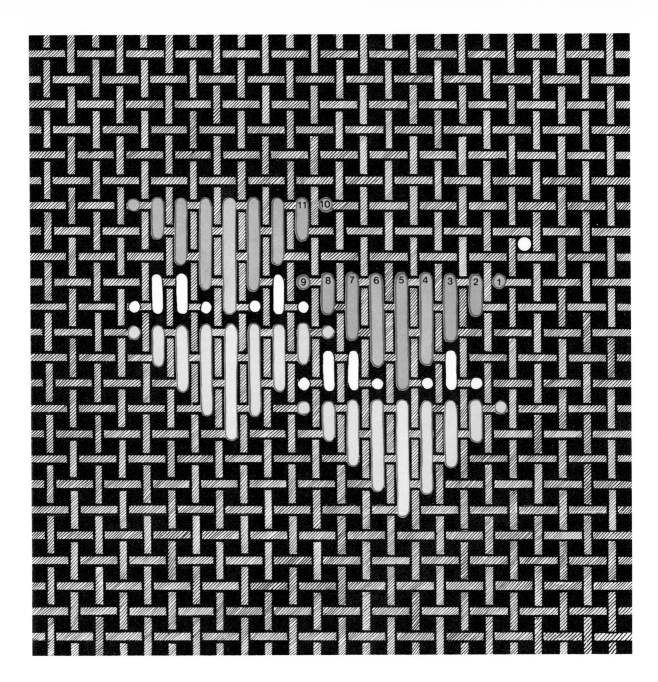

STITCH: FLAT (*Flat*)

DESIGN:[†] Stepped Triangles. From French medieval mosaic pavement study. Rescaling larger would enhance the pattern.

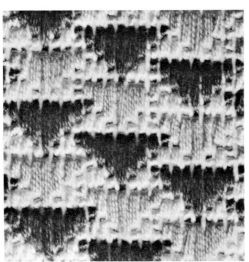

DIAGRAM 8

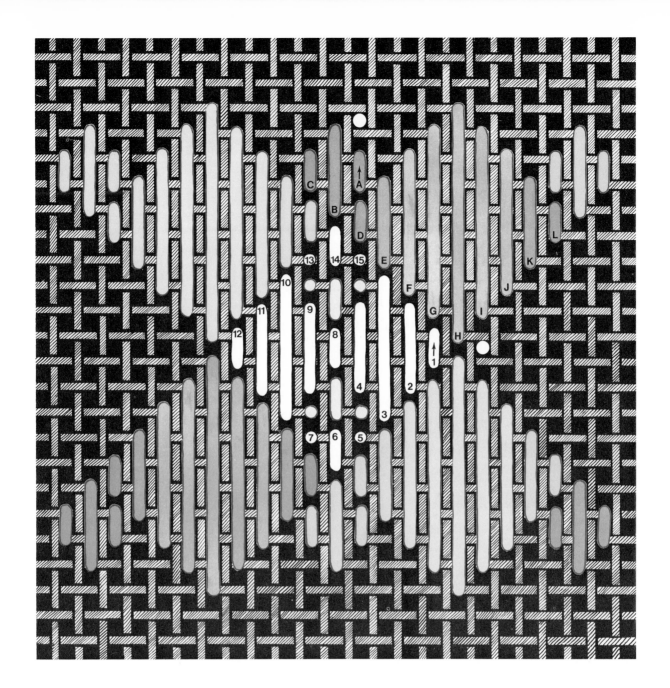

STITCH: FLAT *(Flat)*

DESIGN:[†] Border pattern, Norman-Moorish medieval
pavement mosaic, La Capella di San Pietro, Palermo.

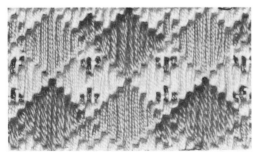

DIAGRAM 9

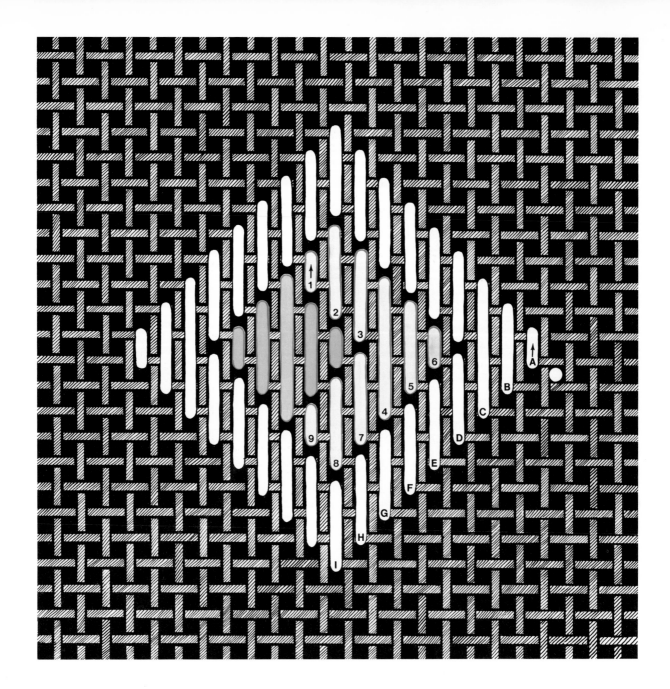

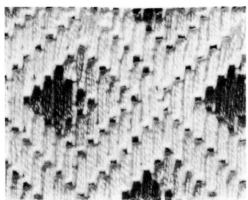

STITCH: FLAT (*Flat*)

DESIGN:[†] 1. From a mosaic pavement design, Pompeii, c. 1st century. It is a handsome diaper pattern but it has no breathing space in the area allowed on my sampler square. More repeats will allow it to develop properly; 2. Khamsa of Nizami, pavement (unshaded), 16th century, Persian manuscript painting, Metropolitan Museum of Art.

DIAGRAM 10

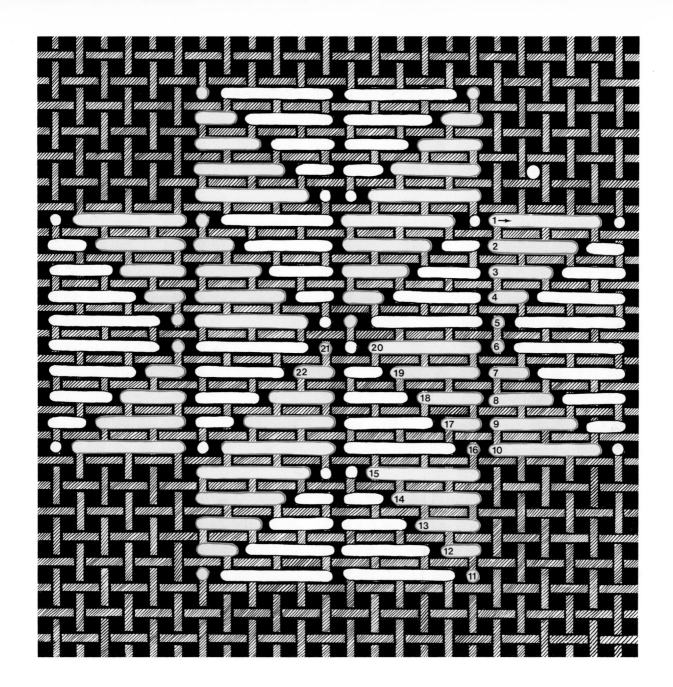

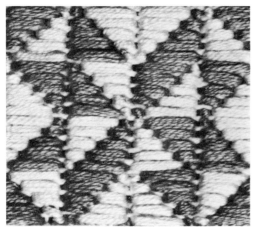

STITCH: FLAT *(Flat)*

DESIGN:[†] French medieval pavement mosaic. In American patchwork quilting this design is known as the Pierced Star.

DIAGRAM 11

STITCH: Flat *(Flat)*

DESIGN:[†] Pavement mosaic in a 14th-century miniature painting by Boucicaut.

STITCH: FLAT *(Flat).* FILLER: CROSS *(Cross)*

DESIGN:[†] An interesting pattern adapted from the wall motif of a French medieval manuscript painting.

DIAGRAM 13

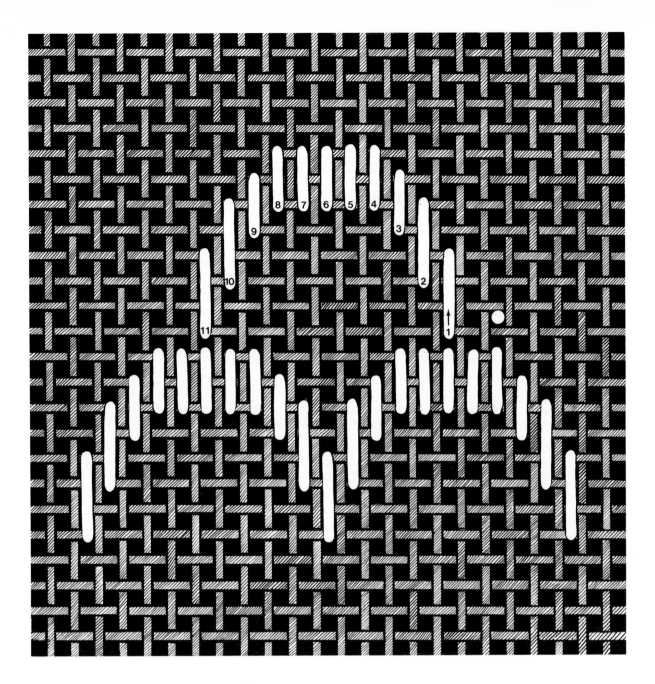

STITCH: FLAT *(Flat)*. FILLER DAMASK DARN *(Flat)*

DESIGN:[†] 1. 1st-century Pompeiian mosaic pavement;
2. Canterbury Arch, England, 12th century; 3. This
pattern is known as Clam Shell in 19th-century patchwork quilting. Other stitches may be used for the filler.
Rescaling is quite simple.

STITCH: FLAT *(Flat)*

DESIGN:[†] 1. Architectural detail, c. 12th–13th century, Rochester Cathedral, Kent; 2. Biblia Pauperum, The Incredulity of St. Thomas, c. 1450, mosaic pavement design, Munich Library; 3. New Caledonian wood-carving pattern.

STITCH: FLAT *(Flat)*. FILLER: CROSS *(Cross)*

DESIGN:[†] Framed Crosses. I cannot remember the specific source for this design, but I adapted it from a wall pattern in a medieval French illuminated manuscript.

                                                          DIAGRAM 16

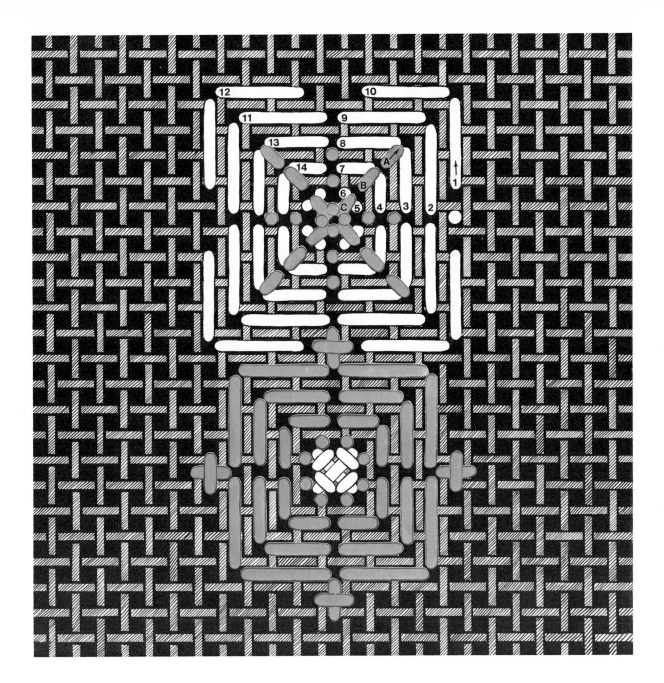

STITCH: FLAT *(Flat)*, CROSSED CORNERS *(Cross)*,
BACK *(Flat)*

The perforations in the paler white Flat Stitch are only
partially Back Stitched. The small white centers in
the dark motif are made with Cross Corners Stitch.
Back Stitches are *always* worked last.

DESIGN:[†] 18th-century Chinese Box, private collection,
Berlin. This pattern is frequently used in Egyptian,
Anatolian-Islamic, and medieval European paintings
and textiles.

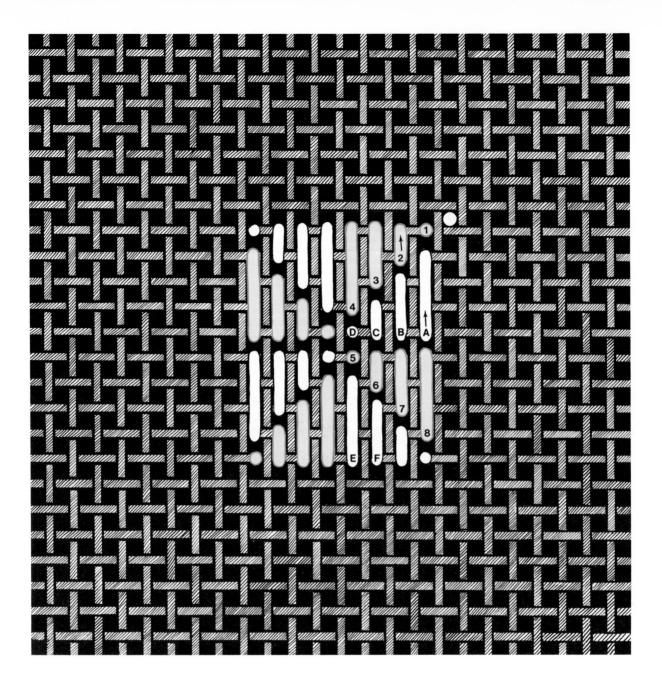

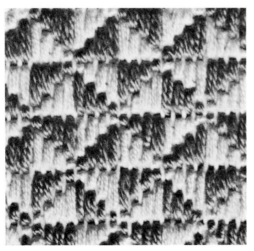

STITCH: FLAT (*Flat*)

DESIGN:[†] A popular and famous mosaic design. 1. The Tournai tapestry, St. Piat, Tournai Cathedral, Order of the Golden Fleece embroidery, pavement pattern, Künsthistorisches Museum collection, Vienna; 2. African textile, Völkerkunde Museum, Berlin; 3. In American patchwork quilting this design is known as Windmills. These uncomplicated counterchange triangle patterns have a surprisingly dynamic effect. They are peculiarly strong and optically memorable—especially in view of their utter simplicity. This particular pattern may be found in medieval and early Renaissance painting throughout Europe.

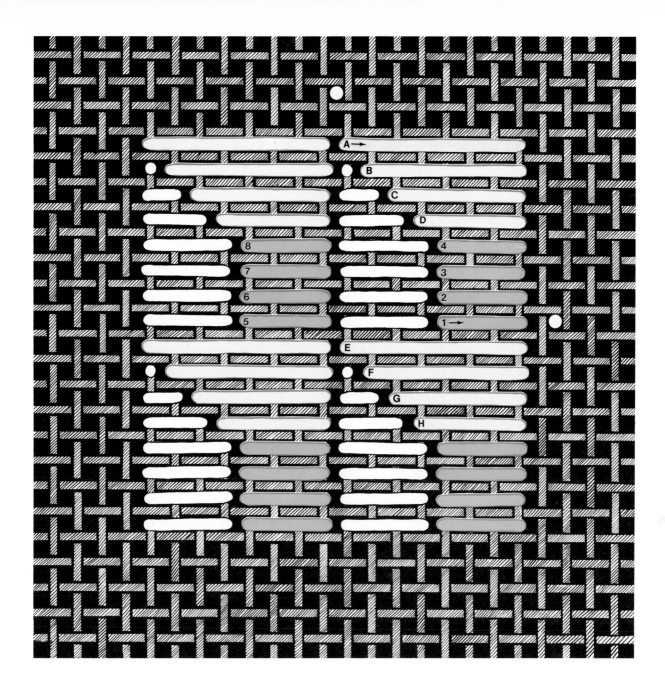

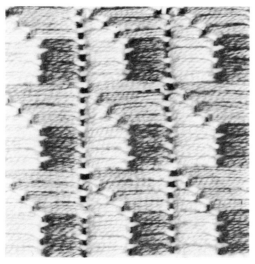

STITCH: FLAT *(Flat)*

DESIGN:[†] Mosaic pavement, 12th-century France. This design has a slight relief effect (boxes) when toned carefully.

DIAGRAM 19

STITCH: FLAT *(Flat)*

DESIGN:[†] Medieval French mosaic pavement.

DIAGRAM 20

Norman-Moorish mosaic pavement.

PLATE 5

St. George and the Dragon pillow.

Medieval interlacement sampler.

PLATE 6

STITCH: RAISED SQUARE *(Cross)*, SQUARE MOSAIC *(Flat)*, and LARGE UPRIGHT CROSS *(Cross)* trebled

DESIGN:[†] 16th-century Russian painted icon. This strongly contrasted pattern entirely covers an ecclesiastical costume fabric. The earlier Byzantine tradition of using geometric design, without regard for body contours or fabric folds, was continued in Russia through later centuries. Many varied and bold diaper patterns may be seen on the costumes in these paintings.

DIAGRAM 21

STITCH: FLAT *(Flat)*

DESIGN:[†] A very common mosaic pattern, also found in almost all the 19th-century needlework geometric motif samplers. The pattern was frequently shaded in pastel floral tones, and four circles were used to represent one flower. This design, when confined to a single row, is known as the Spool border in patchwork quilting.

DIAGRAM 22

STITCH: FLAT *(Flat)*

DESIGN:[†] Counterchange pattern from a French medieval mosaic pavement. It may be shown to better advantage by scaling a little larger.

DIAGRAM 23

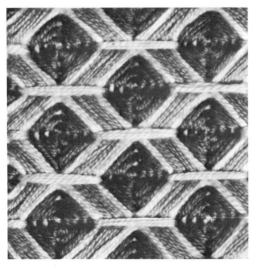

STITCH: FLAT *(Flat)*

DESIGN:† An exact transfer to canvas of a 12th-century Roman mosaic pavement. It illustrates the Roman habit of using optical illusion for relief effect. Amusing to design, but awkward for the balance of the walker. Compare this hexagonal pattern with Diagram 32.

DIAGRAM 24

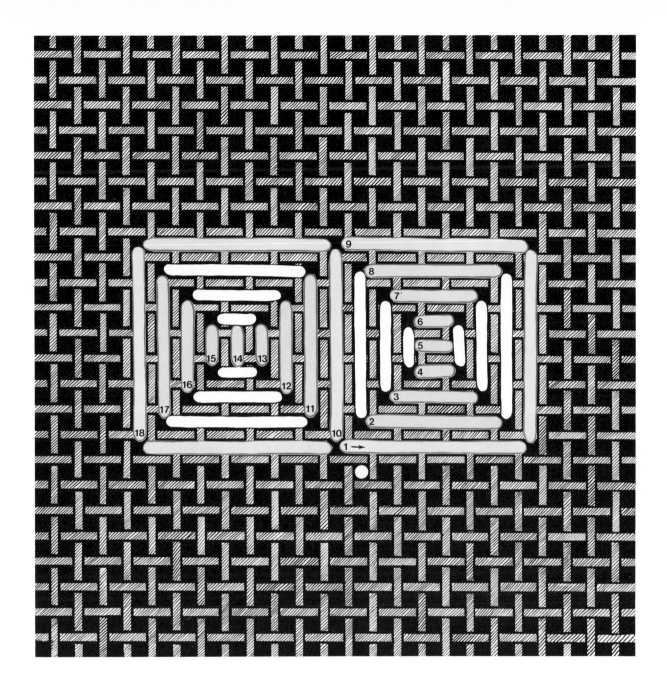

STITCH: FLAT *(Flat)*

DESIGN:† 1. Pompeiian mosaic pavement, c. 1st century; 2. Franco-Flemish embroidery motif, 15th century; 3. In American patchwork quilting it is called Yankee Puzzle. Log Cabin quilts are sometimes arranged in related design. When used in single rows for quilt borders it is called Spools.

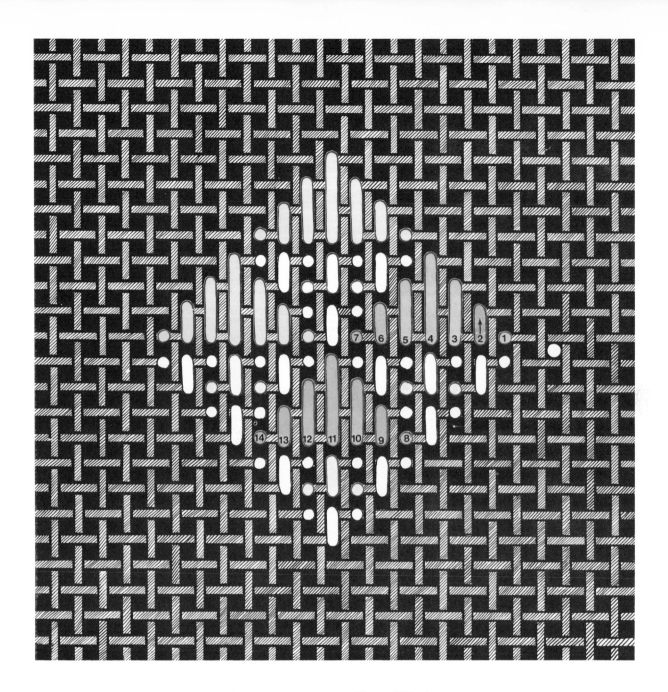

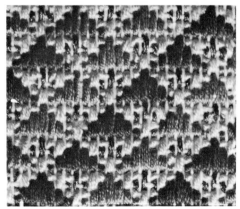

STITCH: Flat *(Flat)*

DESIGN:[†] Norman-Moorish medieval mosaic, La Capella di San Pietro, Palermo. It may be better to make the triangles larger so that the small gold subsidiary triangles (within the white triangle) are more clearly defined.

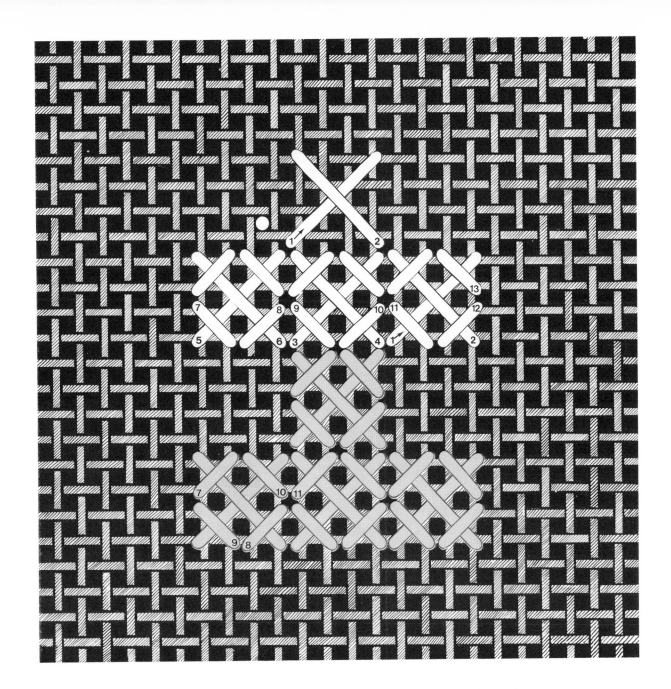

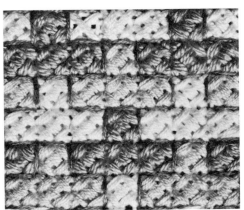

STITCH: CROSSED CORNERS (*Cross*)

DESIGN:[†] Stepped T's from a French medieval pavement mosaic study. Substitute: Sorbello, Raised Square, Double or Single Leviathan, Tent Stitch, Square Mosaic Stitch. Contrasting colors or different tones of the same color may be used. Stitches 7, 8, etc., on top diagram show one method of tying the Cross; 7, 8, etc., on lower diagram show a second.

DIAGRAM 27

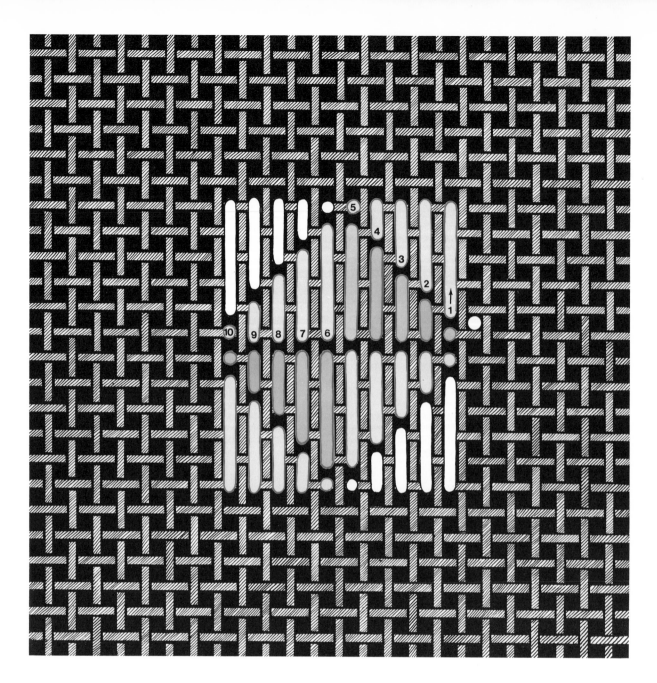

STITCH: FLAT *(Flat)*

DESIGN:[†] Islamic pavement mosaic. Needs wider expanse and more repeats for pattern to develop.

DIAGRAM 28

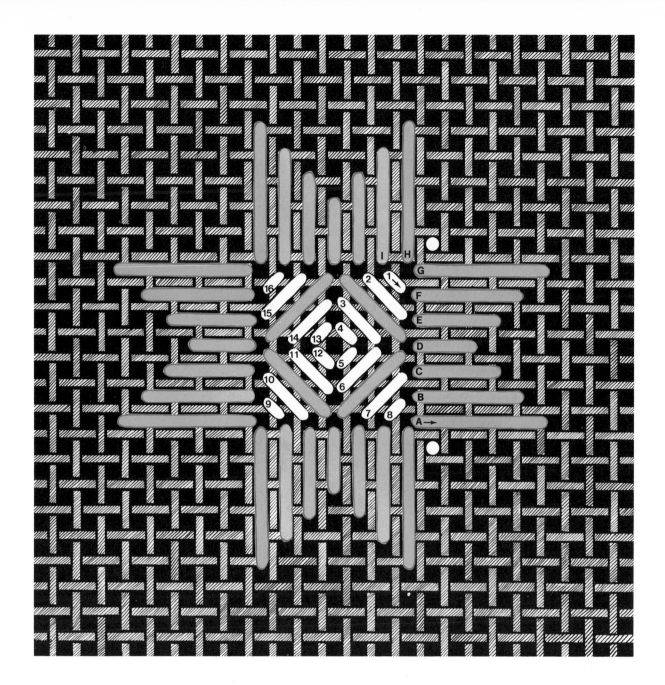

STITCH: FLAT, SQUARE MOSAIC *(Flat)* RAISED SQUARE *(Cross)*

The dark single lines outlining the small Mosaic Stitches (forming one group of white squares) and the Back Stitches around the Raised Squares should be worked last.

DESIGN:[†] Another medieval pavement mosaic, this one painted by Hans Holbein in the 16th century. Of course the mosaics themselves predated their painted representations.

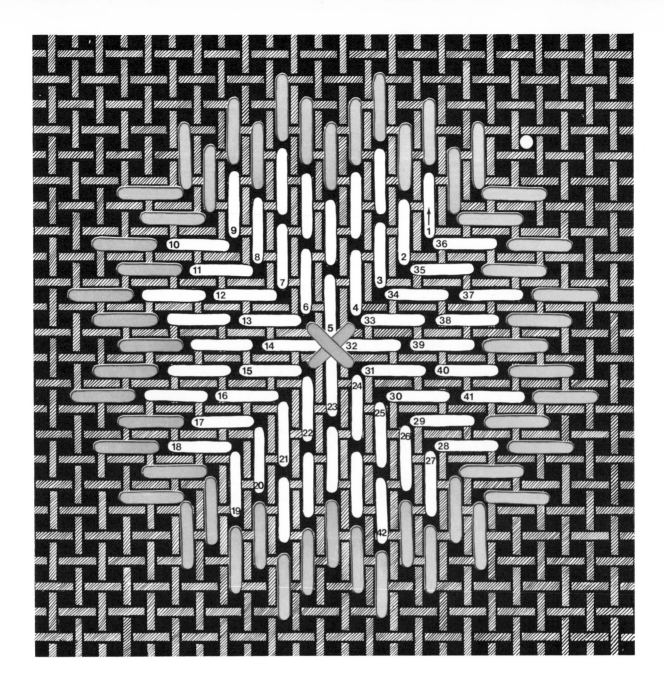

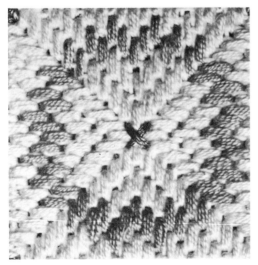

STITCH: FLAT *(Flat)*

DESIGN:† 1. Window pattern, St. Denis Cathedral, France, 12th century; 2. Known in American patchwork quilt design as Star of Bethlehem. *See* Chapter 5 for a photographic history.

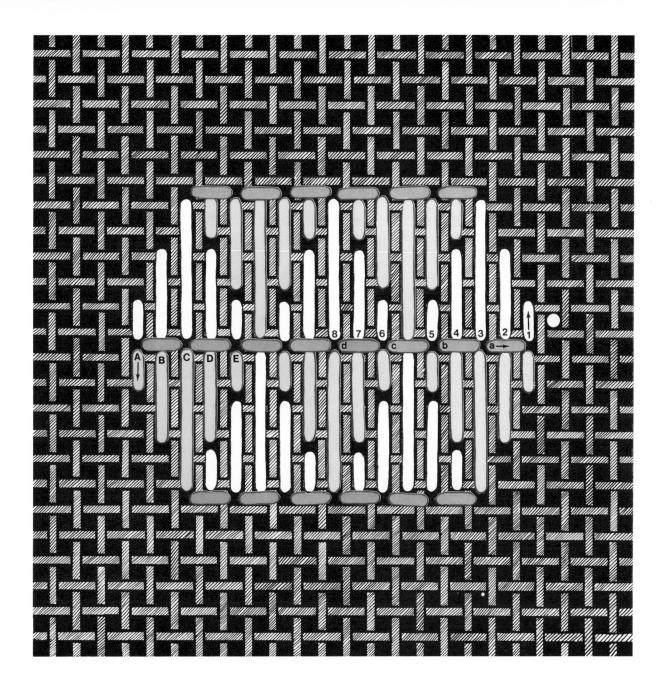

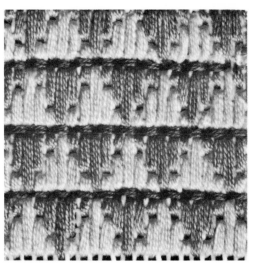

STITCH: FLAT, BACK *(Flat)*

DESIGN:[†] 1. Medieval mosaic pavement (*see* Playing Card hanging, Knave of Spades, Color Plate 11), there are many other historical examples. A curiously effective heraldic organization of a field, and an enduring and interesting pattern, for all its simplicity. *See* Chapter 5 for a photographic history.

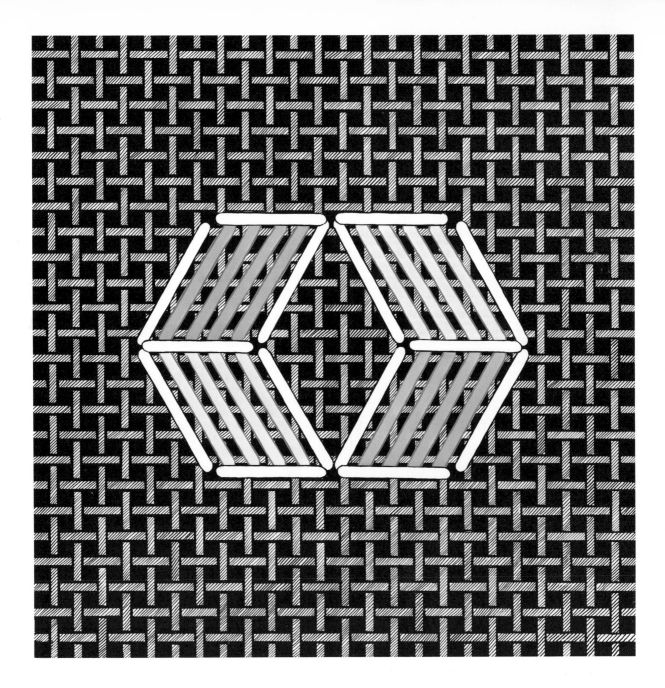

STITCH: FLAT *(Flat)*, ROCOCO *(Loop, Tied)*
See Rococo Diagram 199 for instructions.

DESIGN:[†] 1. Hexagonal box background from the tomb of Bishop John Pecci, Siena, Donatello, sculpture, c. 15th century; 2. Single vertical rows (in ribbon fashion) are frequently used in Anatolian and Persian carpets of the 14th and 15th centuries (*see* the Turkish carpet border sampler, Color Plate 8); 3. American patchwork quilt, Baby Blocks pattern. *See* Chapter 5 for a photographic history.

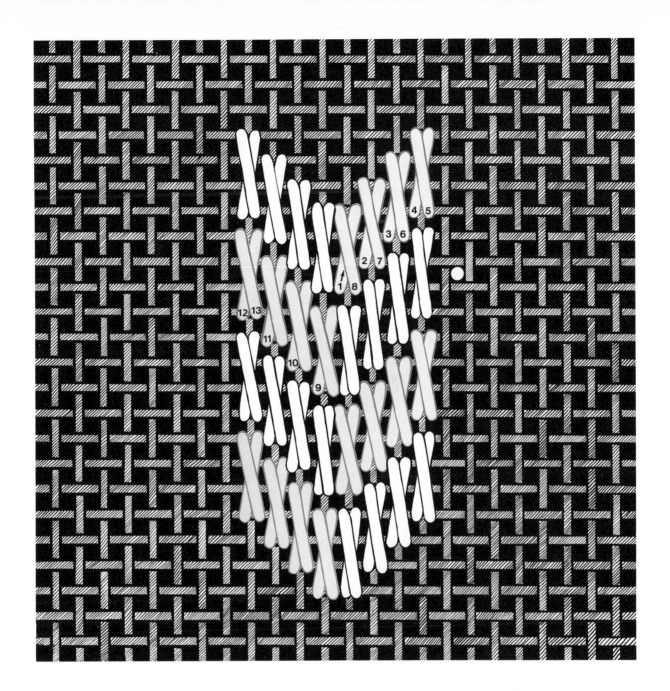

STITCH: Narrow Oblong Cross *(Cross)*

DESIGN:[†] Medieval mosaic. *See* Chapter 5 for a photographic history.

DIAGRAM 33

STITCH: FLAT *(Flat)*

DESIGN:[†] Medieval mosaic. *See* Chapter 5 for a photographic history. *See also* Playing Card hanging, Queen of Diamonds, pavement, Color Plate 11.

DIAGRAM 34

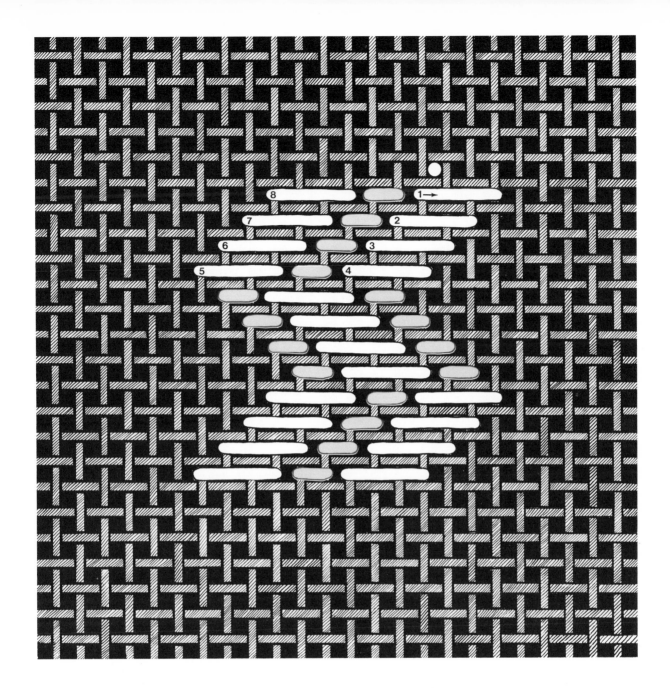

STITCH: FLAT *(Flat)*

DESIGN:[†] Medieval mosaic. *See* Chapter 5 for a photographic history.

DIAGRAM 35

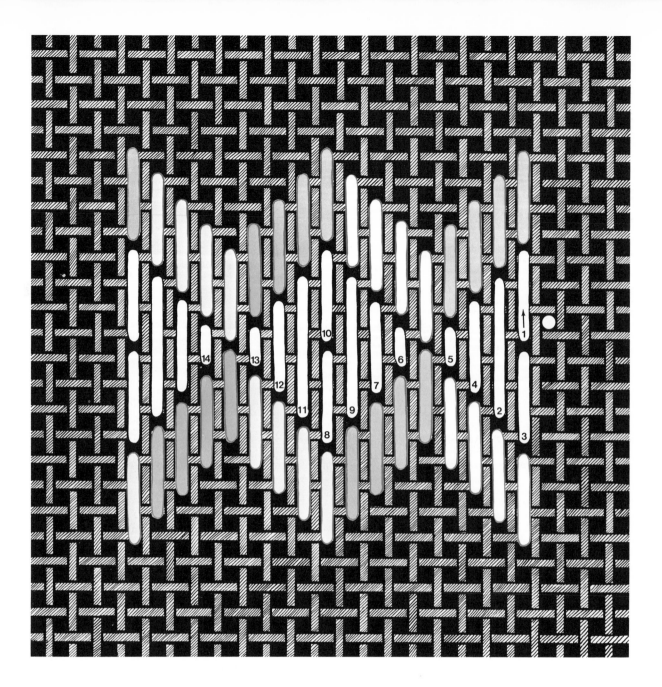

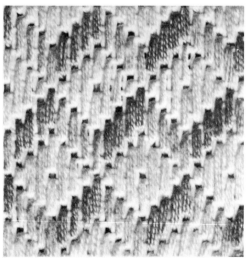

STITCH: FLAT *(Flat)*
The structure is related to Hungarian Ground.

DESIGN: [†] Hexagonal relief ribboning from Byzantine and Roman relief mosaics. There are many examples, for instance, in Ravenna. *See* Chapter 5 for a photographic history.

DIAGRAM 36

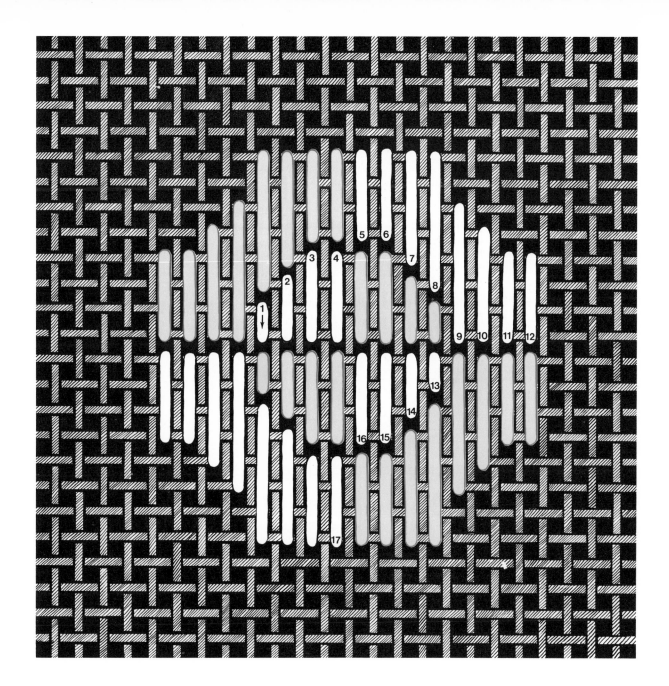

STITCH: FLAT *(Flat)*

DESIGN:[†] 1. From 14th-century Italian marble inlaid mosaic, Victoria and Albert Museum, London; 2. Pavement mosaic, the Baptistery, Florence; 3. American patchwork quilt pattern called Steeplechase. The small "circle" ⊕ is called Jockey Cap in patchwork parlance. *See* Chapter 5 for a photographic history.

DIAGRAM 37

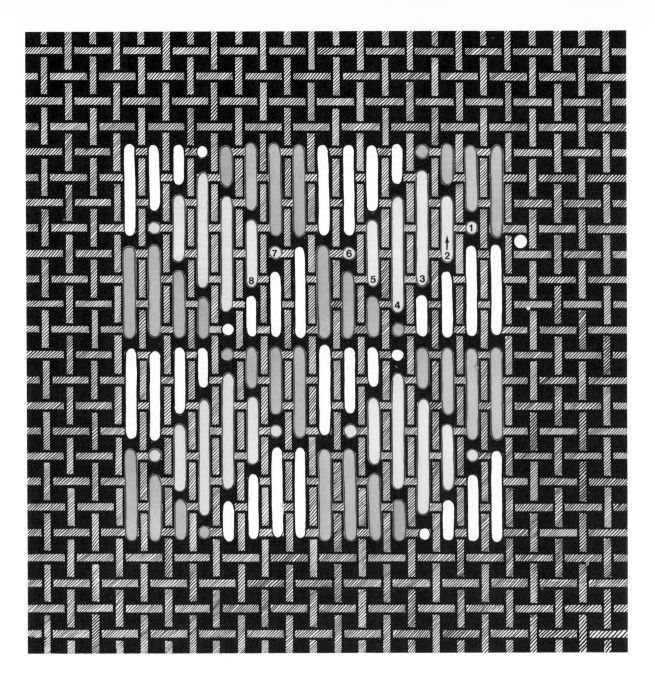

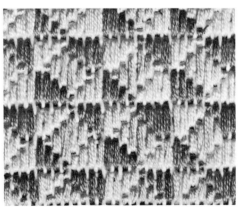

STITCH: FLAT *(Flat)*

DESIGN:[†] 1. 13th-century mosaic pavement, the Baptistery, Florence; 2. Jockey Cap motif.

DIAGRAM 38

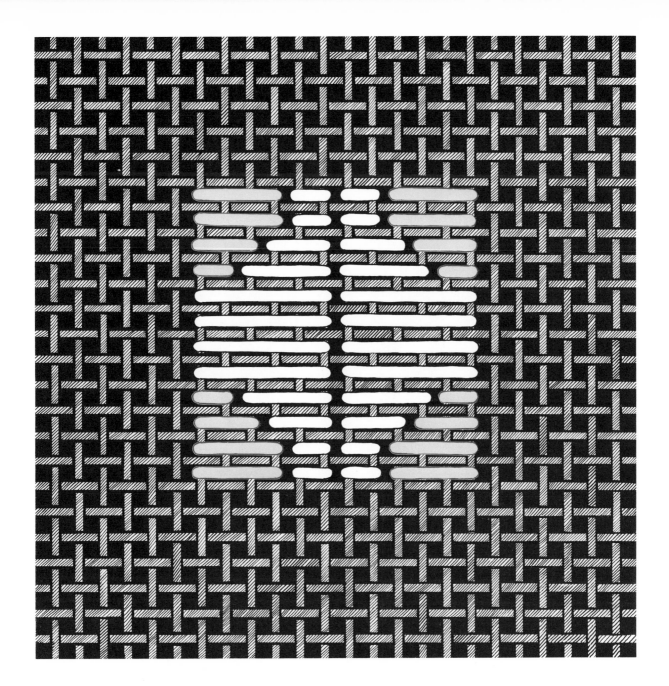

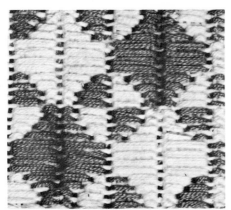

STITCH: FLAT *(Flat)*

DESIGN:[†] 1. 13th-century mosaic pavement, the
Baptistery, Florence; 2. Patchwork quilt design called
Mill Wheels. Jockey Cap motif. Pattern analysis and
additional Jockey Cap patterns follow. *See* Chapter
5 for a photographic history.

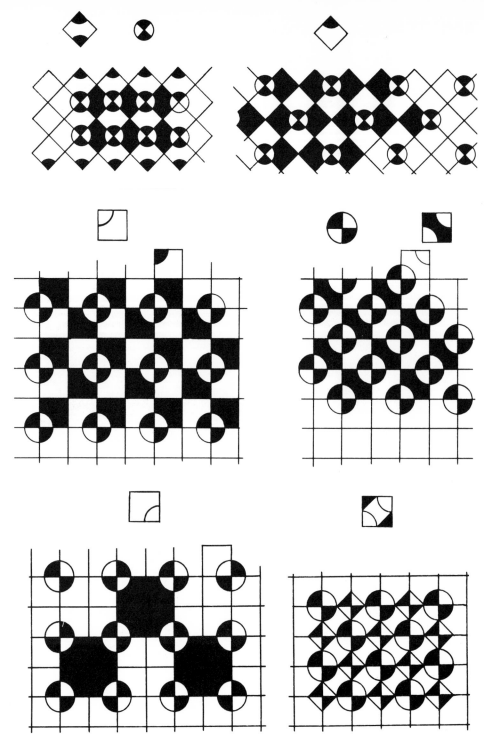

These designs, all of them 13th-century mosaic diaper patterns from the Baptistery, Florence, are outstanding examples of the diversity to be found in strict adherence to geometric form. The basic shape remains constant, but the overall designs appear variegated and are optically enticing.

The first two mosaics show the tipped square (or diamond) invaded by the arc in a counter-change method. The others show the conventional square invaded by the arc. Many other variations are both possible and, I think, inviting.

A number of these mosaics were given renewed life and employment in the patchwork quilts of the 18th and 19th centuries. Whether this was the result of coincidence, conscious or unconscious memory on the part of the worker, or intentional borrowing by the professional designer is disputable. The survival of pattern, whatever the means, is historically interesting. The small particolored circle that emerges when the square is divided in this way came to be known as the Jockey Cap motif amongst quilters. *See* Chapter 5 for a photographic history.

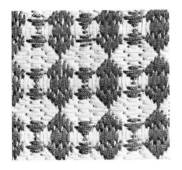

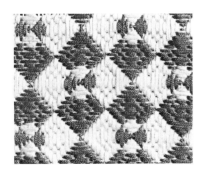

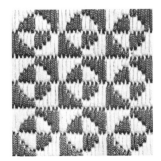

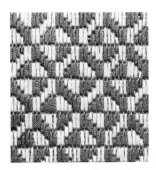

Patchwork quilt design
known as Steeplechase

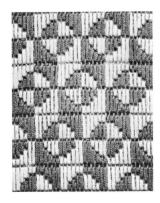

Patchwork quilt design
known as Steeplechase

STITCH: FLAT *(Flat)*

DESIGN:[†] 13th-century mosaic patterns from the Baptistery, Florence.   called Jockey Caps in patchwork quilting. The designer of the mosaics in the Baptistery employed the Jockey Cap formation as a foundation for many interesting geometric variations. The skeleton of the pattern is not immediately discernible to the eye, but nevertheless the use of the same fundamental motif produces unusual harmony. It binds together all these variations which, at first view, seem completely unrelated but particularly well suited to each other.

131

MEDIEVAL GROUNDS

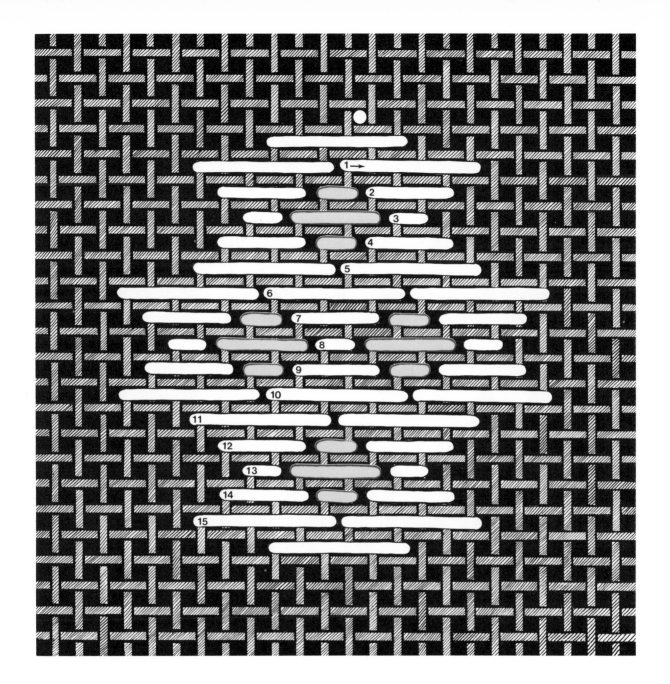

STITCH: FLAT *(Flat)*

DESIGN: Franco-Flemish and German medieval embroidery grounding. This style of patterning was prominent throughout Europe in this period. It was used for background, like modern wallpaper, or for texture detail. The yarns employed were silk, wool, linen, gold silver. Perforations are an essential design element in this work and in the medieval grounds that follow. Tension and stitch direction must be handled with care.

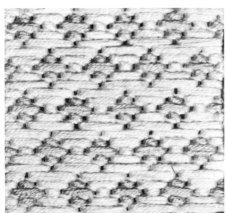

DIAGRAM 40

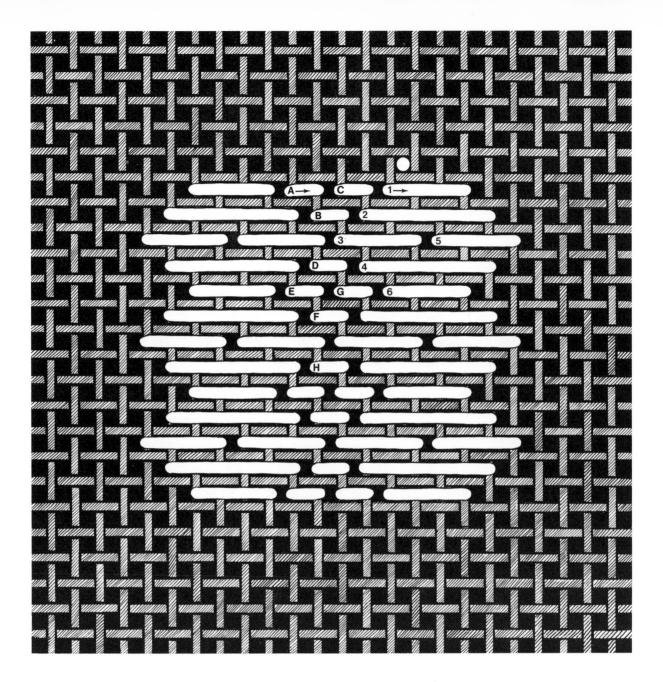

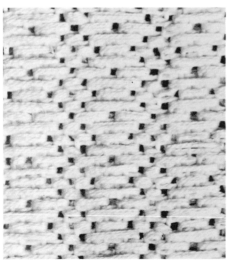

STITCH: FLAT *(Flat)*

DESIGN: Medieval grounding design. Notice how the emphasis on perforation adds to structural enrichment. These medieval geometric patterns are simple, extremely effective, and worth new consideration. The variations you see here are not dramatic, but even modified alteration results in surprising pattern diversity when seen on an expanse slightly larger than the sampler square.

DIAGRAM 41

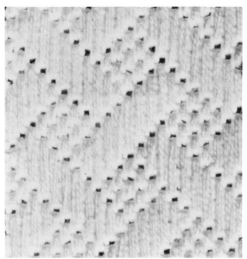

STITCH: FLAT *(Flat)*

Letters show how long blocks may be worked first, triangles last (A, B, C). Numbers (1, 2, 3) show blocks and triangles worked in consecutive order.

DESIGN:† This popular pattern can be found in the work of medieval Spain, France, Germany, Sweden, Flanders and England. 1. Tower base, brick work, Sta. Maria de Villa Major, Spain, 12th century; 2. Embroidered altar frontal of Henry IV of Castile, mid-15th-century, Guadalupe Monastery, Madrid; 3. Franco-Flemish embroidery, Maurus on a Boat, Musée Historique des Tissus, Lyons, 15th century. *See* Playing Card hanging, the Knave of Spades, Color Plate 11.

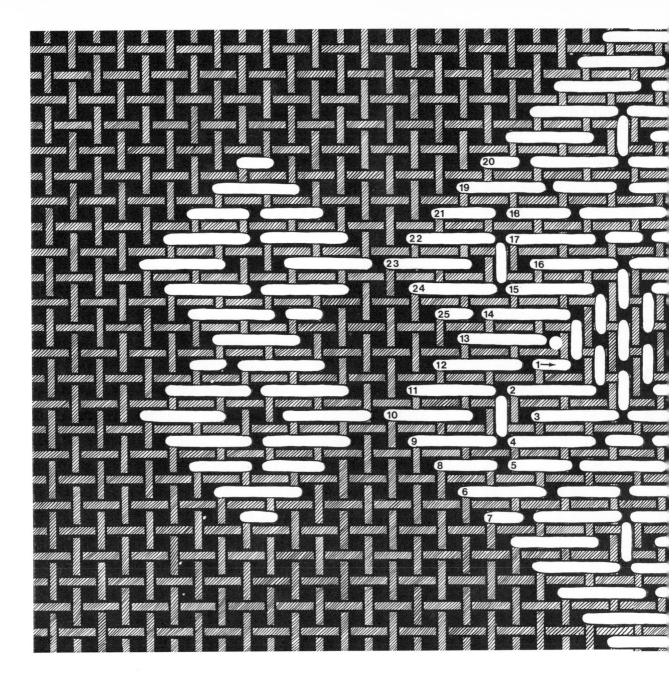

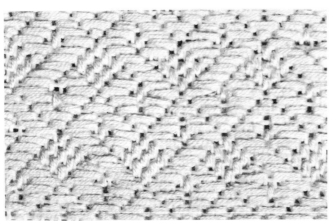

DIAGRAM 43

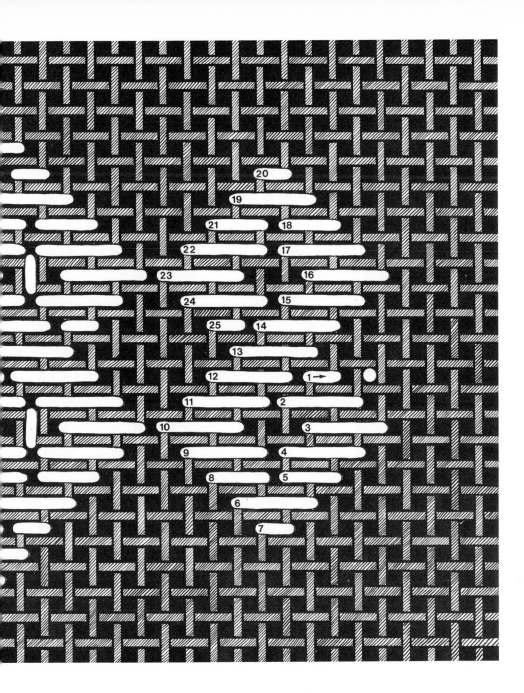

STITCH: FLAT *(Flat)*

DESIGN: * Reversed S ground. The design combines Islamic patterning with medieval European stitching methods. If you wish to highlight the S's use a deeper shade of yarn for the diamonds that separate them.

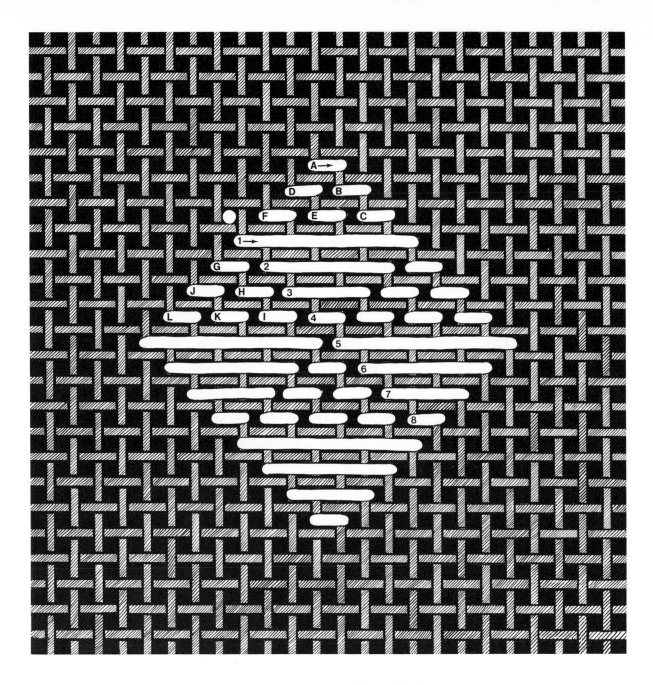

STITCH: FLAT *(Flat)*

DESIGN:[†] Typical medieval grounding. This pattern is adapted from the celebrated St. Martin embroideries, 15th-century Franco-Flemish work (St. Martin with Deacon), Musée Historique des Tissus, Lyons.

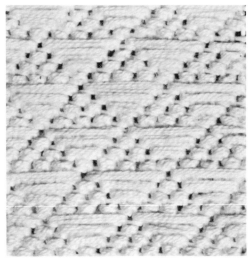

DIAGRAM 44

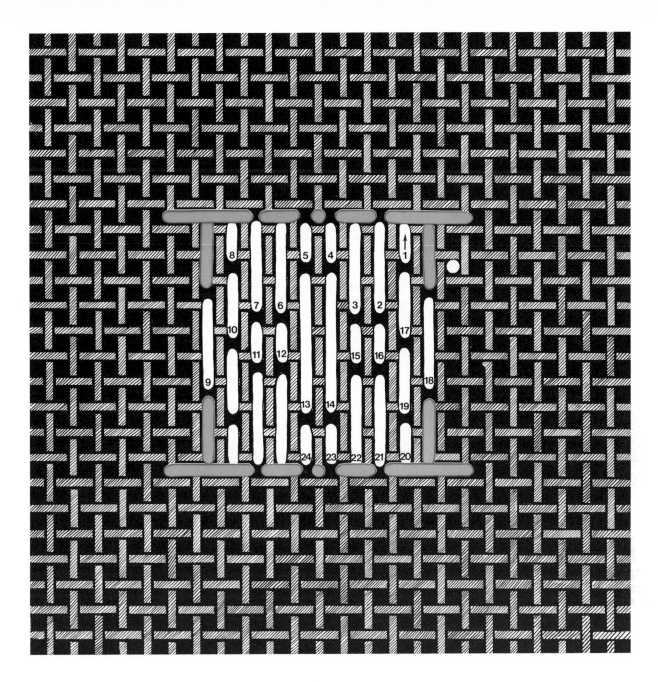

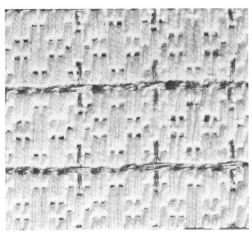

STITCH: FLAT *(Flat)*

DESIGN: Embroidered altar frontal pattern, 1250, Lower Saxony, Kloster St. Marienberg.

DIAGRAM 45

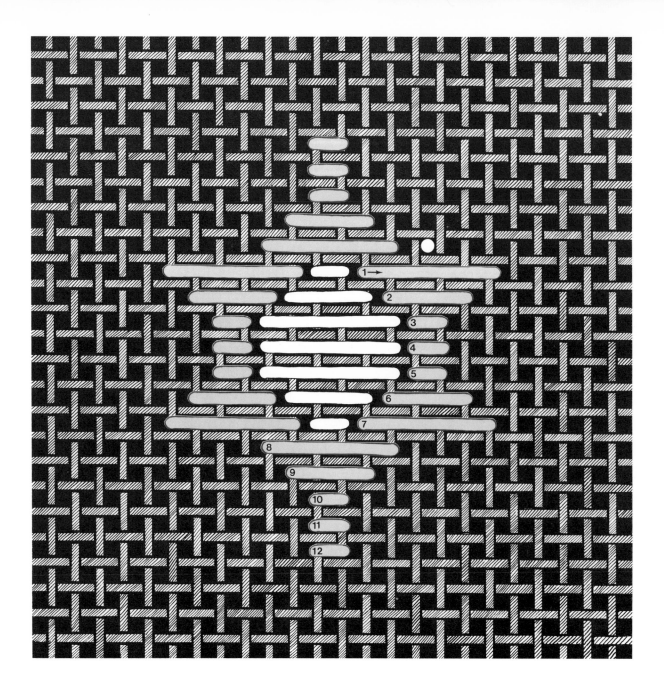

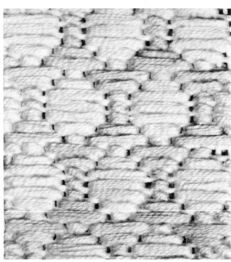

STITCH: FLAT *(Flat)*

DESIGN: German, 15th century, embroidery pattern. Good in monotone or in two colors. This pattern may be seen (in monotone) in the horse's body (Color Plate 12).

DIAGRAM 46

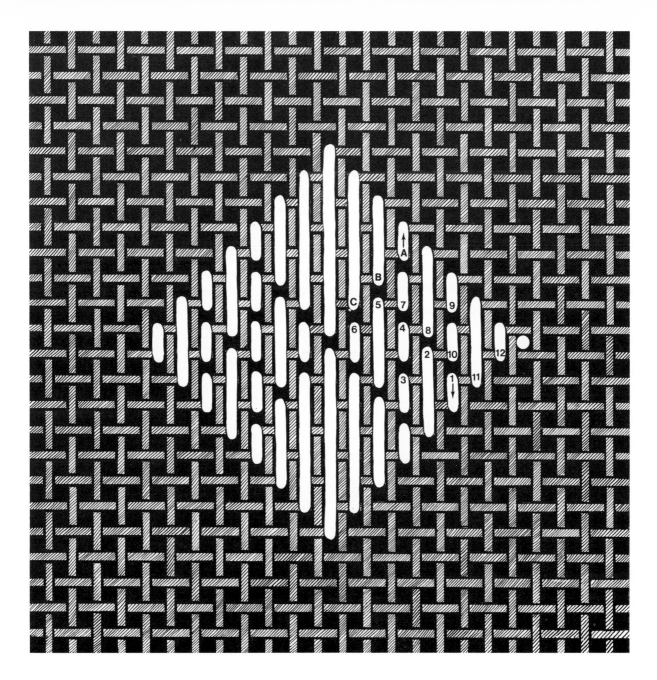

STITCH: FLAT *(Flat)*

DESIGN: Typical medieval pattern—German, Flemish, French, Spanish. It is composed of large and small Hungarian Stitch units.

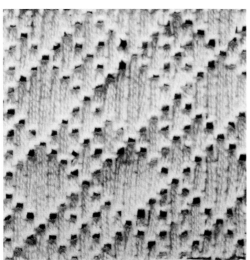

DIAGRAM 47

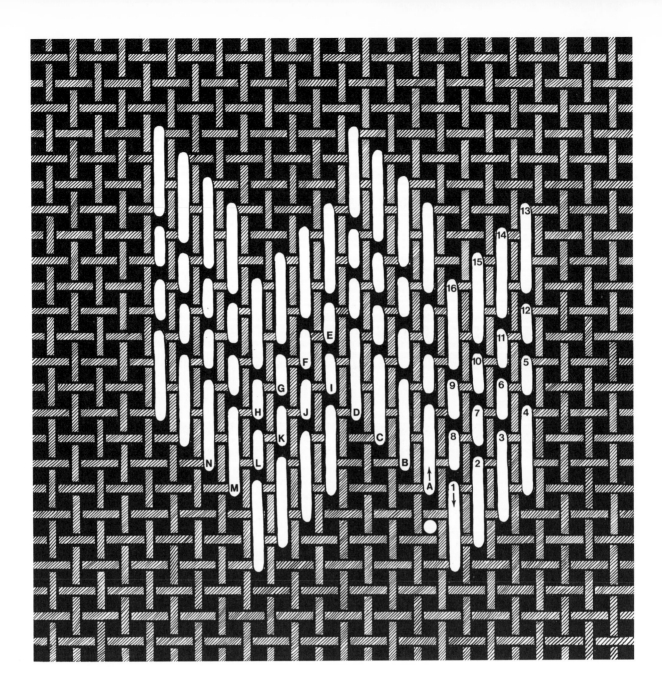

STITCH: FLAT *(Flat)*
The letters and the numerals show two different stitch sequences. Either may be used.

DESIGN: * Variation of Diagram 42; it is also good in two colors.

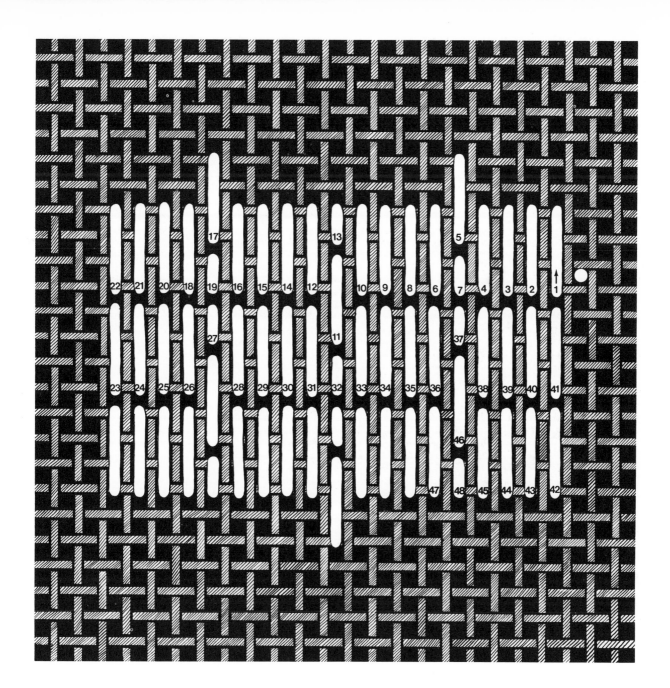

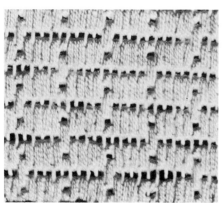

STITCH: FLAT *(Flat)*

NOTE: The diagrams of these perforated patterns have been numbered in what may seem, at first, to be an eccentric fashion. My object is to show how the decorative holes can be made clear and clean.

DESIGN:[†] A unique brick pattern from an embroidered altar frontal depicting the Nativity, reportedly worked by a monk, 15th century, Castile.

DIAGRAM 49

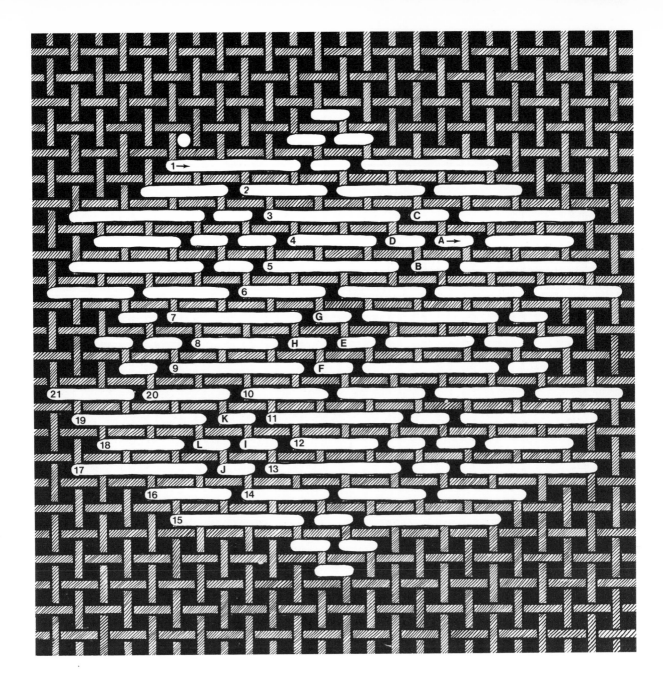

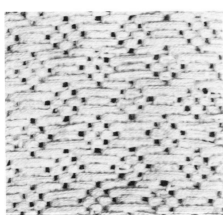

STITCH: FLAT *(Flat)*

DESIGN:[†] 1. Seljuk tomb tower, brick pattern, 11th century, Demavand; 2. Medieval German whitework pattern very frequently used; 3. Medieval Flemish and French gold and silk embroidery pattern.

DIAGRAM 50

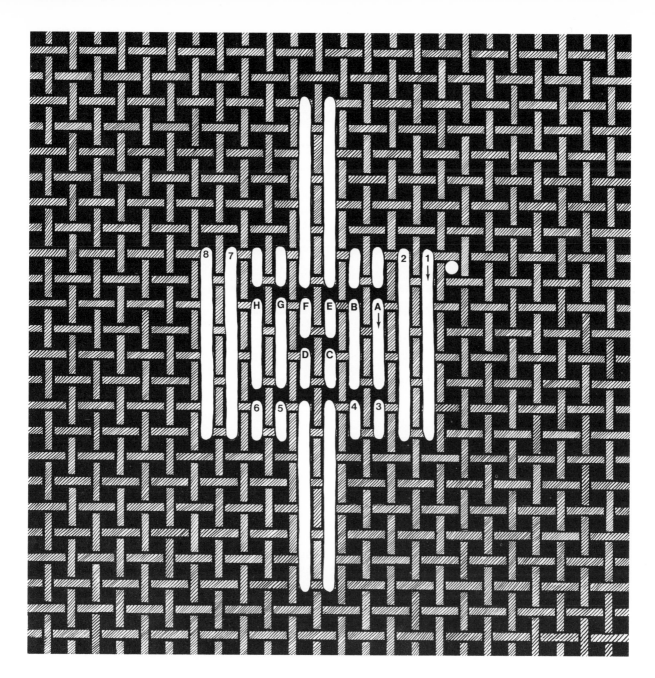

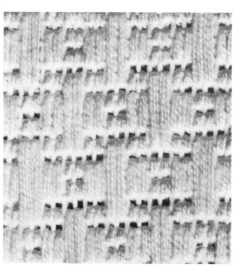

STITCH: FLAT *(Flat)*

Medieval-type grounding, Spanish, German. Colors may be used, perhaps a dark background with a pale Cross. Revived in 19th-century German sampler work.

DIAGRAM 51

STITCH: FLAT *(Flat)*. FILLER: SINGLE LEVIATHAN *(Cross)*

DESIGN:[†] From an altar curtain, late 13th-century, Friauli. In this altar curtain all the costumes were covered by small geometric diaper patterns. This is one of them, or rather, an adaptation. I have seen only a small photograph and even with the aid of a magnifying glass cannot be certain of the original stitch formation. The altar curtain is worked entirely in white geometric patterning in very entertaining variety.

STITCH: FLAT *(Flat)*

DESIGN: Spanish medieval ground pattern.

DIAGRAM 53

STITCH: FLAT (*Flat*). FILLER: CHAIN (*Chain*),
UPRIGHT CROSS (*Cross*)

DESIGN:[†] From a 16th-century Franco-Flemish embroidery. Church of St. Michael, Ghent.

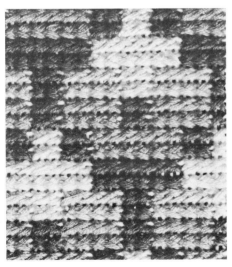

STITCH: LONG-ARMED CROSS *(Cross)*

DESIGN: 12th century Swedish design known as the Trono pattern. I was careful to retain tonal relationships and stitch because they are unusually interesting, visually and historically. The stitch was called Tvistem and it is what we call Long-Armed. This beautiful pattern would make a fine field for cushion or carpet. The surface is durable and dense enough for hard wear. I hope my curtailed example is sufficient to encourage its use. Cross, Single or Double Leviathan Cross, Eye, Sorbello Knot, Tent, Square Mosaic, etc., may be used. Four shades or colors.

ISLAMIC BRICK, TILE, TEXTILE

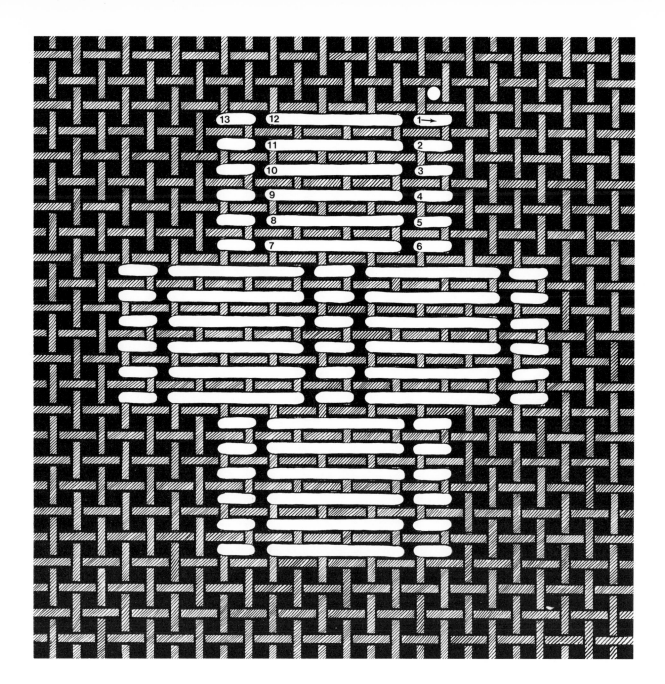

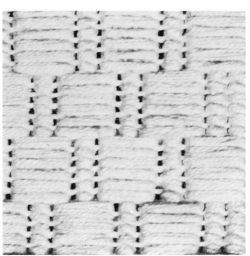

STITCH: FLAT *(Flat)*

DESIGN:[†] 1. Seljuk Islamic brick work, 10th century;
2. Swedish Lace Filling pattern, 18th-century coif.
See Playing Card hanging, Cavalier of Spades, background pattern, rescaled, Color Plate 11.

STITCH: FLAT *(Flat)*. FILLER: TENT or FLAT *(Flat)*

DESIGN:[†] *See* following page.

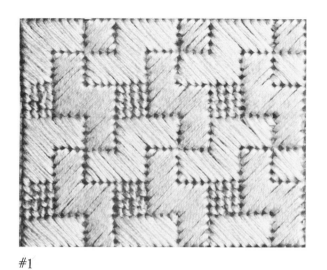

#1

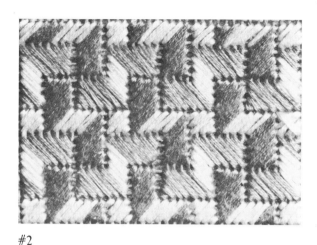

#2

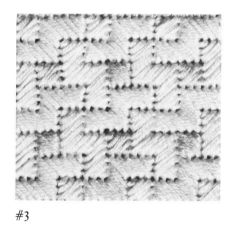

#3

These three photographs illustrate identical patterns. #1 shows the
basic pattern structure clearly. The small squares have been worked
in Tent Stitch. Adapted from an architectural, motif interior of the
mosque of Ahmed-ibn-Tulun, 9th century.

The architectural structure in #2 is exactly the same, although
the scale has been changed slightly. This interesting color arrangement of an Islamic Brick construction is taken from one of the
16th-century Venetian Lace "Esemplario" books. The relationship
may not be immediately perceptible, but the designer simply formed
the Z's in two tones; the center connecting bar of the Z is white
and the arms of the Z are dark. Only one shade of brown was used.
Reflected light caused it to photograph two-toned.

#3 is the same as #1 rescaled and Tent Stitch has been replaced by
a Flat filler in a different color. May be rescaled; many tonal
variations possible.

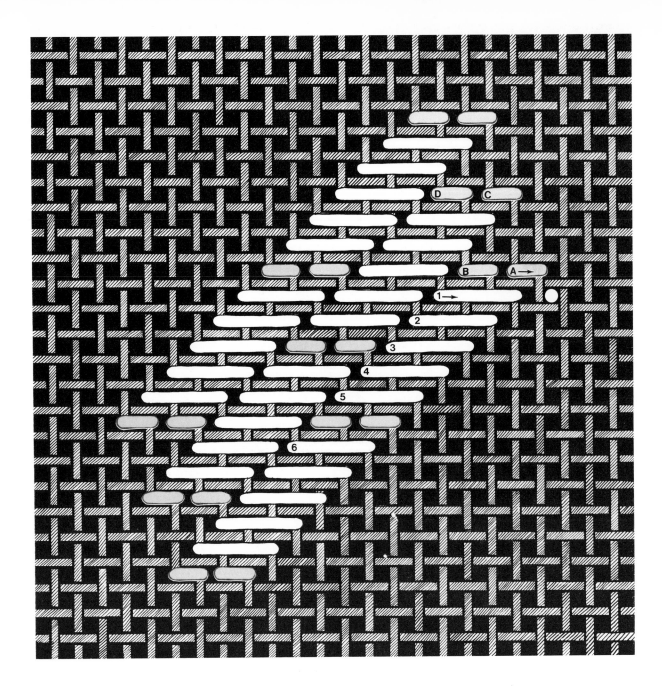

STITCH: FLAT *(Flat)*

DESIGN:[†] Brick wall pattern in a Persian 15th-century manuscript painting. The halfway sectioning, common to brick arrangements, is here worked on the diagonal rather than the horizontal or vertical.

DIAGRAM 58

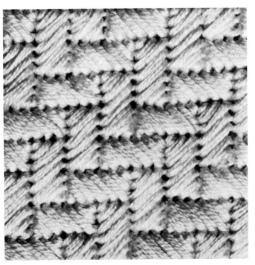

STITCH: FLAT *(Flat)*

DESIGN:[†] 1. Brick pattern in the arch of a Seljuk mosque, 1180 A.D.; 2. Byzantine stone pavement, Torcello, Venice; 3. In English quilting, this patterning is called Splint.

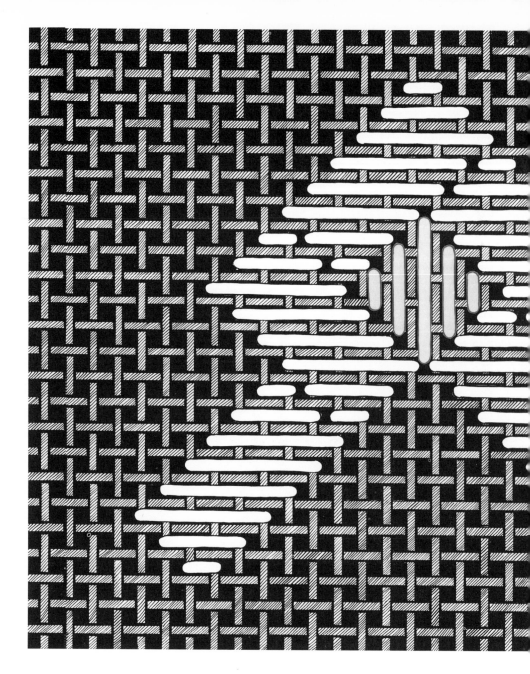

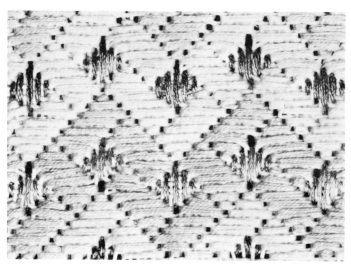

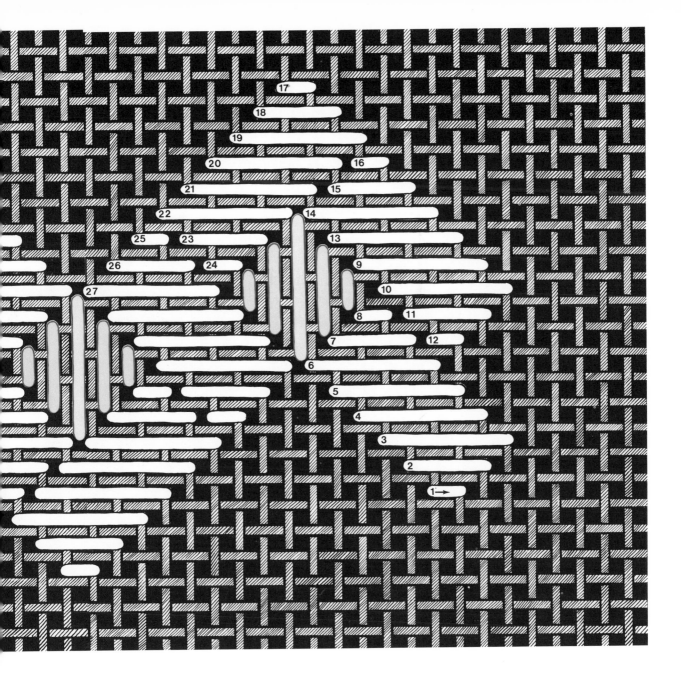

STITCH: FLAT *(Flat)*

DESIGN:[†] From an early Egyptian mosaic pavement, Cairo. It is here transferred with fidelity of scale. This pattern may be worked in Tent, Brick, Diamond Cross, Hungarian Stitch, Rococo or Barred Diagonal Upright. See Playing Card hanging, Queen of Diamonds, background, Color Plate 11.

DIAGRAM 60

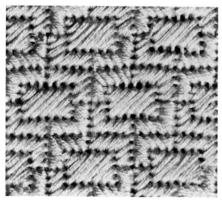

STITCH: FLAT *(Flat)*

DESIGN:[†] Persian miniature painting, brick wall pattern, Firdusi's Shah-Nameh, 1430, Gulestan Palace library, Teheran.

DIAGRAM 61

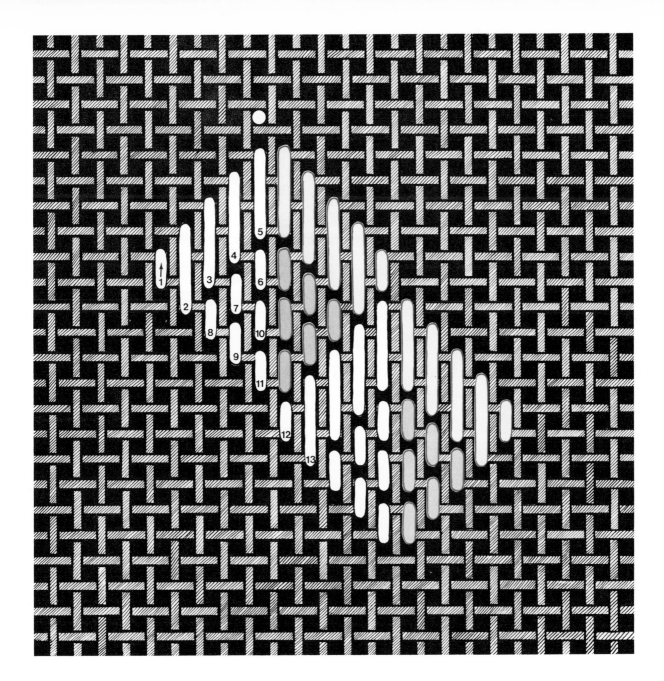

STITCH: FLAT *(Flat)*

DESIGN:[†] Islamic (Seljuk) brick pattern; Konya, 13th century.

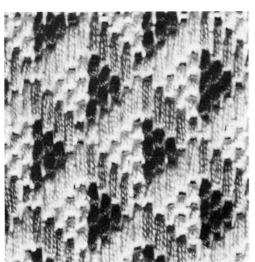

DIAGRAM 62

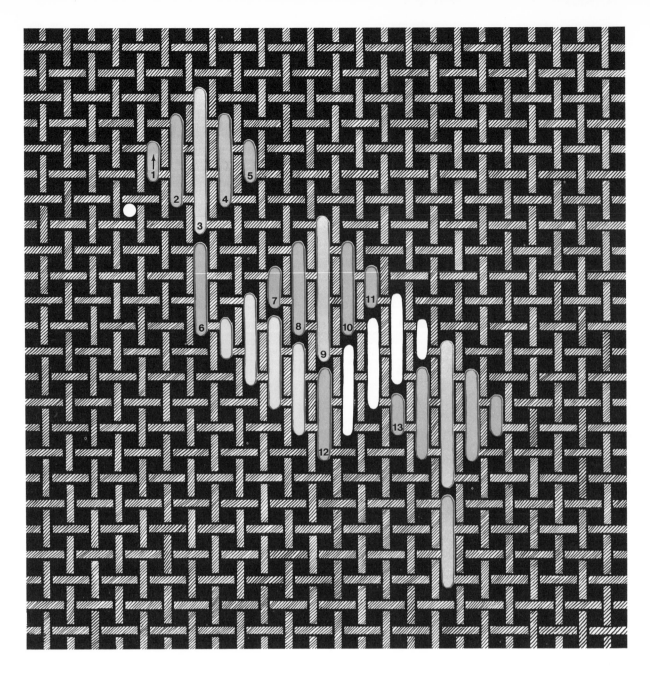

STITCH: FLAT *(Flat)*

DESIGN: * Boxes. Variation on a Seljuk brick pattern.

DIAGRAM 63

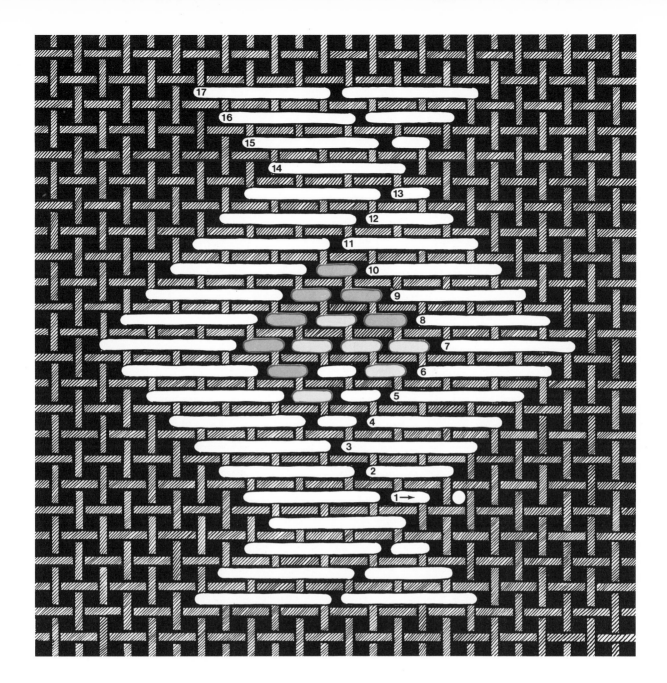

STITCH: FLAT *(Flat)*

DESIGN:† 1. Seljuk tomb tower, brick pattern, 11th century, Demavand; 2. Architectural detail, column, Chartres Cathedral, 12th century.

DIAGRAM 64

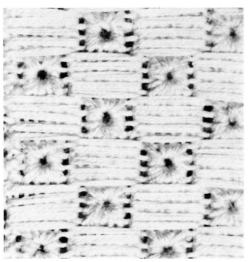

STITCH: FLAT *(Flat)*, EYE *(Pulled Yarn)*

DESIGN:[+] A brick pattern from a 12th-century Seljuk mosque, Konya.

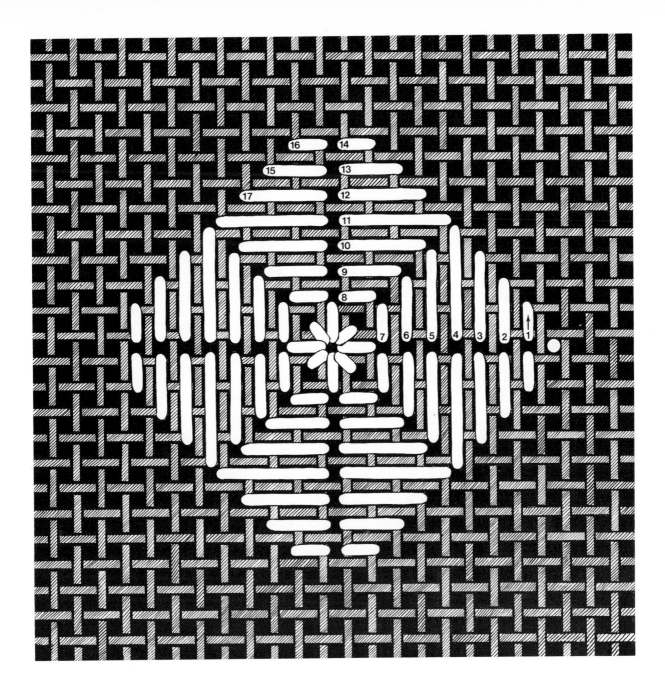

STITCH: Flat *(Flat)*. FILLER: Diamond Eye *(Pulled Yarn)*

DESIGN:[†] Windowpane pattern, medieval drawing, Master of Flémalle, Louvre, Paris.

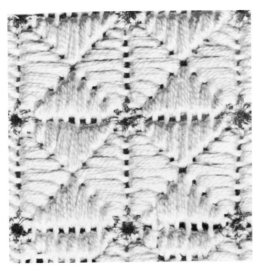

DIAGRAM 66

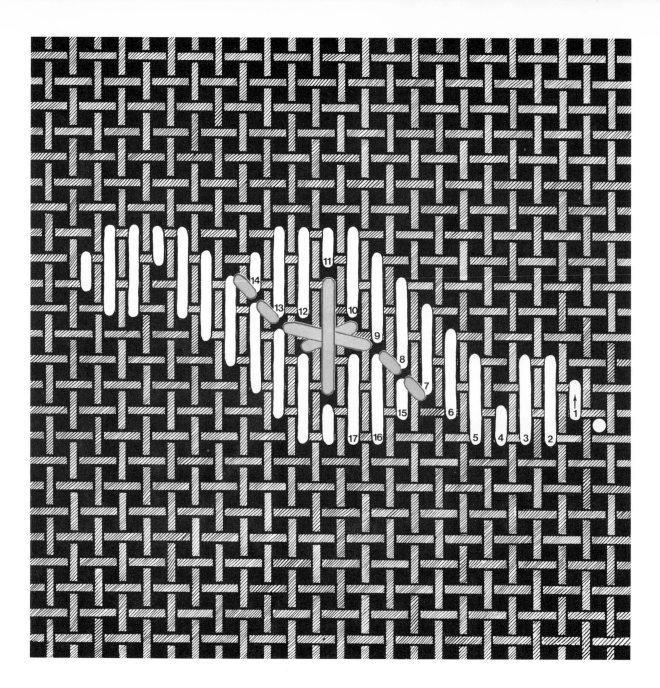

STITCH: Flat *(Flat)*. FILLER: Brick *(Flat)*, Uneven Cross

DESIGN:[†] Islamic Link pattern, 13th-century Syrian textile.

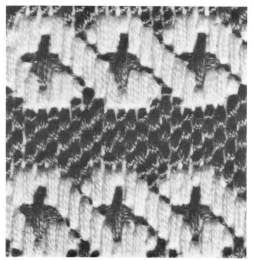

DIAGRAM 67

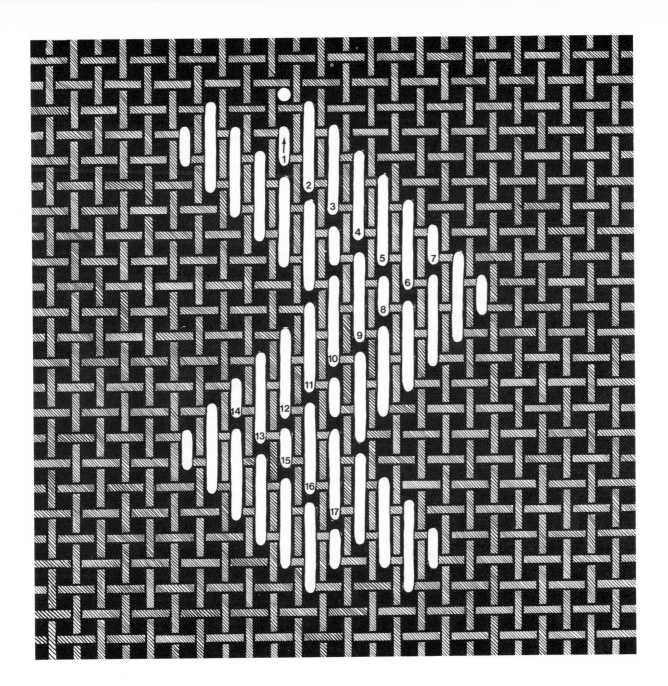

STITCH: FLAT *(Flat)*

DESIGN:[†] Brick work, Qal'ah-i mosque, 12th century, Afghanistan.

DIAGRAM 68

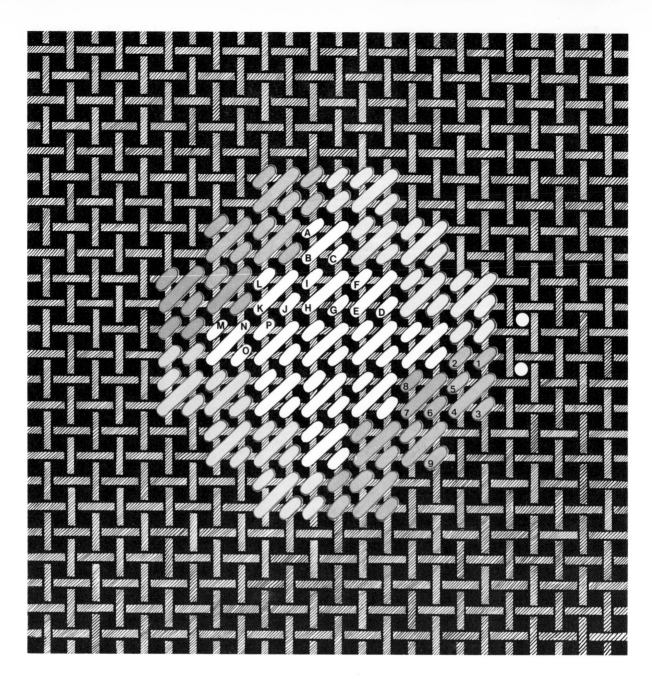

STITCH: Sᴏ Mᴏsᴀɪᴄ *(Flat)*

DESIGN:[†] A Turcoman carpet pattern. The adaptation is very exact. This design is handsome in Tent Stitch.

166

DIAGRAM 69

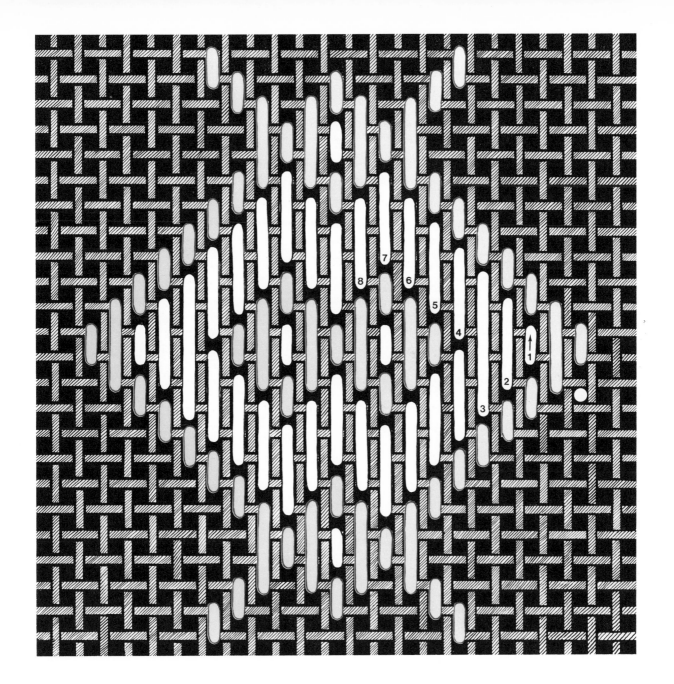

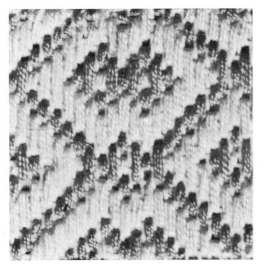

STITCH: FLAT *(Flat)*

DESIGN:[+] A good European medieval diaper pattern, greatly influenced by Islamic tile and textile design. In the original Islamic patterns of this style, the diagonal lines were arranged or shaded to give the appearance of interlacement.

DIAGRAM 70

STITCH: FLAT *(Flat)*

DESIGN:[†] 13th-century Seljuk textile pattern.

DIAGRAM 71

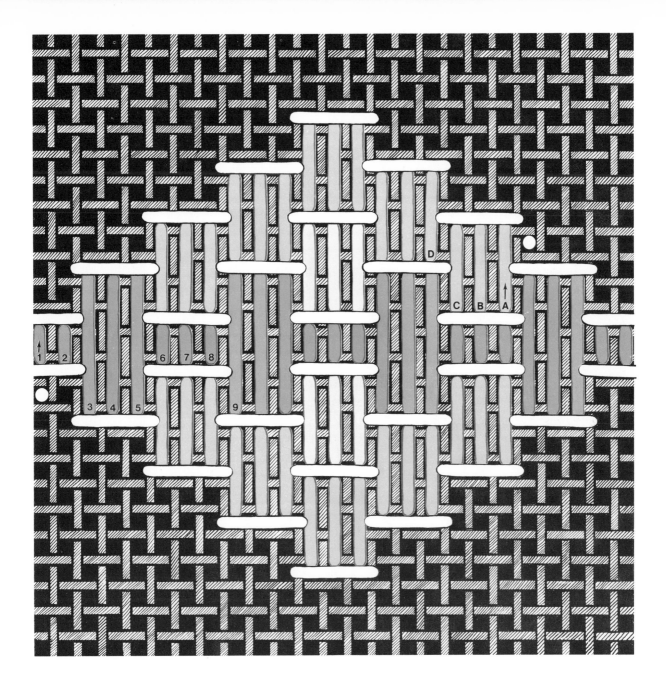

STITCH: FLAT *(Flat)*

DESIGN:[†] Central motif in a 19th-century embroidered Turcoman saddlebag. The architecture shows an interesting kinship with Victorian embroidery of the same period. Note the horizontal lines covering perforation.

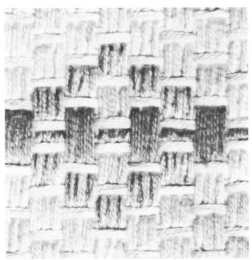

DIAGRAM 72

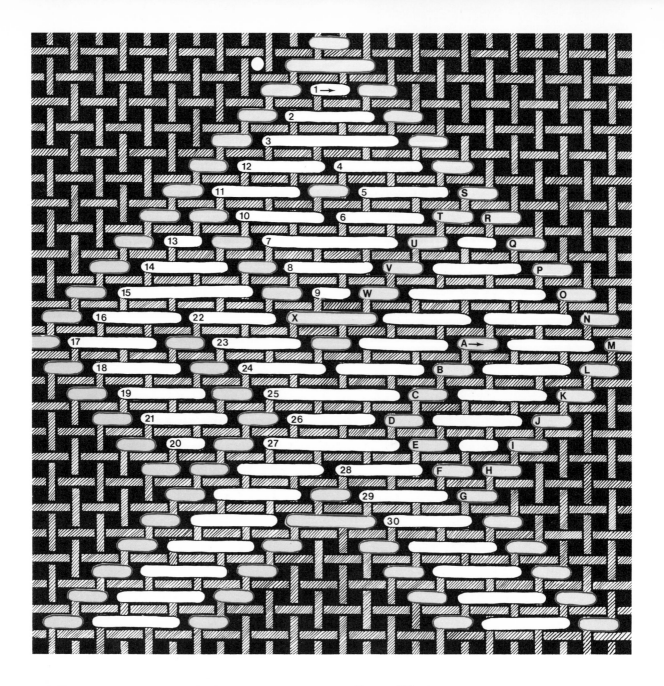

STITCH: SATIN *(Flat)*

Satin Stitch is the name given to long lengths of Flat Stitch. The surface must be kept smooth.

DESIGN:[+] From Seljuk brick, carpet, textiles, etc. Used extensively in Europe.

See Chapter 5 for a photographic history.

See the following page for sampler squares showing how to substitute stitches in geometric patterns.

#1 Brick (*Flat*)†

#2 Rococo (*Loop, Tied*)†

#3 Satin (*Flat*)†

#4 Tent (*Flat*) Carpet Border

These photographs illustrate how one geometric pattern may be carried out in various stitches. The Tent Stitch example is from the Turkish carpet border sampler, Color Plate 8. It is entertaining to see how dramatic the textural and compositional changes are when you substitute stitches. More importantly, it is vital to replace long Flat Stitches with hardier stitches such as Tent if you wish to employ diaper patterns (mosaic, Islamic brick, etc.) for needlepoint carpets or upholstery. (The Persian Bakhtiari carpet on the following page shows one possible way of dividing a field. Almost all the geometric designs in the sampler squares would lend themselves beautifully to such an arrangement.) This particular Seljuk pattern may also be executed in Upright Diagonal-Barred Cross, small Upright Cross, Oblong Cross (barred or simple), French Double Tie, Hungarian Stitch, Cross, Diamond Cross, Diamond Eye, Renaissance, French Stitch. Experiments with some of these, preferably after having followed the four photographed examples, will help overcome difficulties with other repeat designs. The choice of stitch gives individuality to work, just as choice of design and color does, and these interesting exercises will aid in suiting texture to function.

171

The example of the famous Persian Bakhtiari squared garden
carpets, photographed above, shows a divided field that could
pleasantly accommodate the diaper patterns in the sampler squares.
The stitch selected must be hardy enough to withstand hard wear:
Tent, Cross, Long-Armed Cross, French, Crossed Corners, etc.

HISTORICAL SAMPLER PATTERNS

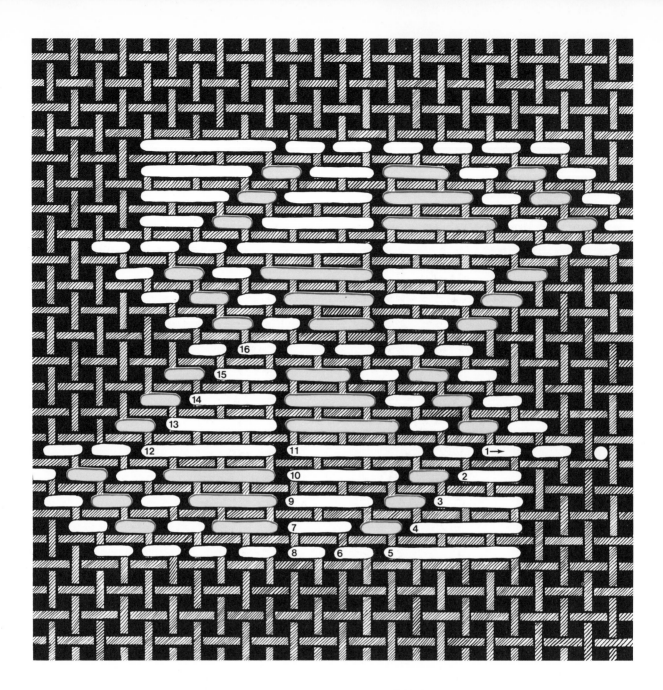

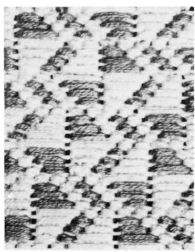

STITCH: FLAT *(Flat)*

DESIGN:[†] From a Japanese sampler, early 20th century,
Cooper-Hewitt Museum, New York.

DIAGRAM 74

Islamic-Turkish design carpet (in work).

PLATE 7

Turkish carpet border sampler hanging.

Moroccan motif sampler pillow.

PLATE 8

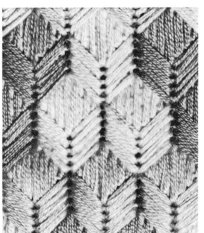

STITCH: FLAT (*Flat*)

Do all Diamond shapes first, then follow with the diagonal lines. That is the neat but not the easy method. It is simpler to work in sequence, as in the diagram, finishing each hexagon in turn. If you follow this second method you will have to snug under your needle. By snug, I mean that part of the hole is covered by previous stitching and subsequent stitches will have to be fitted under previously worked yarn.

DESIGN:[†] From a mid-19th-century English sampler, Victoria and Albert Museum, London.

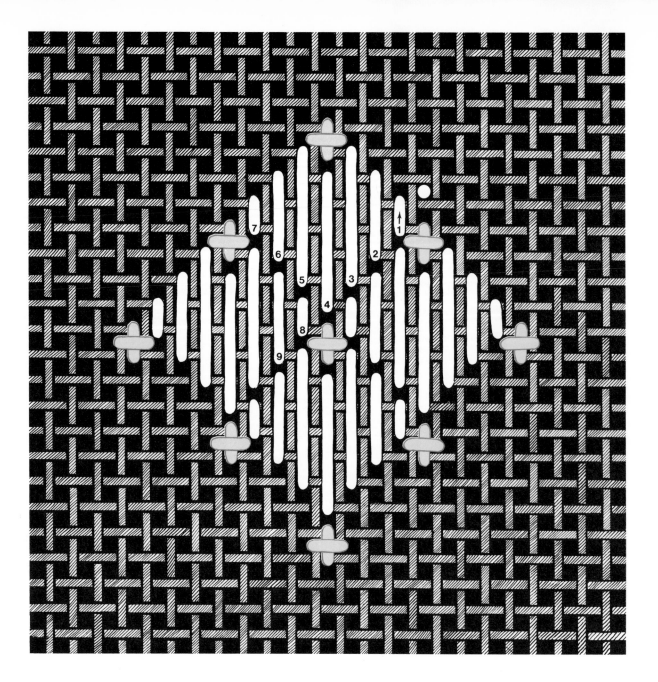

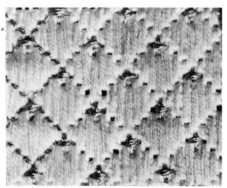

STITCH: FLAT *(Flat)*. FILLER: SMALL UPRIGHT CROSS *(Cross)*

DESIGN: Austrian sampler, 1864, Cooper-Hewitt Museum, New York.

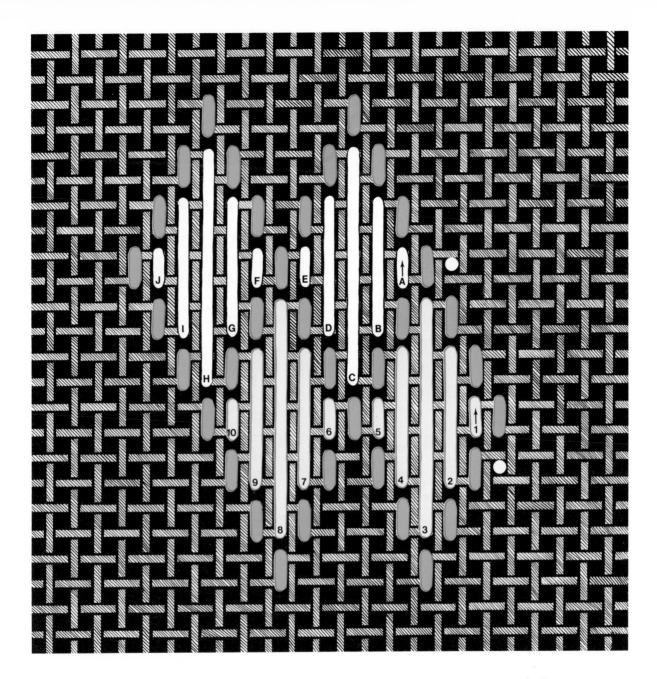

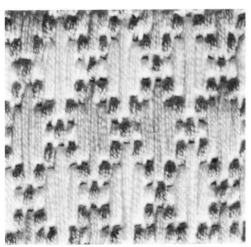

STITCH: FLAT *(Flat)*

DESIGN:[†] Long Diamond Ground adapted from 19th century German and Austrian samplers. Many tonal variations possible for geometric patterning.

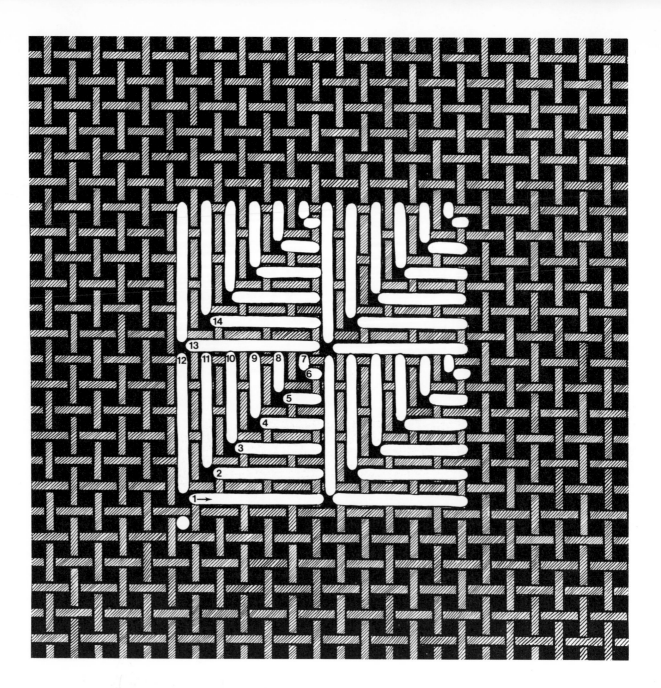

STITCH: FLAT *(Flat)*

Must be worked from lower left corner as shown.

DESIGN: Ground from an English sampler, 1841, Philadelphia Museum of Art. Should feature perforations to be interesting.

DIAGRAM 78

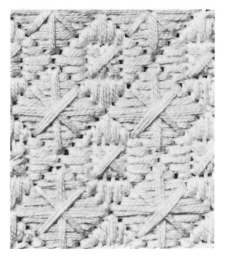

STITCH: FLAT *(Flat)* X CROSS *(Cross)*
Best in monotone.

DESIGN:[†] From an English sampler, 1841, Philadelphia
Museum of Art.

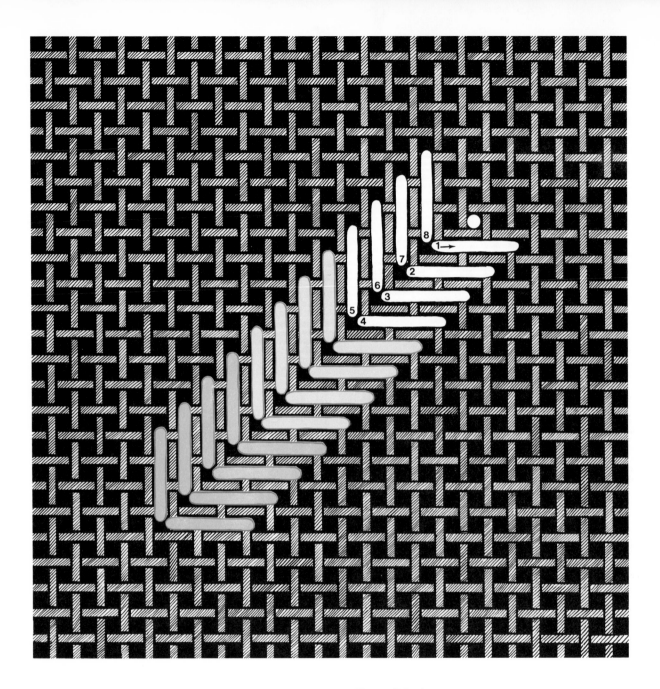

STITCH: FLAT *(Flat)*

DESIGN: 19th-century German sampler, Newark Museum of Art. The design is determined by the placement of shading.

DIAGRAM 80

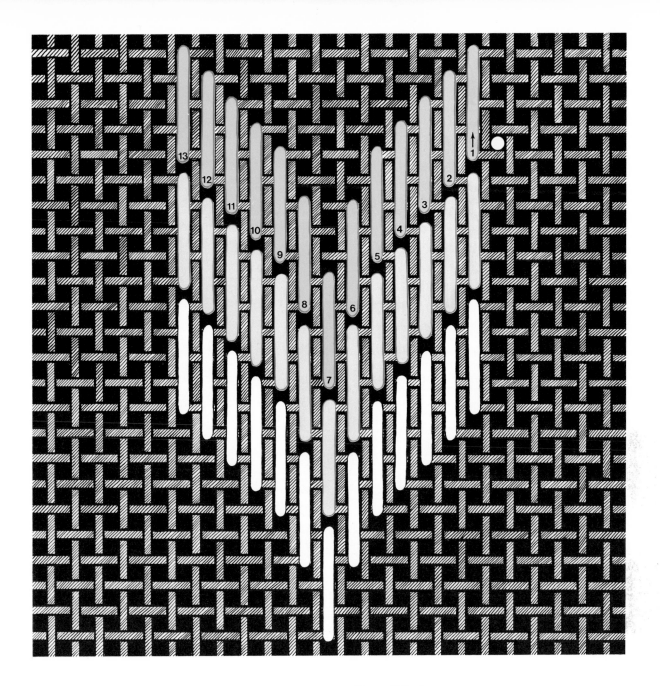

STITCH: Flat *(Flat)*

DESIGN: Typical 19th-century patterning, this one from an Austrian sampler, 1859, Lerman-Foy Collection, New York. It is a vertical strip design which may be bordered by other vertical designs. It may also be continued as a field pattern—in V form.

DIAGRAM 81

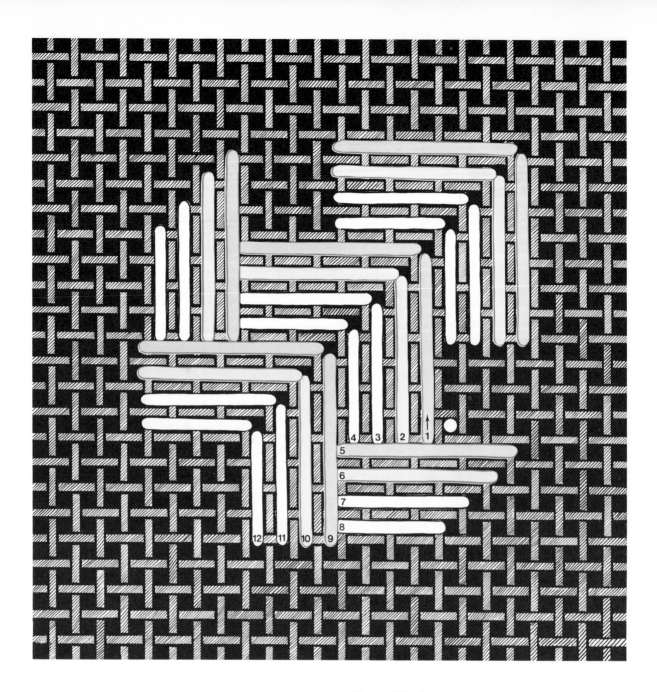

STITCH: FLAT *(Flat)*

DESIGN:[+] From an English sampler, 1841, Philadelphia Museum of Art.

DIAGRAM 82

Islamic-Turkish design carpet (in work).

PLATE 7

Turkish carpet border sampler hanging.

Moroccan motif sampler pillow.

PLATE 8

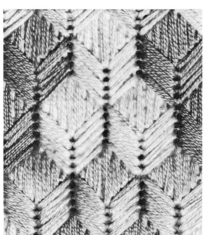

STITCH: FLAT *(Flat)*

Do all Diamond shapes first, then follow with the diagonal lines. That is the neat but not the easy method. It is simpler to work in sequence, as in the diagram, finishing each hexagon in turn. If you follow this second method you will have to snug under your needle. By snug, I mean that part of the hole is covered by previous stitching and subsequent stitches will have to be fitted under previously worked yarn.

DESIGN:[†] From a mid-19th-century English sampler, Victoria and Albert Museum, London.

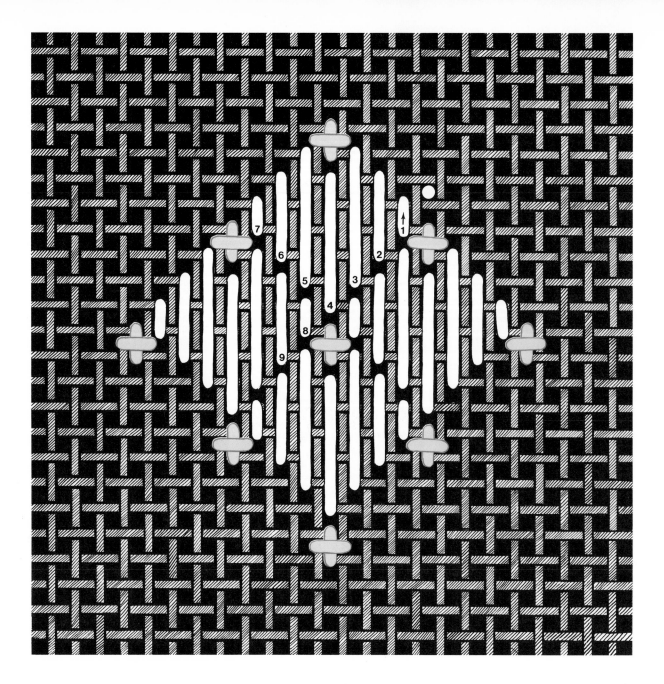

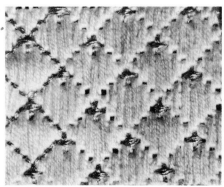

STITCH: FLAT *(Flat)*. FILLER: SMALL UPRIGHT CROSS *(Cross)*

DESIGN: Austrian sampler, 1864, Cooper-Hewitt Museum, New York.

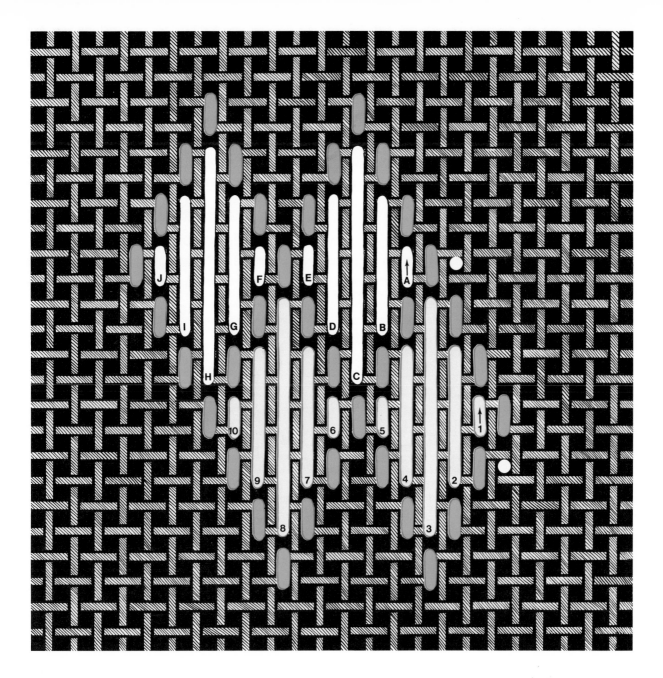

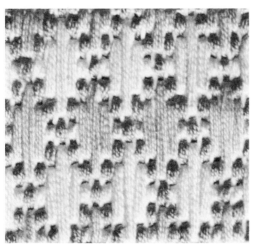

STITCH: FLAT *(Flat)*

DESIGN:[†] Long Diamond Ground adapted from 19th
century German and Austrian samplers. Many tonal
variations possible for geometric patterning.

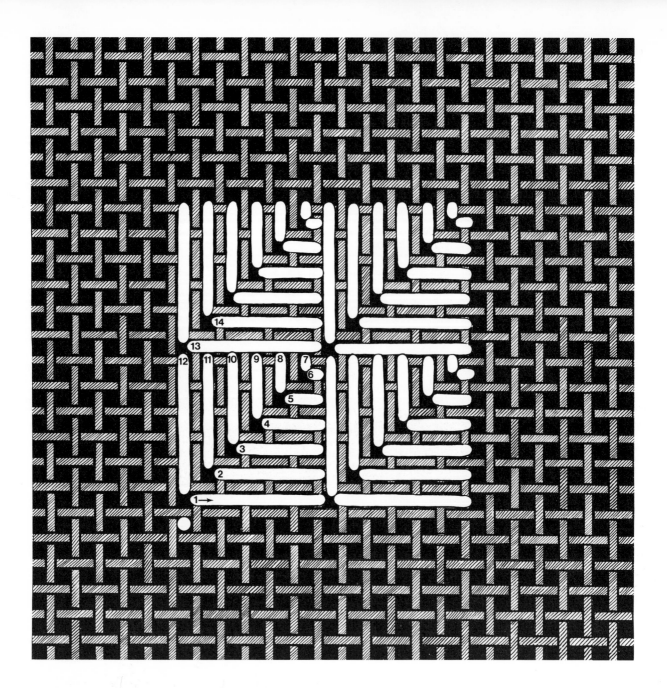

STITCH: FLAT *(Flat)*

Must be worked from lower left corner as shown.

DESIGN: Ground from an English sampler, 1841, Philadelphia Museum of Art. Should feature perforations to be interesting.

DIAGRAM 78

STITCH: FLAT *(Flat)* X CROSS *(Cross)*
Best in monotone.

DESIGN:[†] From an English sampler, 1841, Philadelphia
Museum of Art.

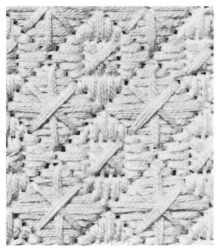

DIAGRAM 79

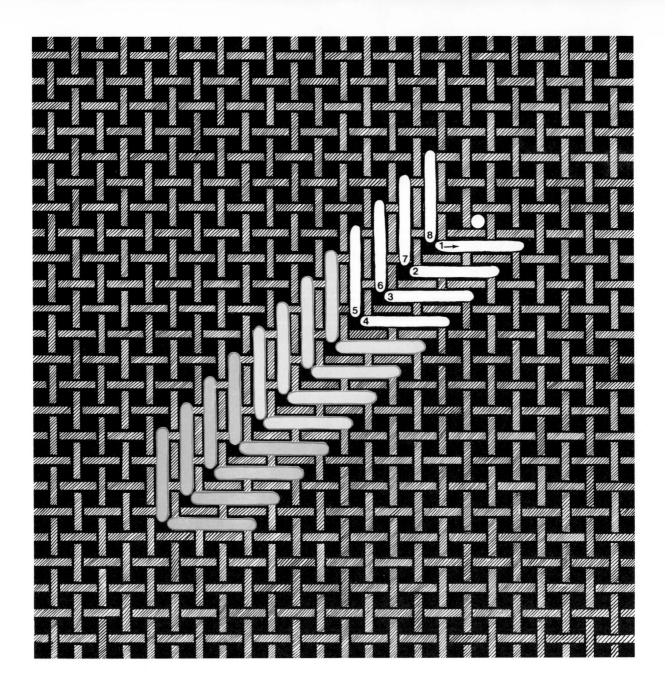

STITCH: Flat *(Flat)*

DESIGN: 19th-century German sampler, Newark Museum of Art. The design is determined by the placement of shading.

DIAGRAM 80

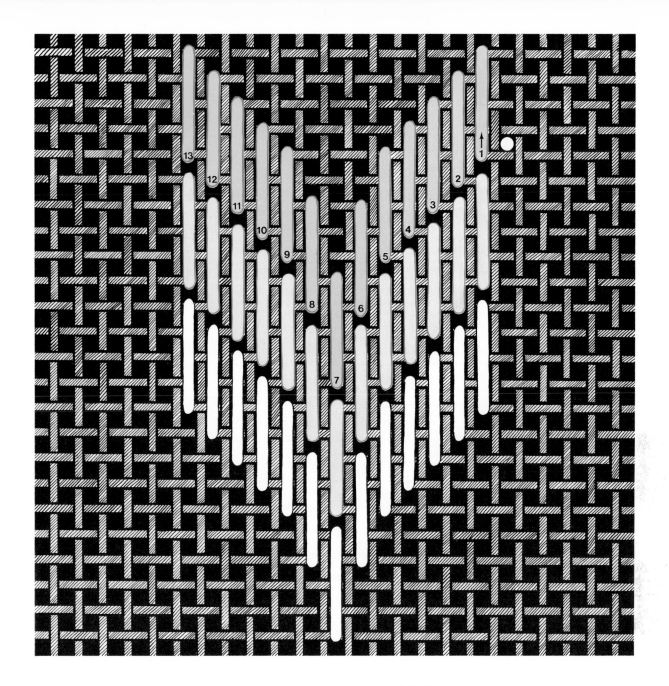

STITCH: FLAT (*Flat*)

DESIGN: Typical 19th-century patterning, this one from an Austrian sampler, 1859, Lerman-Foy Collection, New York. It is a vertical strip design which may be bordered by other vertical designs. It may also be continued as a field pattern—in V form.

DIAGRAM 81

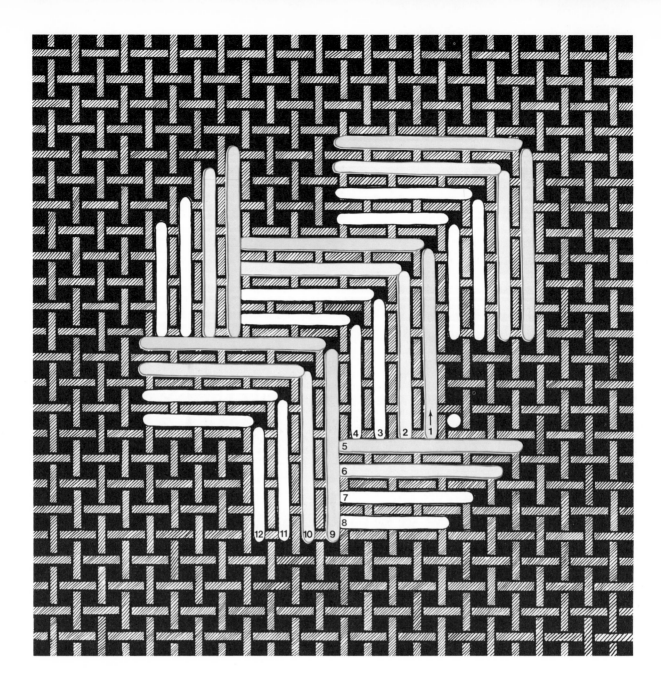

STITCH: FLAT *(Flat)*

DESIGN:[†] From an English sampler, 1841, Philadelphia Museum of Art.

DIAGRAM 82

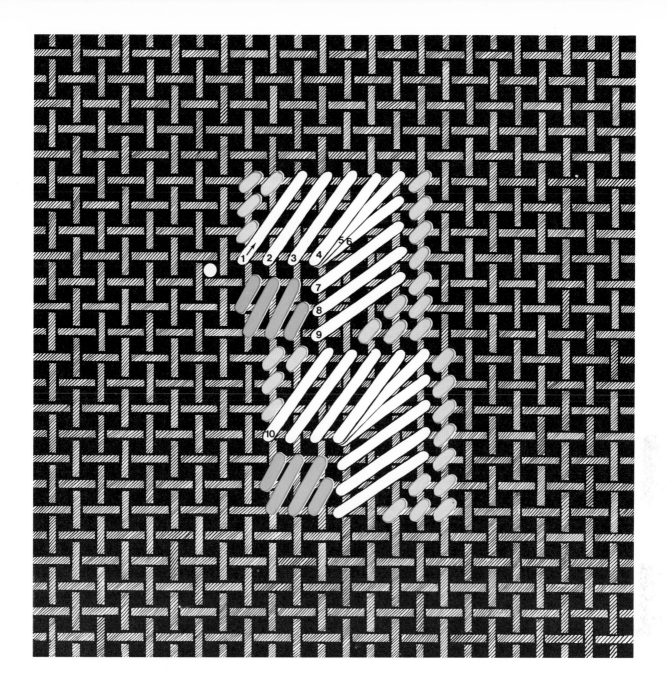

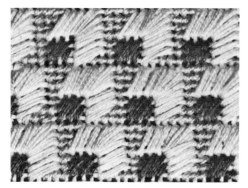

STITCH: FLAT *(Flat)*. FILLER: TENT *(Flat)*

DESIGN:[†] From a mid-19th-century English sampler, Victoria and Albert Museum, London.

DIAGRAM 83

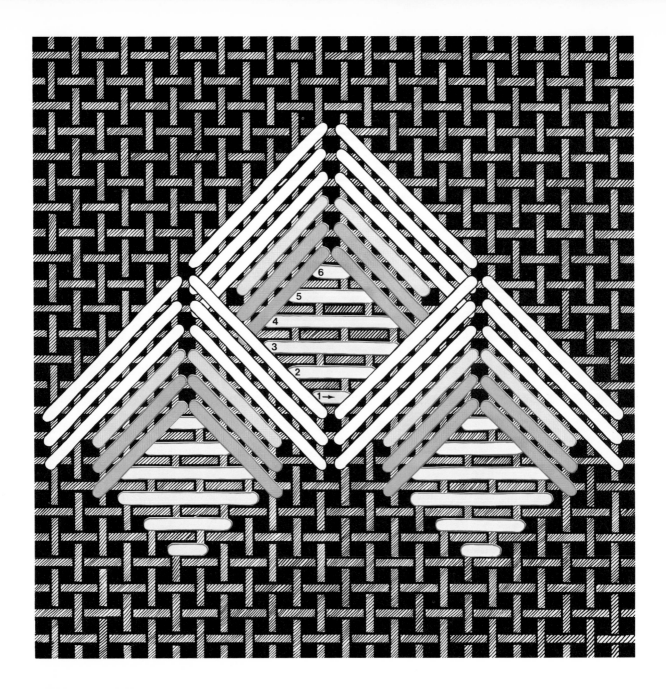

STITCH: Flat *(Flat)*

DESIGN:[†] From mid-19th century English sampler, Victoria and Albert Museum, London. I should point out that, although my structure may be similar to the original needlework to be found in these samplers, I have not always seen the actual embroidery, and many adaptations were made from photographs.

DIAGRAM 84

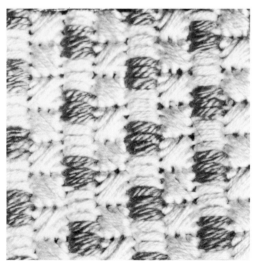

STITCH: FLAT *(Flat)*

DESIGN:[†] From an English sampler, 1841, Philadelphia Museum of Art.

DIAGRAM 85

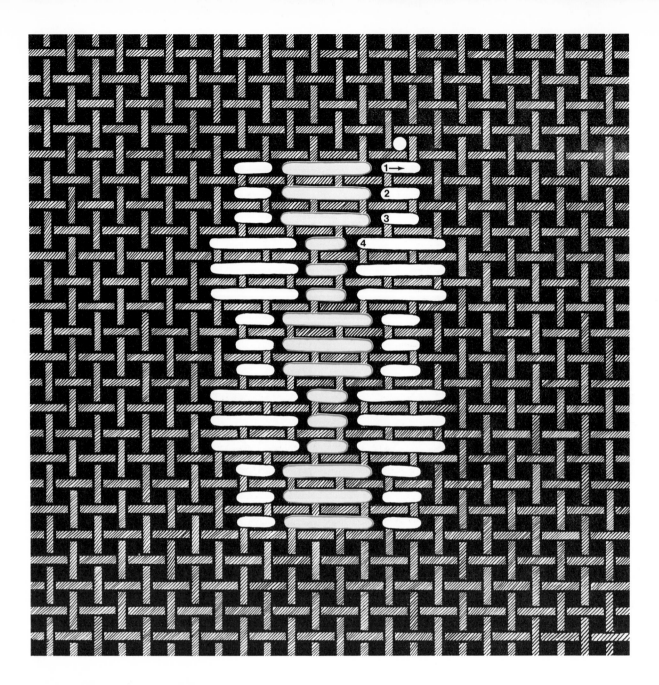

STITCH: FLAT *(Flat)*

DESIGN:[†] East African basket pattern, Private collection, Berlin.

DIAGRAM 86

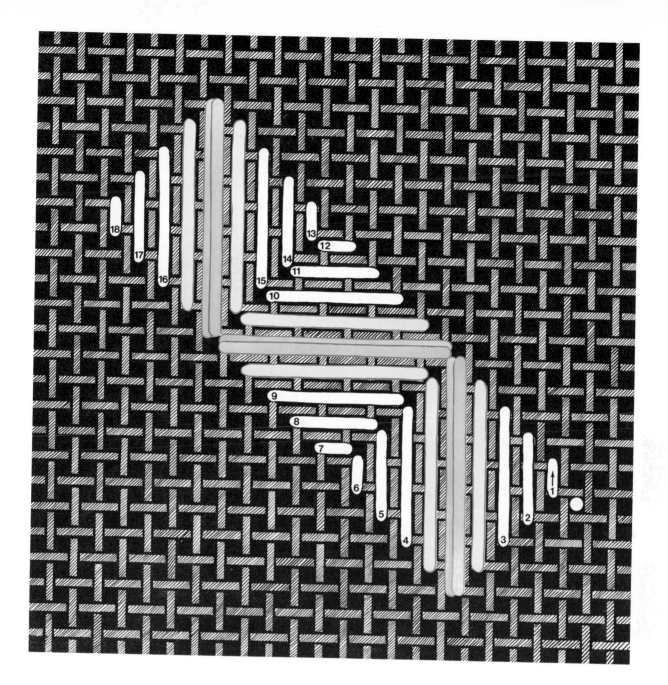

STITCH: FLAT *(Flat)*

DESIGN:[†] From an 1841 English sampler, Philadelphia Museum of Art. Composed of simple Diamonds, the distribution of color in the center gives the appearance of a Step design. Color experiment would be interesting: try reversing the dark and light tones; varying the tones in diagonal or triangular units; shading diagonally.

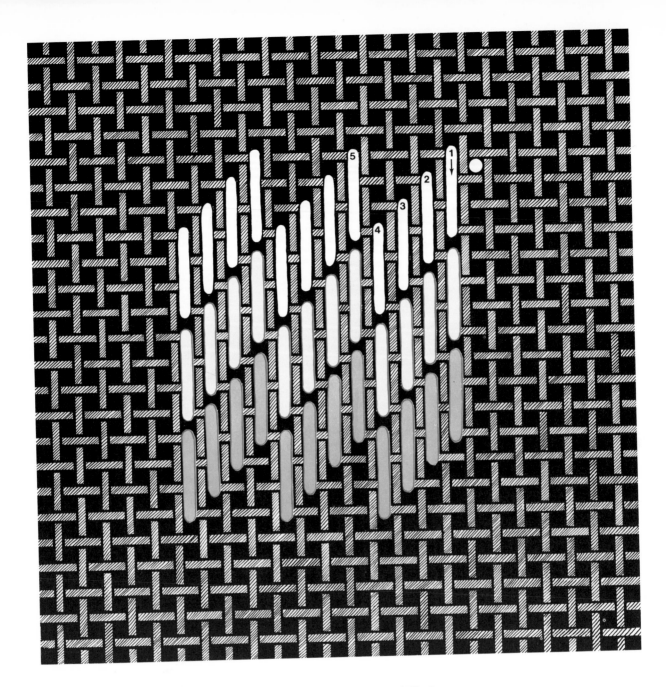

STITCH: FLAT *(Flat)*

DESIGN:[†] From an English sampler, 1841, Philadelphia Museum of Art. The pattern depends entirely on shading distribution. Many other tonal arrangements are possible.

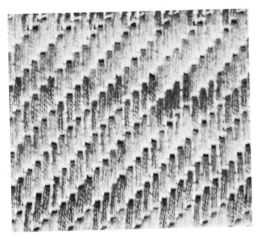

DIAGRAM 88

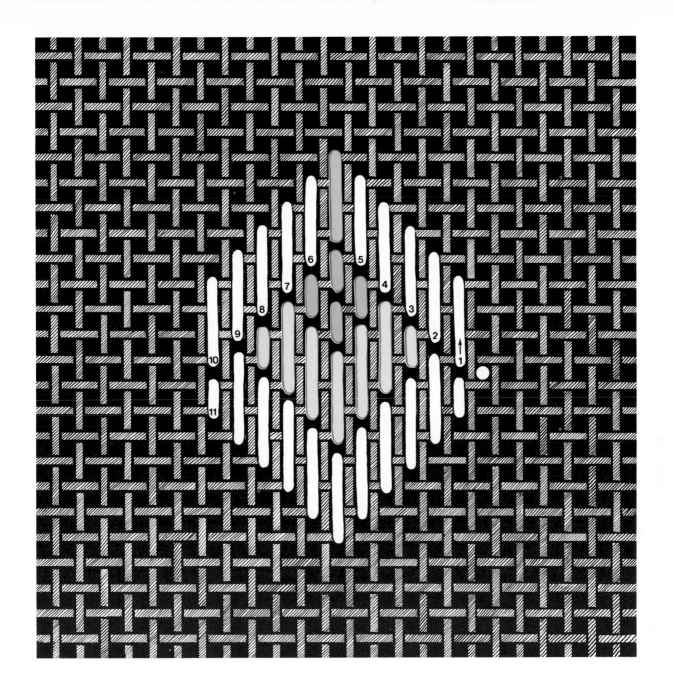

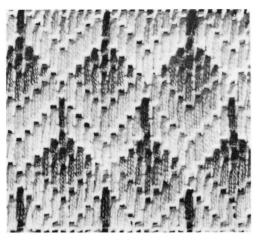

STITCH: FLAT (*Flat*)

DESIGN:[†] This pattern appears in similar form on many of the 19th-century geometric motif samplers. Except for the long dark stitch rising out of the center Diamond, it is a duplication of a Pompeiian pavement design. Color experiment would be very interesting.

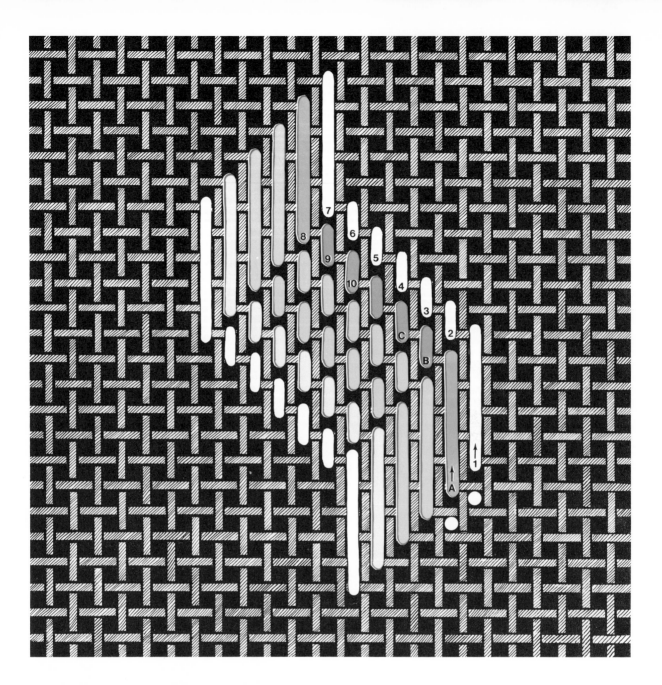

STITCH:[†] VICTORIAN STEP 1 *(Flat)*
The numbers 8, 9, 10, show how to proceed if monotone yarn is used, A, B, C, show start of second-shade stitching.

DESIGN:[†] From an English sampler, 1841, Philadelphia Museum of Art.

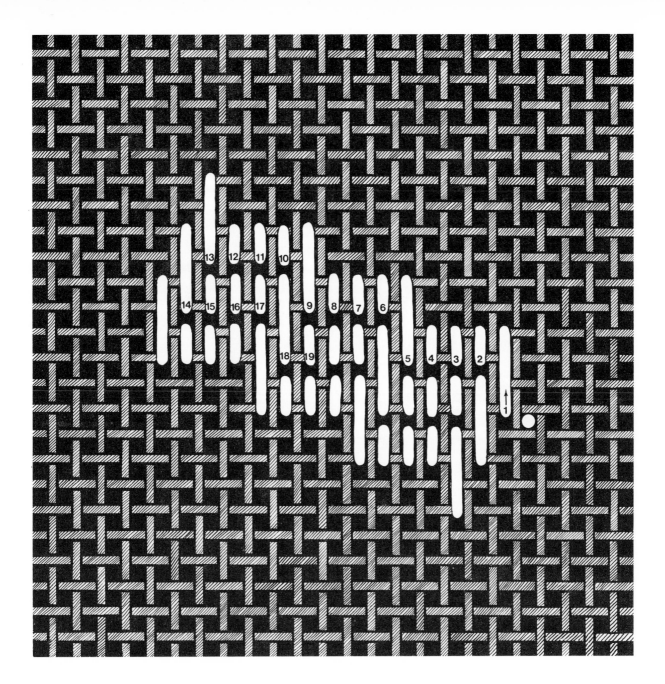

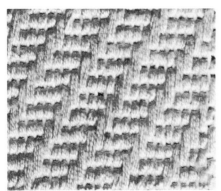

STITCH: VICTORIAN STEP 2 *(Flat)*
From a mid-19th-century German sampler, Metropolitan Museum of Art, New York. Shading or different colors may be used.

DIAGRAM 91

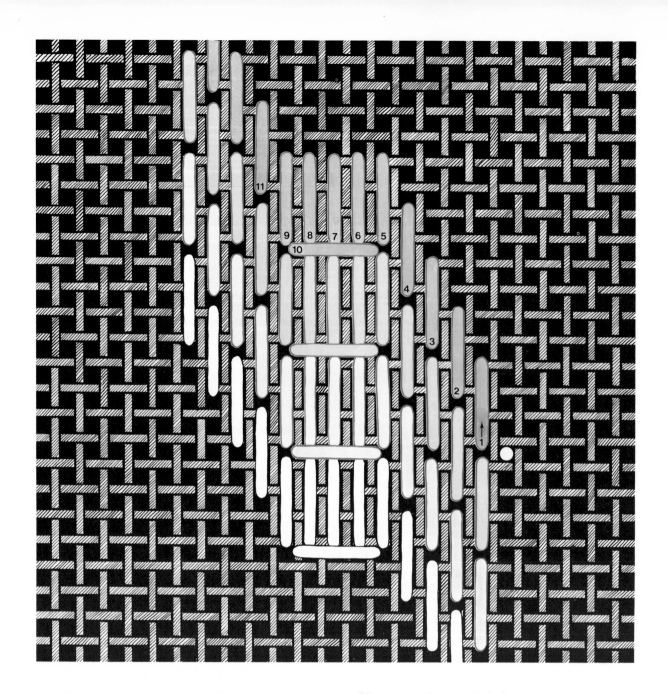

STITCH: VICTORIAN STEP 3 *(Flat)*

DESIGN: Another Step formation from 19th-century sampler work, in this case an Austrian example, 1859, Lerman-Foy Collection, New York.

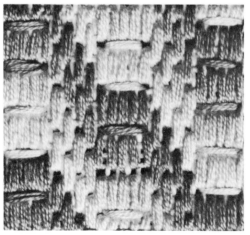

DIAGRAM 92

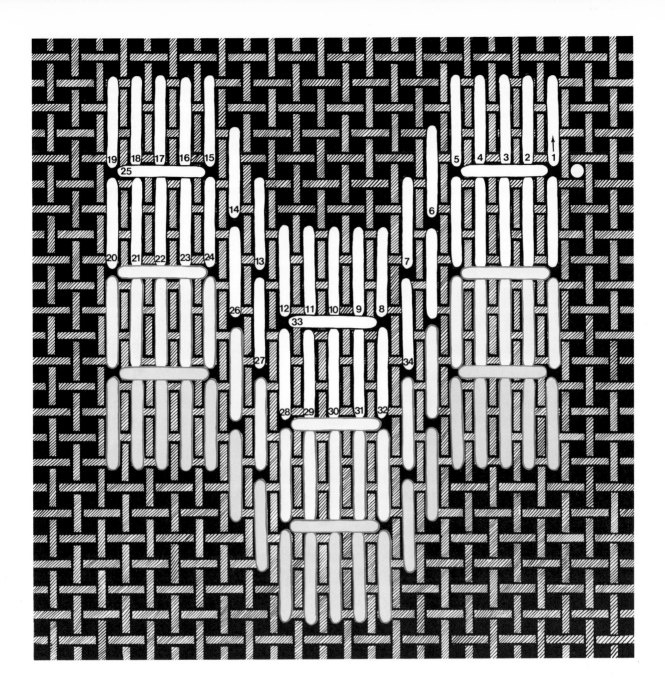

STITCH: FLAT *(Flat)*

DESIGN:[+] 1. From a Bavarian sampler, late 18th century;
2. Also mid-19th-century German sampler, Metropolitan Museum of Art, New York.

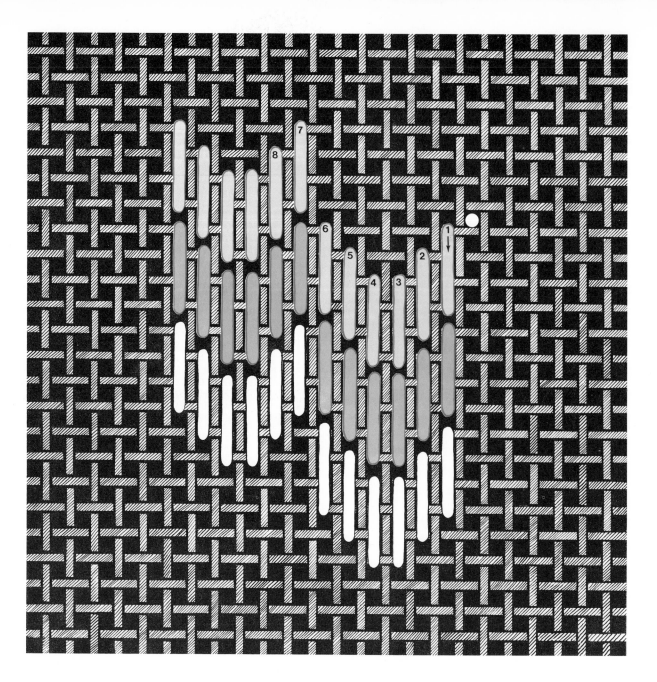

STITCH: FLAT *(Flat)*

DESIGN: Typical 19th-century German sampler pattern, Metropolitan Museum of Art Collection, among others.

DIAGRAM 94

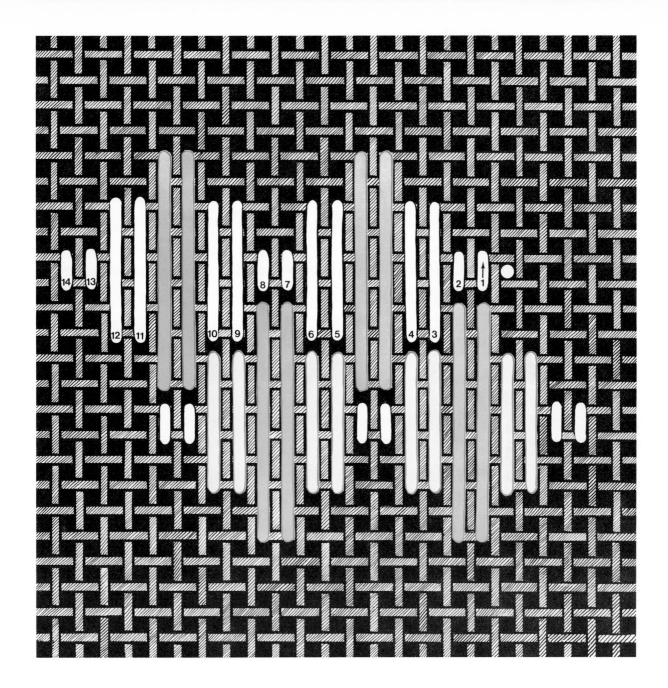

STITCH: FLAT *(Flat)*

DESIGN:[†] From an English sampler, 1841, Philadelphia Museum of Art. H pattern.

DIAGRAM 95

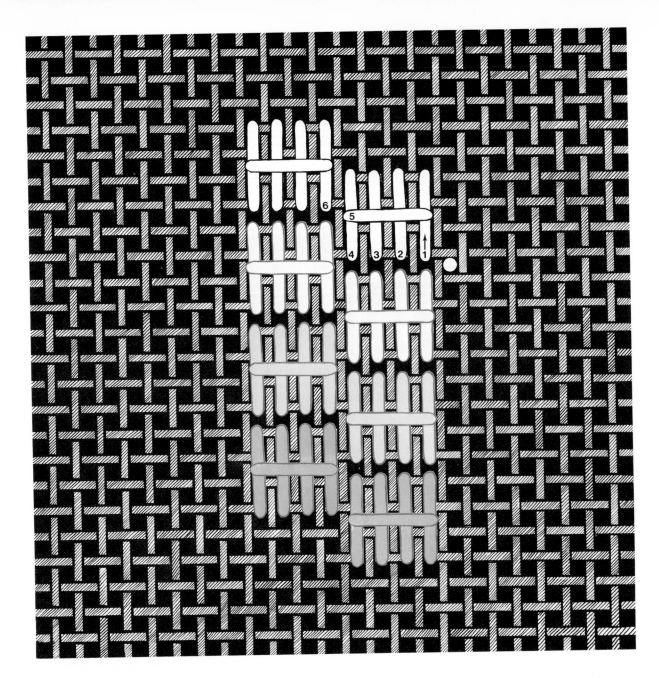

STITCH: Tied Bundles (*Loop, Tied*)

DESIGN:[†] From mid-19th century English sampler, Victoria and Albert Museum, London.

A change in color distribution will give many possibilities for geometric designs.

DIAGRAM 96

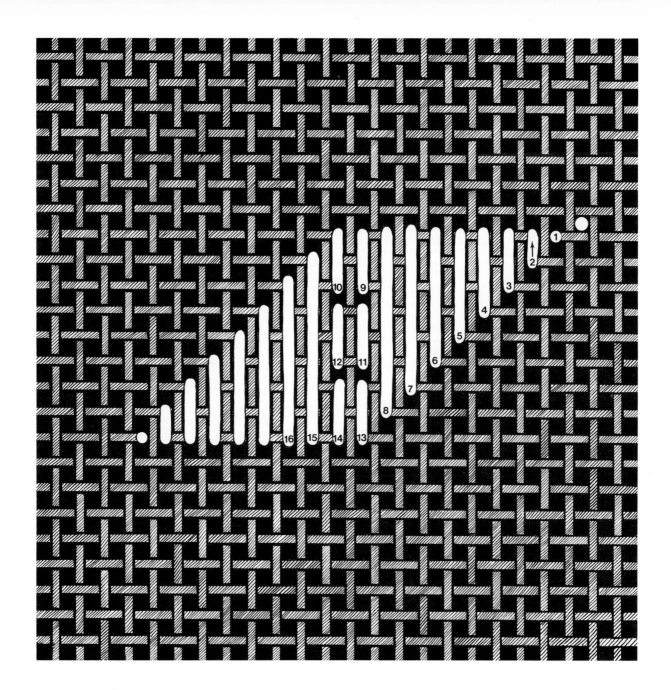

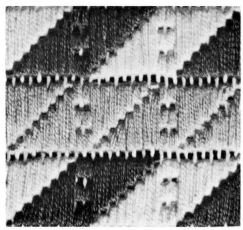

STITCH: FLAT *(Flat)*

DESIGN:[†] From an English sampler, 1841, Philadelphia Museum of Art. The effect, after sufficient repeats, should be that of horizontal ribbons crossing on top of striped diagonal ribbons. This pattern offers very interesting opportunities for tonal experiment. Follow the numbering carefully so as to reveal perforations. The moves are arranged for this specific purpose.

DIAGRAM 97

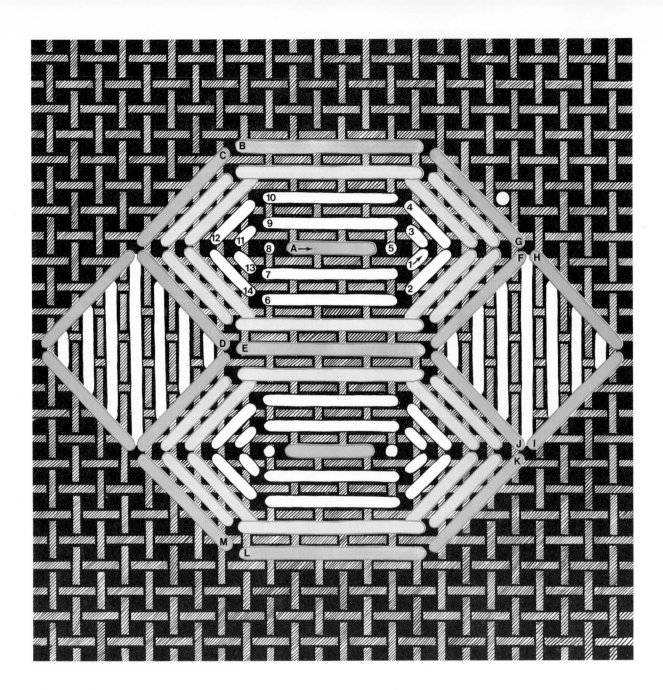

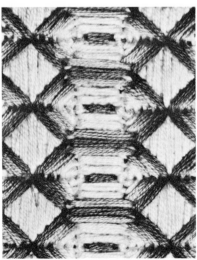

STITCH: FLAT *(Flat)*
The tonal values in this pattern may be reversed. It also looks interesting turned on its side.

DESIGN:[†] From a mid-19th-century English sampler, Victoria and Albert Museum, London.

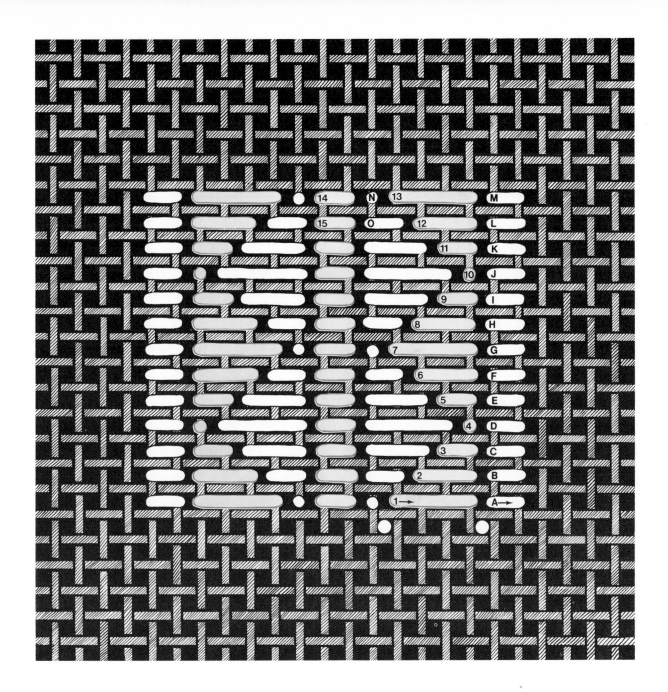

STITCH: FLAT *(Flat)*

DESIGN:[†] Austrian, German, and English motif samplers of the 19th century almost all show variations of this pattern. From a Victorian German sampler in the Newark Museum of Art. The scale and distribution of color may be changed.

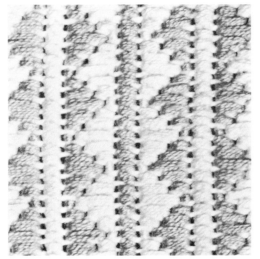

DIAGRAM 99

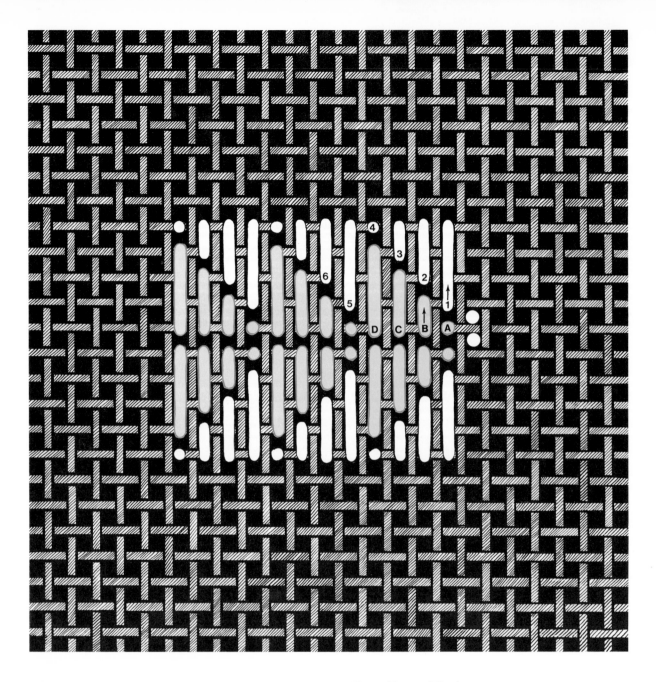

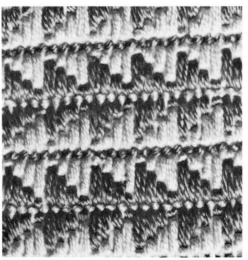

STITCH: Flat, Back *(Flat)*

DESIGN: 19th-century German sampler, similar to American patchwork quilt pattern called Wild Goose Chase.

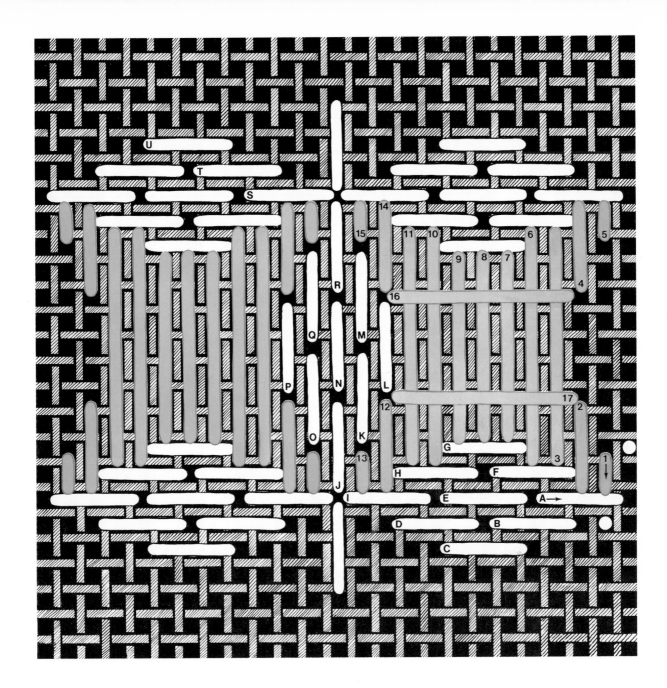

STITCH: FLAT *(Flat)*

DESIGN: From a 19th-century sampler, Philadelphia Museum of Art. *See* Chapter 5 for a photographic history.

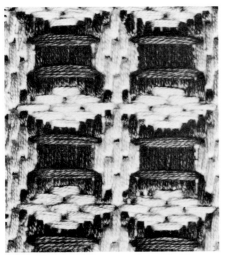

DIAGRAM 101

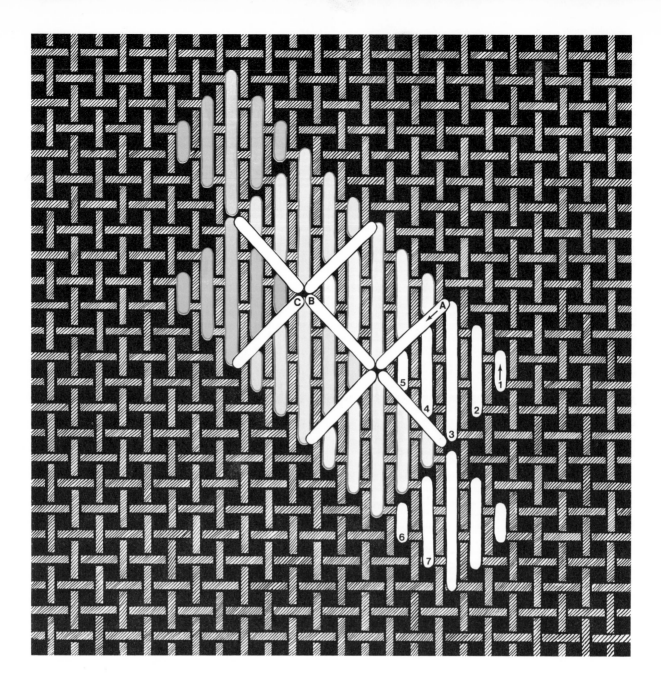

STITCH: FLAT *(Flat)*

The Hungarian Stitch (type) diamonds are worked first. The outline stitch is back-stitched in chevron V formation as the final step.

DESIGN: It appears in many Victorian samplers. The perforations are hidden by overstitching. Change of color distribution can make many geometric patterns of the stained-glass type: the V's can be used like lead strips.

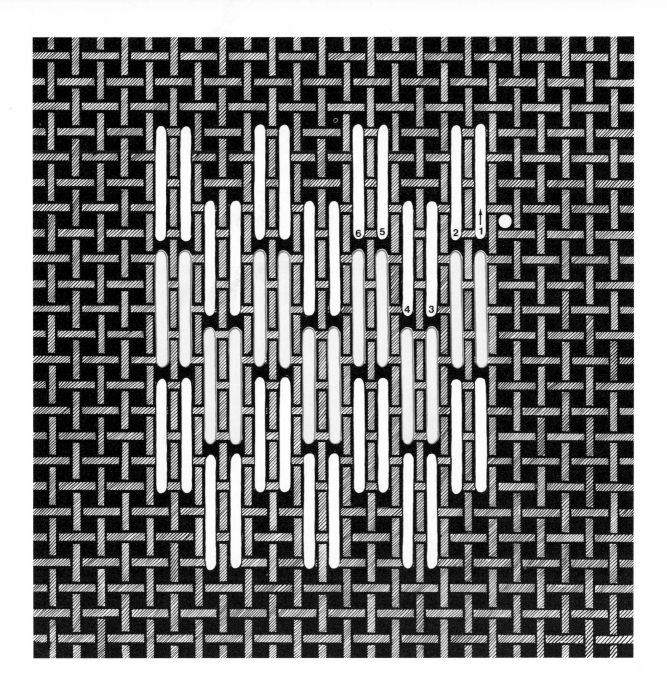

STITCH: VICTORIAN GROUND *(Flat)*

DESIGN: This is a common pattern in Victorian samplers. Sometimes the color groups are made wider, or the individual blocks thicker. Or a wider range of tones may be used.

It is not a Brick Stitch pattern because the stitch falls over five threads and the block is not divisible in the center.

DIAGRAM 103

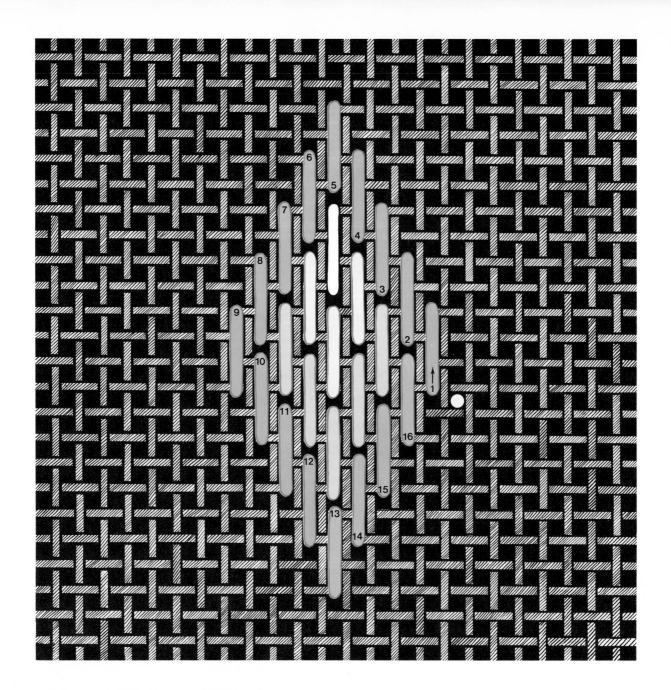

STITCH: FLAT *(Flat)*

DESIGN: A typical 19th-century small-scale motif.
Florentine-type arrangements of tone and flat stitches.

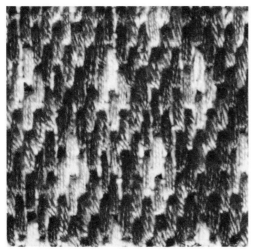

DIAGRAM 104

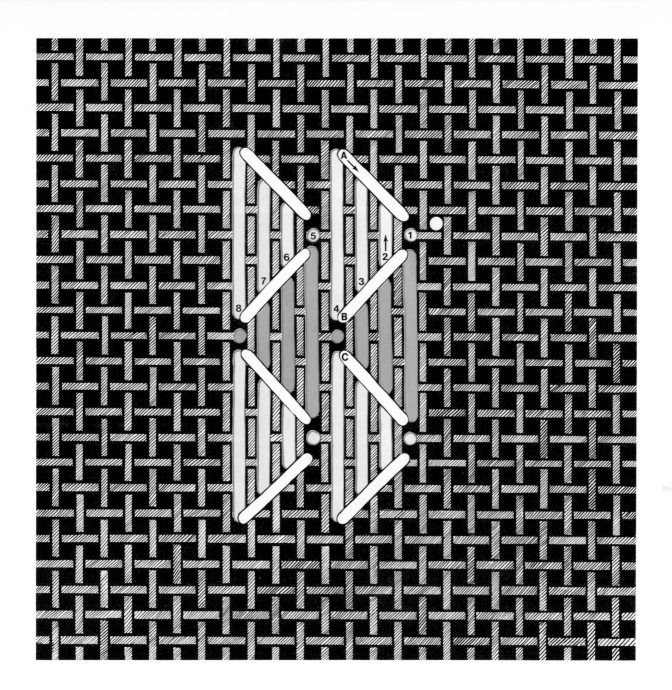

STITCH: FLAT *(Flat)*

DESIGN:[+] From many Victorian samplers. Typical of its period, the final threads conceal perforations.

DIAGRAM 105

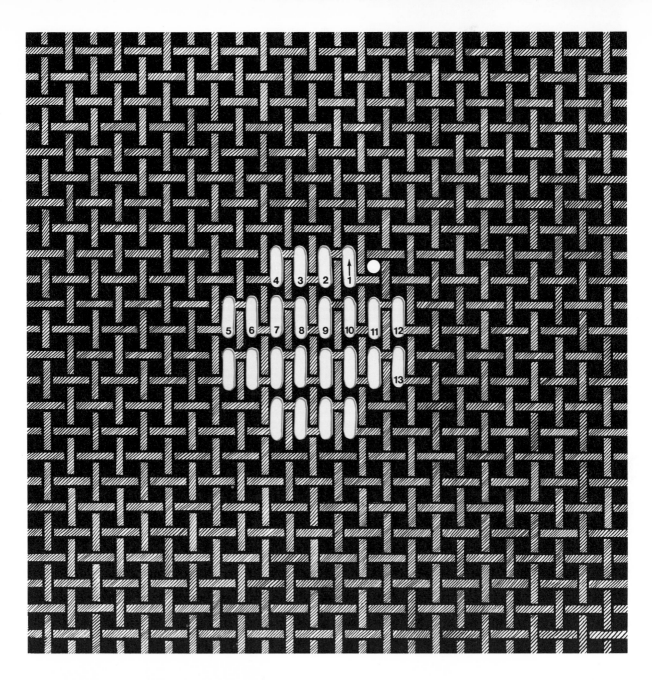

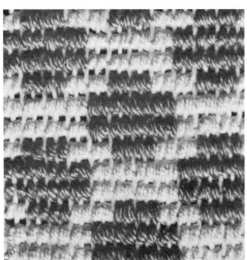

STITCH: STRAIGHT GOBELIN *(Flat)*

DESIGN:[†] From a 19th-century Austrian sampler, 1864, Cooper-Hewitt Museum, New York.

DIAGRAM 106

Antique Moroccan carpet, adaptation.

PLATE 9

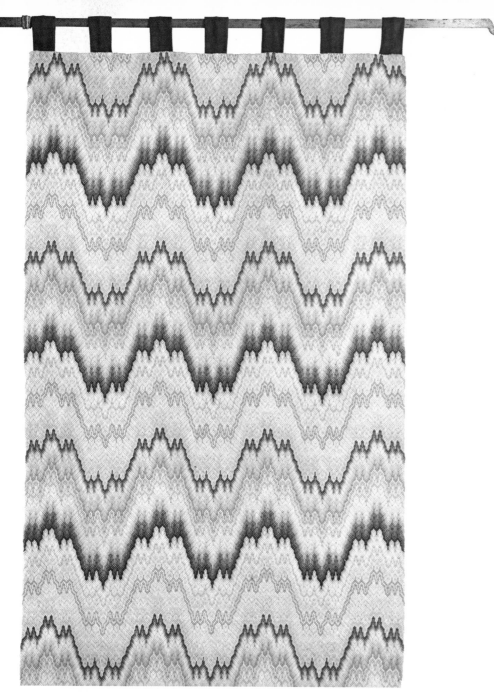

Hungarian Point wall hanging.

Hungarian Point pillow.

PLATE 10

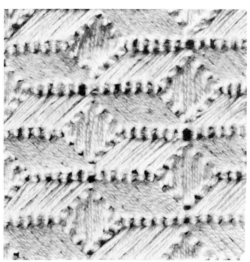

STITCH: Fʟᴀᴛ, Bᴀᴄᴋ *(Flat)*

DESIGN:[†] From English 18th- and 19-century samplers. Contrasting colors in the diamonds, or shading by horizontal row, may be used. Remember that Back Stitches are always worked at the very end.

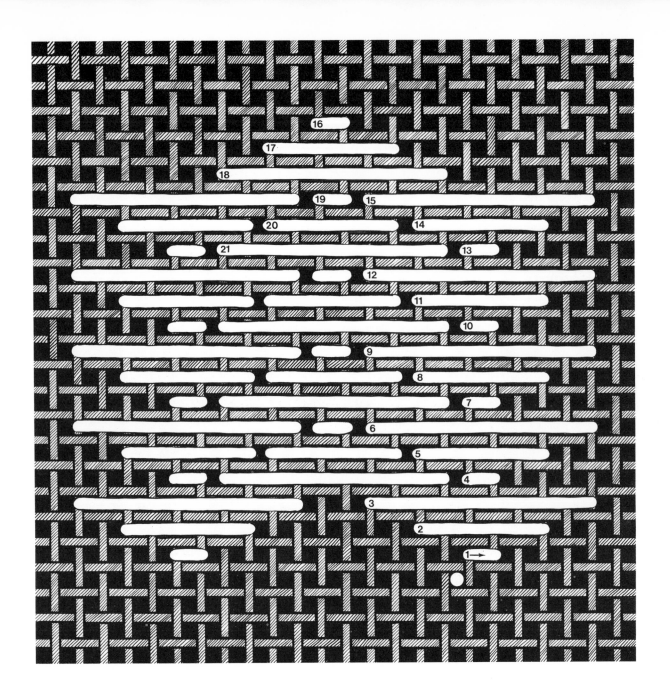

STITCH: FLAT *(Flat)*

DESIGN:[†] 18th-century German embroidery ground.

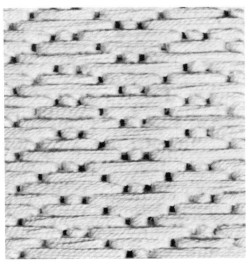

DIAGRAM 108

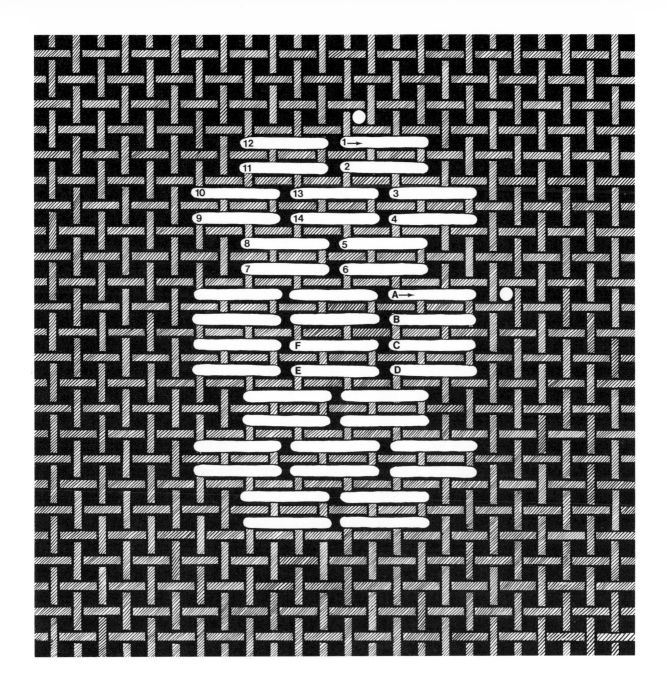

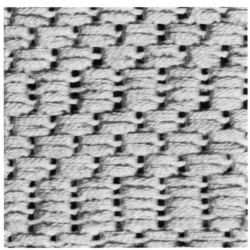

STITCH: FLAT *(Flat)*

DESIGN:[†] From an 18th-century Swedish sampler ground pattern. In the photograph of my sampler square, one group of blocks shows five stitches and another shows four. This is an error: either one will do. The original uses five.

DIAGRAM 109

STITCH: FLAT *(Flat)*, EYE *(Pulled Yarn)*

DESIGN:* Stepped Eyes, based on 18th-century type needle work.

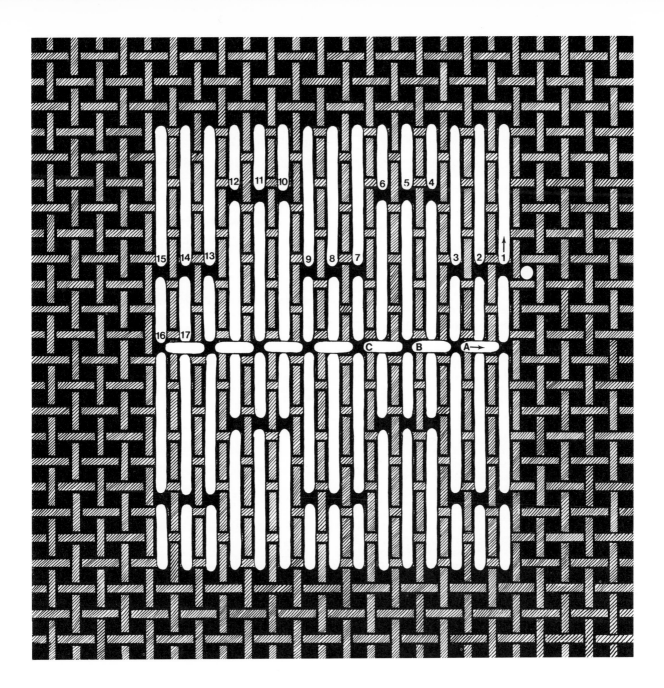

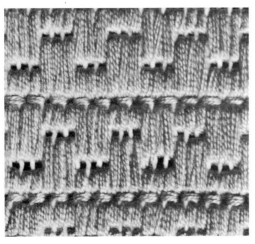

STITCH: FLAT, BACK (Flat)

DESIGN: 18th-century German sampler, border or grounding.

DIAGRAM 111

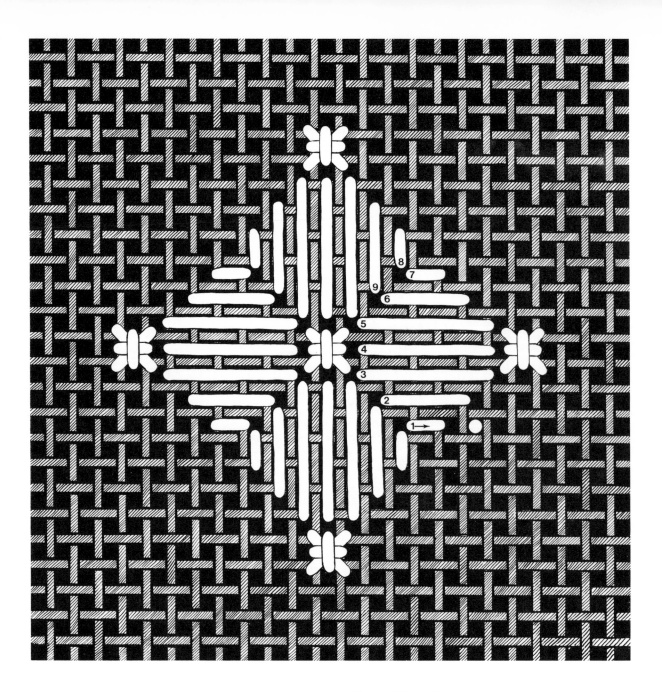

STITCH: Flat *(Flat)*, Single Leviathan *(Cross)*

DESIGN:[†] 18th-century embroidery grounding, German sampler. *See* Playing Card hanging (Color Plate 12), the pattern is used in the body of the horse.

STITCH: OBLONG CROSS, BARRED AND TIED *(Cross)*

DESIGN:[†] From a Danish Sampler, 1751, Victoria and Albert Museum, London.

DIAGRAM 113

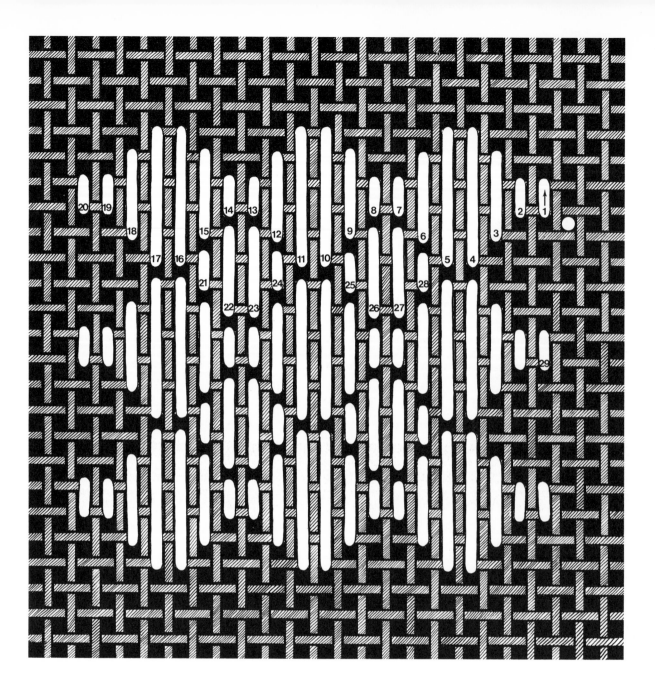

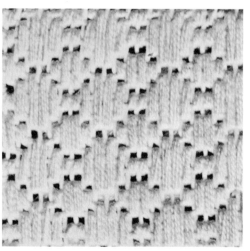

STITCH: FLAT *(Flat)*

DESIGN:[†] From a 17th-century European sampler, Cooper-Hewitt Museum, New York. *See* Playing Card hanging (Color Plate 12), pattern used in the body of the horse.

12) Stitches

CROSS

In their more simple form, Cross Stitches are the best choice for the beginner. They are easily grasped, lend themselves to geometric ground and pattern with ease, and, with few exceptions, give a good, stable, and durable surface. They combine well with one another in construction and in appearance. Cross Stitches differ from Plait or Interlace because the point of meeting is usually, but not always, in the center. In fact, a case could be made for moving Cross Stitches that do not intersect in the center to the Plait Group. I have left them where they are in deference to custom rather than logic. Most Cross Stitches are built on the even thread count, covering 2, 4, 6, 8, and so on. I have experimented with odd numbers and you will find them on the diagram pages.

Technically, Cross Stitches are modest in demand. Your count, as in all stitches, must be meticulous and you must be aware of direction so that your final threads have a uniform slant, unless you consciously plan to vary this. If the slant is altered by error rather than intention, it will destroy textural rhythm.

They accommodate all yarns well.

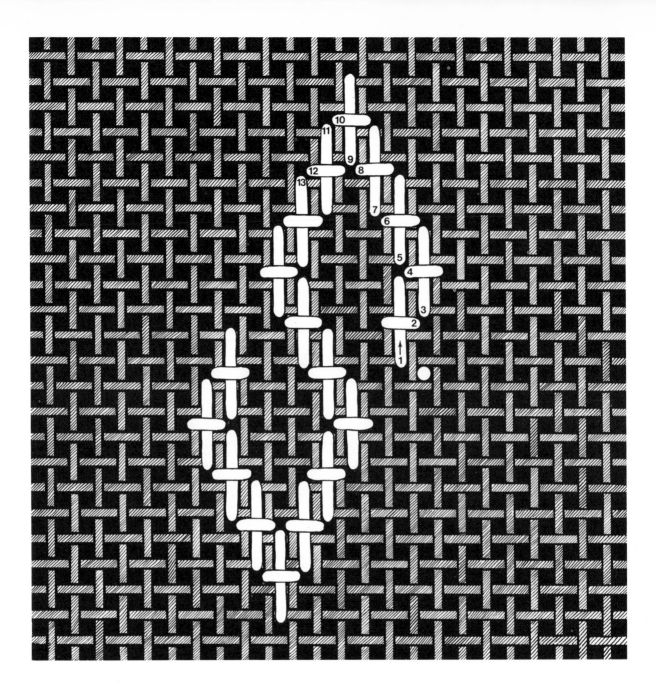

STITCH: UPRIGHT CROSS *(Cross)*

DESIGN:[†] From a 19th-century Persian saddlebag. This pattern may be worked in almost any Cross Stitch or in Rococo, French, Sorbello Knot, Diagonal-Barred Cross, Diamond Eye, Tent, Renaissance, etc.

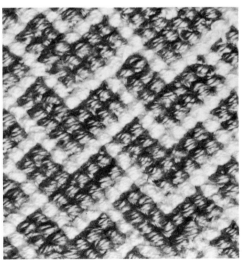

STITCH: SMALL UPRIGHT CROSS *(Cross)*

DESIGN: † From a Danish sampler, 1751, Victoria and Albert Museum, London. This may be worked in many stitches: Brick, Rococo, Diamond Eye, Oblong Cross, Diamond Cross, Diagonal-Barred Cross, French, French Double Tie, etc.

DIAGRAM 116

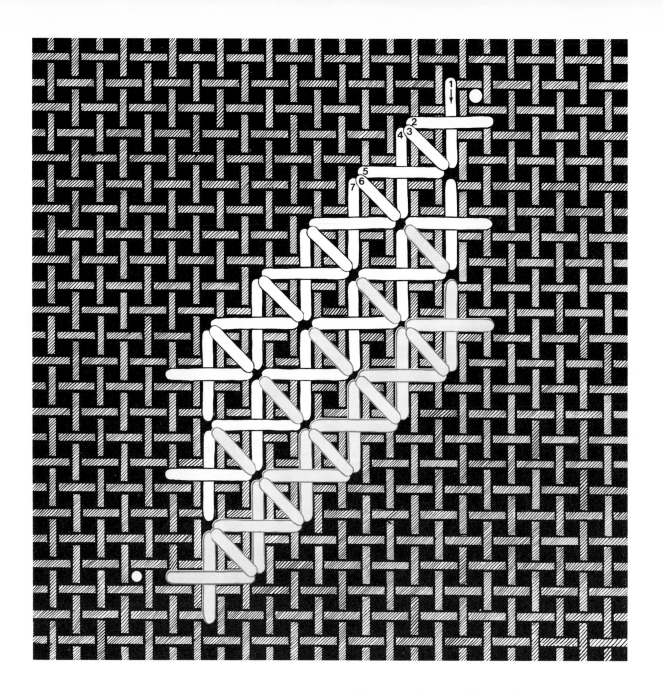

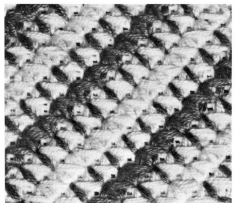

STITCH: DIAGONAL-BARRED CROSS *(Cross)*

DESIGN: * It may appear more complex, but only Diagonal-Barred Cross was used for this pattern. The design is formed, and may be altered, by the distribution of color in cross and bar.

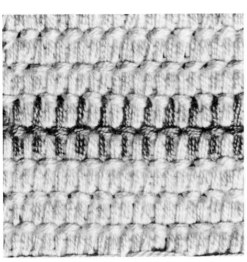

STITCH: UPRIGHT CROSS, HALF-DROPPED *(Cross)*
This stitch resembles French Double Tie (Diagram 204) but it is constructed quite differently. It is worked in horizontal rows, in single stitching, and the perforation is less marked.

DIAGRAM 118

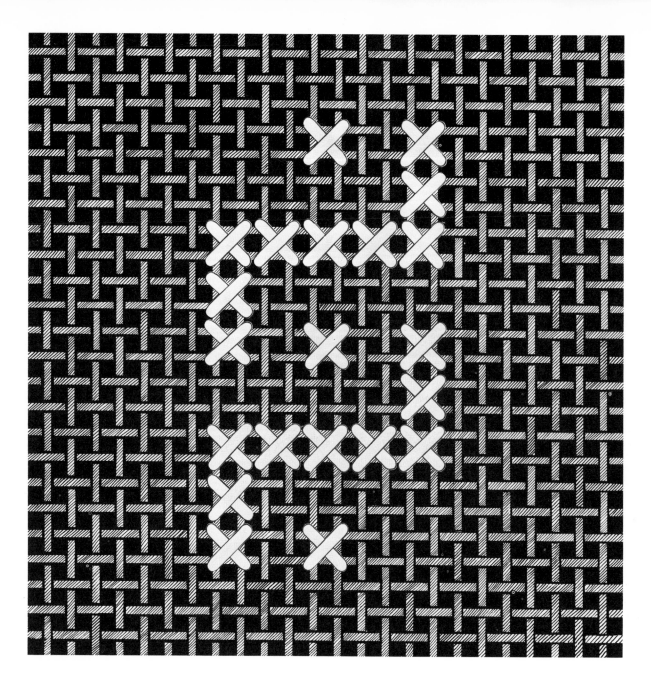

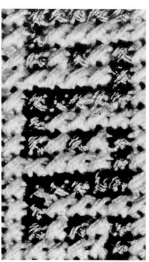

STITCH: CROSS *(Cross)*

DESIGN:[†] Border design from 13th-century altar curtain, The Annunciation, Syria. Osterreichisches Museum, Vienna.

The white Cross Stitches form a boxed-link design. The dark Cross Stitches form the background, which may be stitched first as in the diagram. This design requires additional dark Cross Stitch borders worked vertically on both sides to take proper shape. Typical Islamic fret pattern.

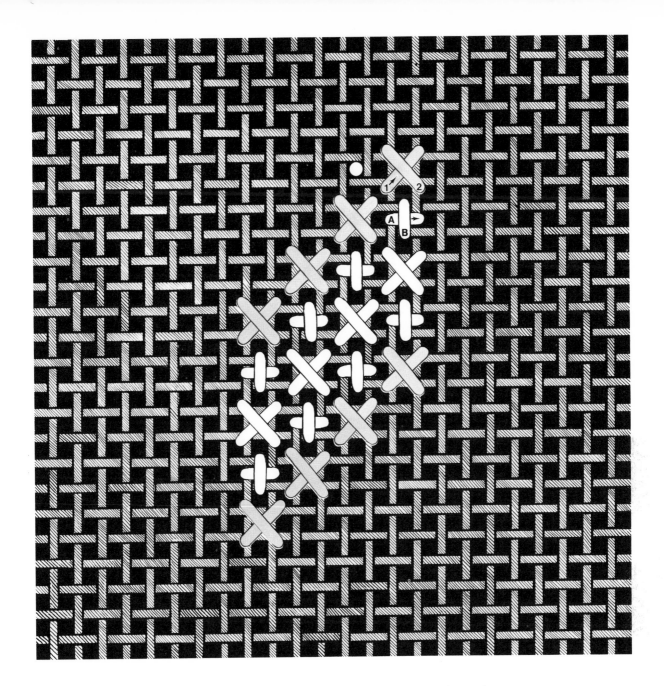

STITCH: SAINTS' CROSS *(Cross)*
Usually called the St. George and St. Andrew Stitch;
a cumbersome name for a small stitch. It is composed
of one small upright and one X shaped Cross placed
alternately. Here I used it for a toned design, but it is
most frequently worked in monotone or in checkerboard shading.

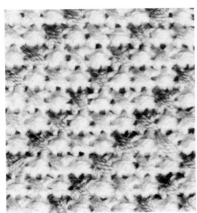

STITCH: LARGE X CROSS *(Cross)*. FILLER: SMALL
UPRIGHT CROSS *(Cross)*

As with Crossed Corners Stitch (Diagram 123), color
distribution can be employed to form many geometric
patterns. It is fine for textural interest when worked
in monotone.

DIAGRAM 121

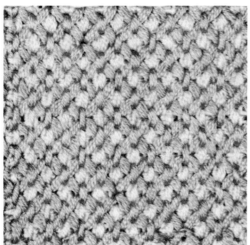

STITCH: * LARGE X CROSS, TIED *(Cross)*. FILLER: SMALL
UPRIGHT CROSS *(Cross)*
May be tied vertically or horizontally. Fastening down
the Large Cross gives it a harder, more stable surface.

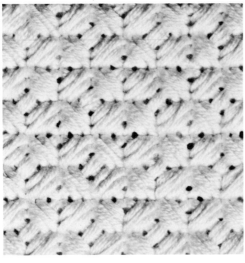

STITCH: * CROSSED CORNERS, VARIATION *(Cross)*
Good in monotone and polychrome shading.
For basic Crossed Corners *see* Diagram 27.

STITCH: DOUBLE LEVIATHAN
See following page description and for a design making use of this stitch.

DIAGRAM 124

STITCH: DOUBLE LEVIATHAN and SINGLE LEVIATHAN CROSSES (*Cross*)

These are also called Smyrna, Double and Single, in some books. The large square is the Double, the smaller is the Single Leviathan.

DESIGN:[†] Adapted from an illustration in a book devoted to French medieval pavement mosaics. Unfortunately, no provenance accompanied the drawings. I based a few squares on the designs in the book nevertheless. Stitches such as Raised Squares, Palestrina Knot, Sorbello Knot, Crossed Corners, Square Mosaic, or other stitches with square outlines may be substituted for this design. Remember, virtually all toned geometric designs may be easily worked out in Tent Stitch.

DIAGRAM 125

STITCH: TRIPLE LEVIATHAN *(Cross)*
Simple to work, its pattern resembles that used for many medieval wall designs in illuminated manuscripts. The foundation Cross may be formed by working stitches into the center hole (A in diagram) instead of running them full length. The last Cross (7, 8) will cover the hole.

DESIGN: I adapted this pattern from a wall-detail in a 14th-century mural painted by Ambrogio Lorenzetti, Siena, and only later discovered that it was a full-fledged proper-name stitch. Monotone or use contrast.

DIAGRAM 126

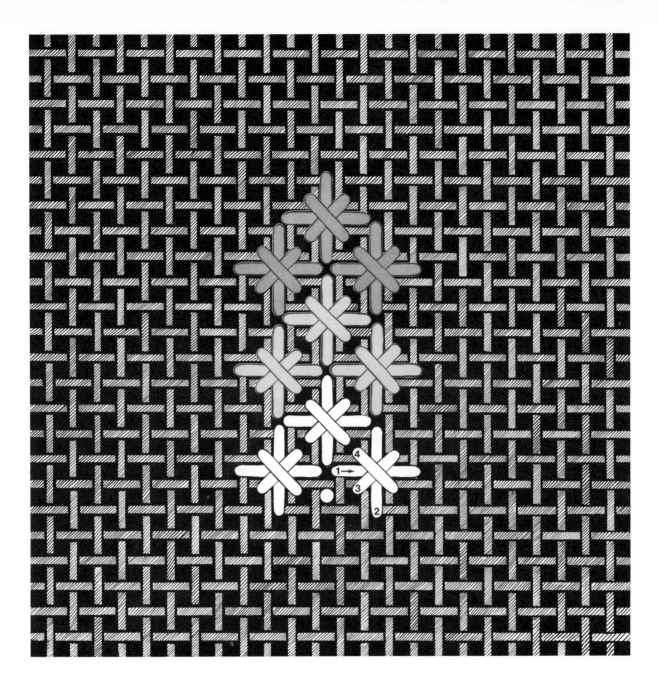

STITCH: DIAMOND CROSS *(Cross)*

Although it is sometimes called Double Cross, Diamond Cross gives a clearer picture of its architectural function in pattern (it is, of course, a tipped square). Related to the Leviathans.

DESIGN:[†] INVERTED V's

From a medieval French pavement mosaic study. Tent, Hungarian Stitch, Diagonal Cross, Rococo, French, Renaissance or Diamond Eye may be substituted.

STITCH: *FLOWER CROSS (*Cross*). FILLER: DIAMOND CROSS (*Cross*)

DESIGN:[†] This small repeating motif can be found in a 14th-century painting of the Madonna by Jacopo di Cione in the design of the mosaic pavement floor, St. Apostoli Church, Florence.

STITCH: LONG DIAMOND CROSS *(Cross)*

DESIGN: * I discovered this stitch in a 19th-century German sampler in the Metropolitan Museum of Art collection. It can be used for many geometric pattern variations by changing the color distribution.
Stitches that take the shape of diamonds or squares cooperate well with geometric diaper designs. This one forms elongated true diamonds, rare in needlework structures, and can replace Rococo, Diamond Cross, Diamond Eye, etc. Its angle will alter the geometric pattern significantly and interestingly. Thicker yarn required.

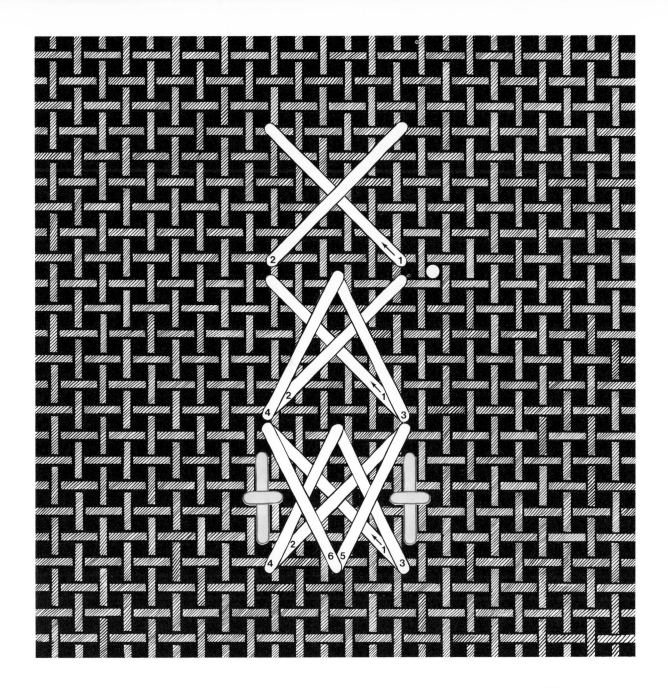

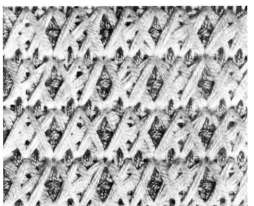

STITCH: Triple Cross *(Cross)*. FILLER: Upright Cross
An embroidery stitch adapted for canvas. It may be
used for patterning, in two or more shades or in monotone for textural interest.

DIAGRAM 130

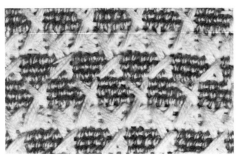

stitch: * Single Insertion Ground *(Cross)*. filler:
Tent *(Flat)*

An embroidery stitch converted to a ground pattern
by combining it with Tent Stitch.

DIAGRAM 131

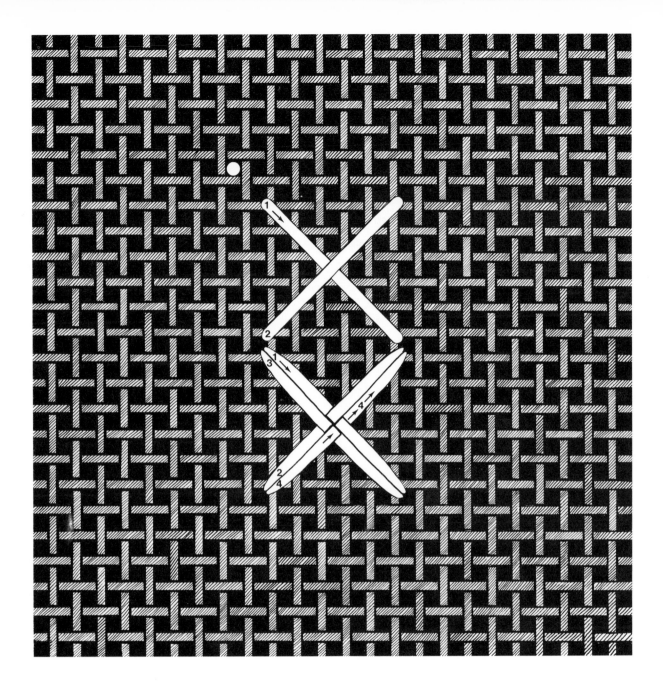

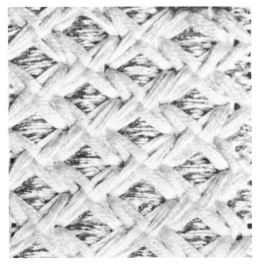

STITCH: * INTERLACED CROSS *(Cross)*. FILLER: UPRIGHT
CROSS
An Upright Cross may be worked in similar structural
sequence. Follow the same numerical procedure, using
perpendicular and horizontal instead of slanted
stitches.

233   DIAGRAM 132

STITCH: ZIG ZAG CROSS *(Cross)*

DESIGN: * *See* following page.

DIAGRAM 133

#1

#2

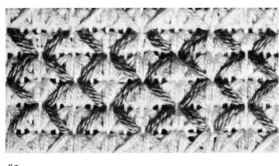

#3

STITCH: Zig Zag *(Cross)*

DESIGN: These three structures are identical in stitch and scale. A very simple color change was made in each to illustrate how minute alteration will bring a surprising metamorphosis to pattern. One shade of brown and one of white were used for all.

The pattern for #2 was adapted from an embroidery of The Nativity, 1485, Guadalupe Monastery, Castile.

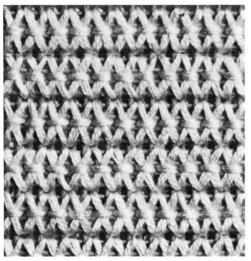

STITCH: OBLONG CROSS, TIED (*Cross*)
This stitch is often back-stitched (barred), top and bottom, as well as tied in the center. It may also be worked without the center tie.

DIAGRAM 134

STITCH: [+] OBLONG CROSS, BARRED AND HALF-DROPPED
(*Cross*)
Bars may be made in contrasting colors.

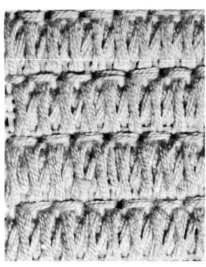

STITCH: Narrow Oblong Cross *(Cross)*, Back-Stitched. FILLER: Cross *(Cross)*, BACK *(Flat)*
The filler Cross Stitch may be lengthened by one canvas thread, top and bottom, as in stitched sampler square.

DIAGRAM 136

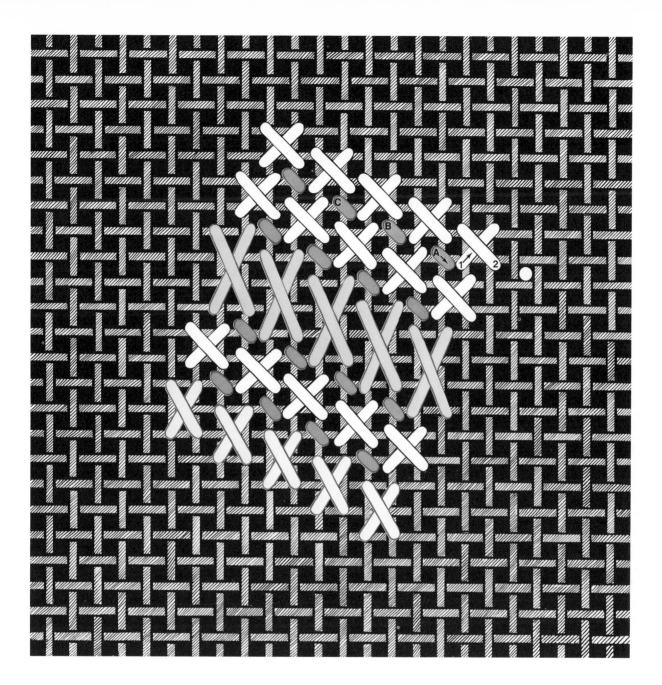

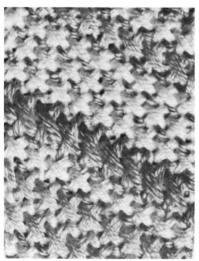

STITCH: OBLONG CROSSES, CROSS *(Cross)*. FILLER:
REVERSED TENT *(Flat)*

DESIGN: * CROSS MEDLEY
The pattern is composed of three Cross Stitches with
Reversed Tent Stitch filler.

DIAGRAM 137

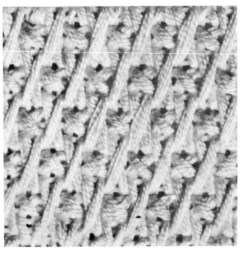

STITCH: DOUBLE STITCH *(Cross)*
This stitch can be given tonal and pattern variation by contrasting the larger with the smaller Crosses or by using contrast in the small Crosses. One example of a composite formation, or stitches given a new name because of habitual coupling.

DIAGRAM 138

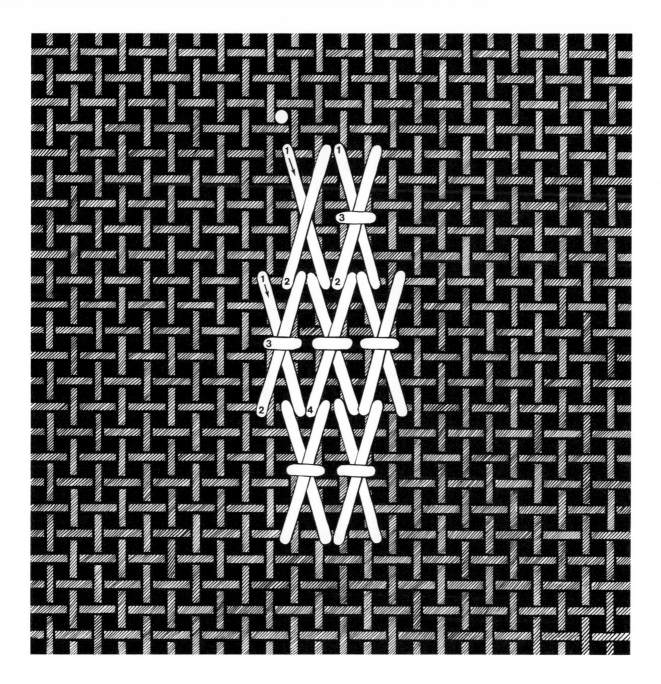

STITCH: OBLONG CROSS, TIED, ENCROACHED (*Cross*)

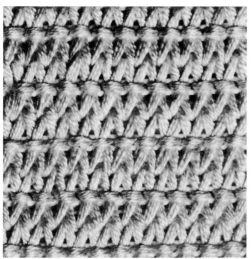

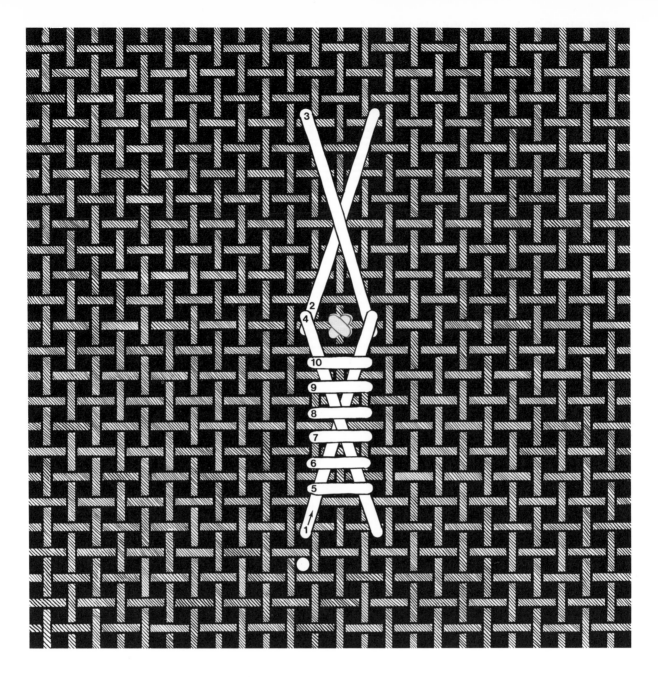

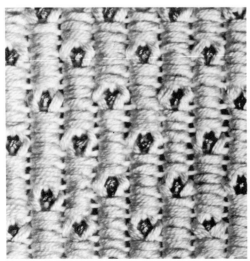

STITCH: * NINE CROSS *(Cross)*. FILLER: CROSS *(Cross)*
This and the four stitches following are the result of experiments with odd-number thread count Cross Stitches. Though all have a strong kinship, they may be used for diverse surfaces and patterns. Nine Cross may be worked horizontally for a quite different effect. The filler may be lengthened as in stitched square.

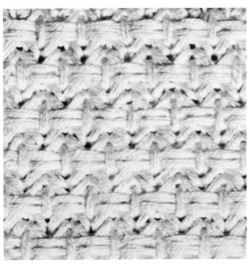

STITCH: * RIBBON CROSS, ENCROACHED (*Cross*)
Another experiment made with odd-number Crosses.
The surface has the appearance of ribboning through
bars.

DIAGRAM 141

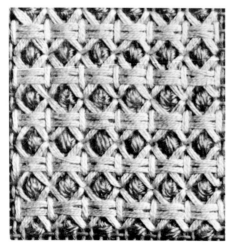

STITCH: * RIBBON CROSS *(Cross)*. FILLER: UPRIGHT
CROSS

The same Cross as preceding, but not encroached.
For a different effect the horizontal stitches may be
worked first and the Cross Stitches over them.

DIAGRAM 142

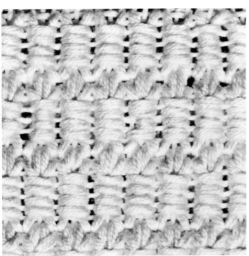

STITCH: * SEVEN CROSS *(Cross)*
The space under the Crosses may be filled with a narrow Oblong Cross.

DIAGRAM 143

STITCH: * SEVEN CROSS, VARIATION *(Cross)*
The same basic structure as shown in the preceding
diagram. In addition to the color change in alternate
stitches, a final vertical stitch has been added.

DIAGRAM 144

STITCH: RAISED SQUARE *(Cross)*, SINGLE LEVIATHAN *(Cross)*, FLAT *(Flat)*.

DESIGN:[†] From an English sampler, 1841, Philadelphia Museum of Art. I had taken this pattern from a French medieval mosaic before seeing the Philadelphia sampler; the colors maintain the tonal arrangement of the earlier design.

STITCH: * RAISED X CROSS *(Cross)*
Offshoot of Raised Square.

DIAGRAM 146

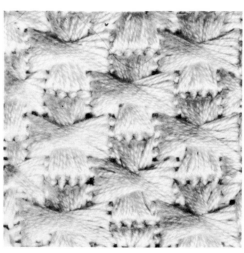

STITCH: * RAISED MALTESE CROSS, HALF-DROPPED
(*Cross*)
Offshoot of Raised Square.

DIAGRAM 147

STITCH: * RAISED MALTESE CROSS *(Cross)*. FILLER: CROSS *(Cross)*, BACK *(Flat)*

DESIGN: * MALTESE CROSS GROUND
Inspired by a medieval English illuminated manuscript pattern.

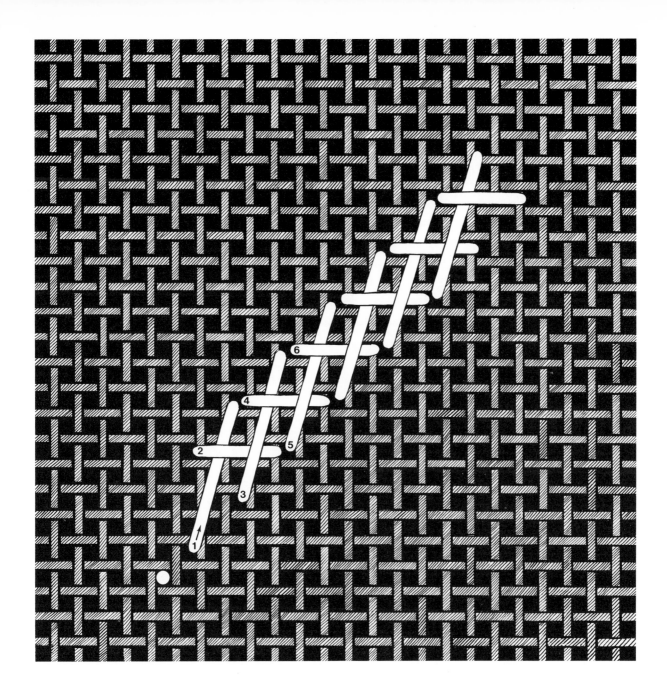

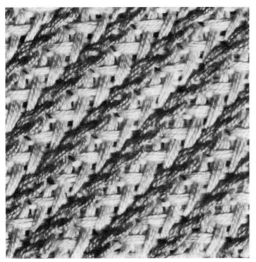

STITCH: DIAGONAL LONG-ARMED CROSS *(Cross)*.
FILLER: DIAGONAL CABLE CHAIN *(Chain)*
Diagonal Long-Armed Cross may also be worked as a
ground without the intercepting Chain Stitch. For
basic Long-Armed Cross *see* Diagram 55.

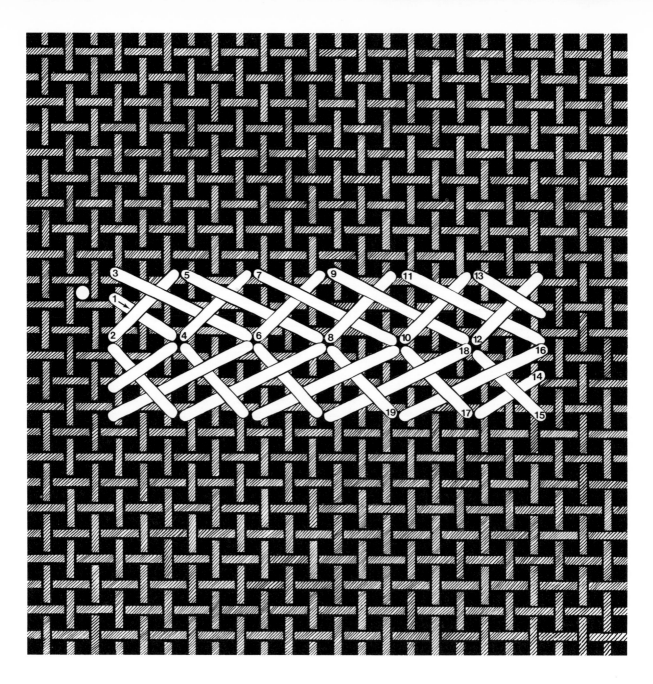

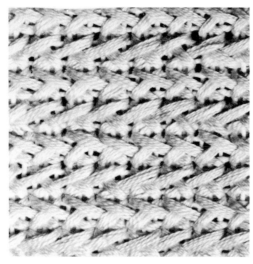

STITCH: GREEK CROSS *(Cross)*

The usual method is to reverse the direction of alternate lines as arranged in the stitched square. It may also be worked in one direction only as a Long-Armed Cross by starting each row from the left side.

DIAGRAM 150

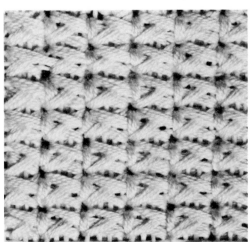

STITCH: MONTENEGRIN CROSS *(Cross)*
The scale for this stitch may be changed very easily.
Alter the number of strands in the yarn to provide
adequate coverage. It is best worked in monotone.

DIAGRAM 151

PLAITED–INTERLACED

Plaiting has had a curious fascination for man throughout the ages. It has involved the mind and hand in basketry, braiding, carpet and textile design, macramé, metalwork, architectural fret, and strapwork. It has been explored by the peoples of all lands, most notably the Chinese, Japanese, Persians, Turks, Greeks, and Celts. These last developed it to a point of almost maniacal intricacy. Whether it is simulated in paint or textile or actually laced as in stitching or basketry, it exerts a peculiarly atavistic magnetism; it seems to be related to ancient mysteries which we respond to but do not fully understand. It is simultaneously dynamic and anachronistic. In fact it is a true spellbinder.

This strange quality makes the stitches in this group exceptionally interesting to explore. Even when their structures are completely known, one finds a certain unaccountable mystery in them. They are very rewarding and interesting to work. In the beginning, you may wish to learn the stitches by using them in one shade or in very simple patterns. You can experiment later when you have sufficient mastery to concentrate on design rather than structure. Follow diagram directions carefully and keep your yarn untwisted.

All yarns may be used.

STITCH: FERN and FERN DIAGONAL *(Plaited-Interlaced)*
Originally I worked the diagonal pattern (in the center) as a duplication of a Seljuk, 11th-century, brick design. Its structural resemblance to vertical Fern (outside rows) suggested a coupling for comparison.

DIAGRAM 152

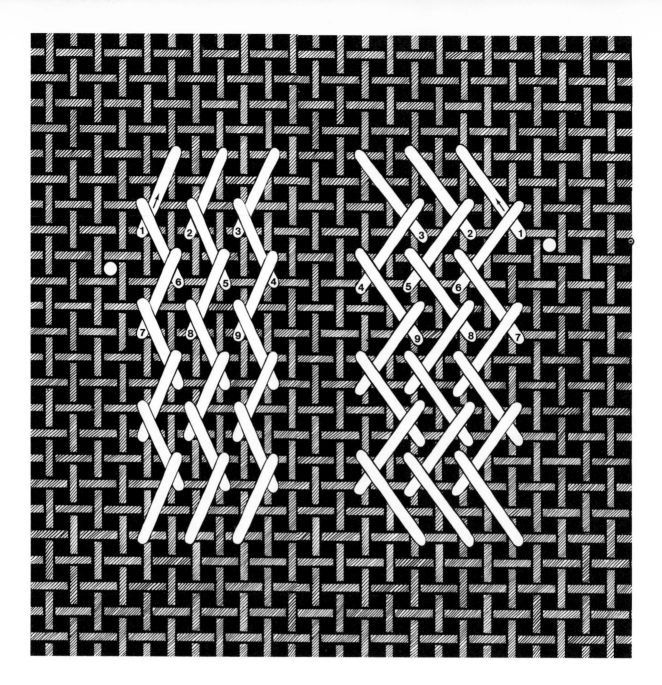

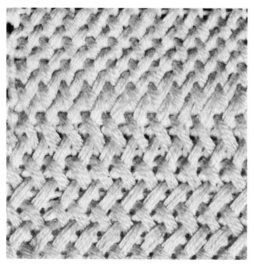

STITCH: PLAITED GOBELIN *(Plaited-Interlaced)*
The sampler square is stitched in various scales and
slants. There is no need to be confined to only one.
Adjust the thickness of the yarn for correct coverage.

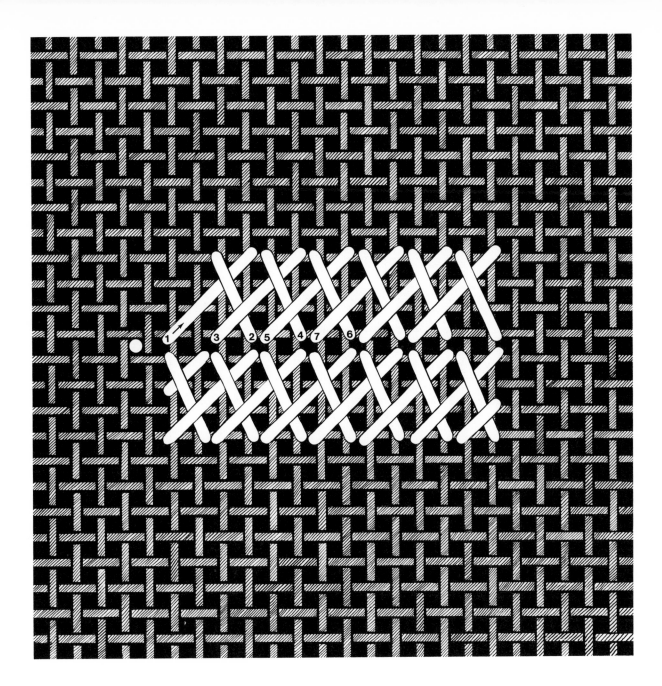

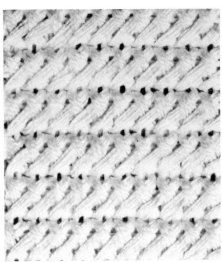

STITCH: PLAIT *(Plaited-Interlaced)*
May be rescaled. This looks the same as some Herring-bone formations but the back will show vertical instead of horizontal stitches.

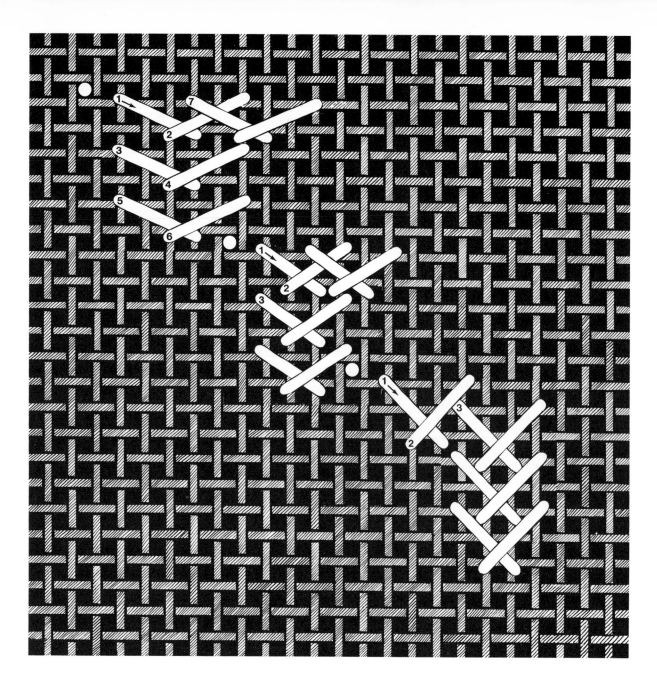

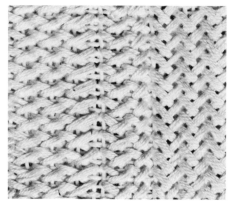

STITCH: PLAITED *(Plaited-Interlaced)*
Worked in various scales.

DIAGRAM 155

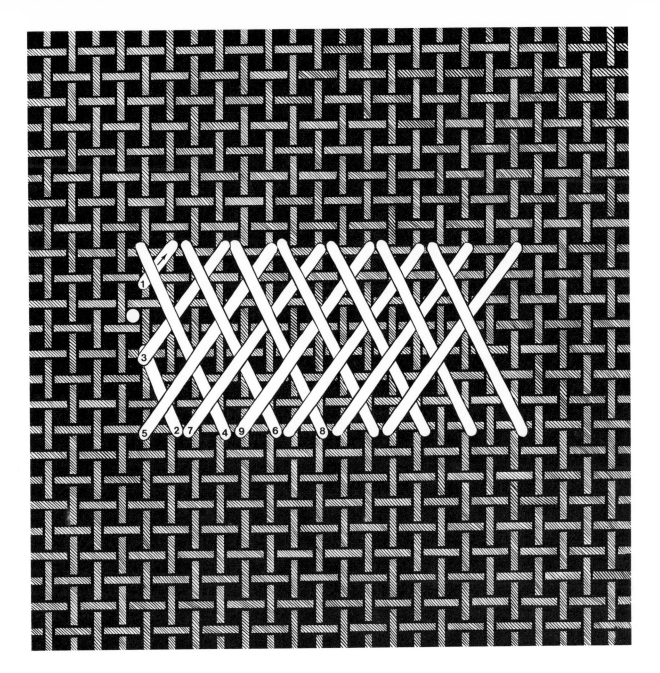

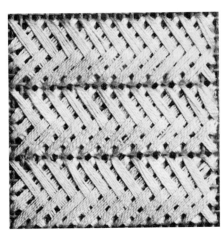

STITCH: DANISH PLAIT *(Plaited-Interlaced)*
This handsome Plait comes from an old Danish stitch
book. It is called Renaissance Stitch in Denmark.
The first stitch (1) may commence from one square
below the starting dot, as shown in the photograph
of the stitched square.

DIAGRAM 156

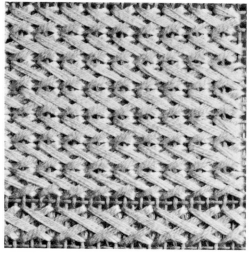

STITCH: KNITTING *(Plaited-Interlaced)*
May be rescaled.

DIAGRAM 157

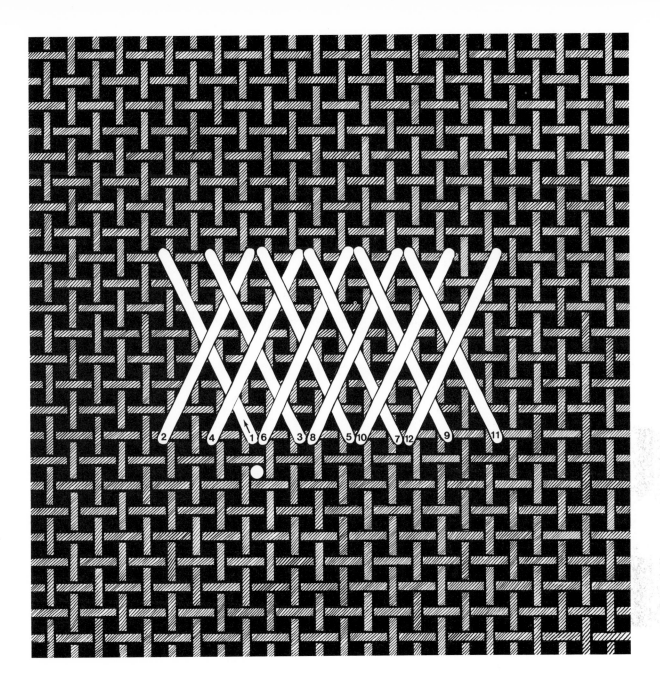

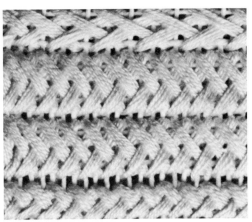

STITCH: BASKET *(Plaited-Interlaced)*
May be rescaled in height but not in width.

DIAGRAM 158

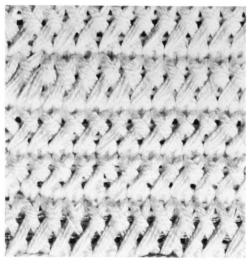

STITCH: HERRINGBONE *(Plaited-Interlaced)*
Herringbone rows in varied scales. Herringbone is known as the Hex or Witches' Stitch in most North European countries. The name is probably derived from the peculiar fascination of interlacement or knots, and its connection with magical ancient rites including those of marriage and medicine.

STITCH: Victoria and Albert Herringbone *(Plaited-Interlaced)*

From a Victoria and Albert Museum Handbook of Stitches. It makes a more interesting texture than conventional Herringbone Stitch.

DIAGRAM 160

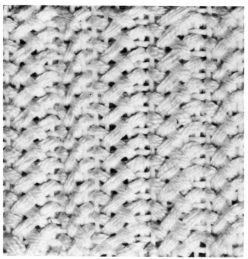

STITCH: * VICTORIA AND ALBERT HERRINGBONE
(*Plaited-Interlaced*)
Varied scales.

DIAGRAM 161

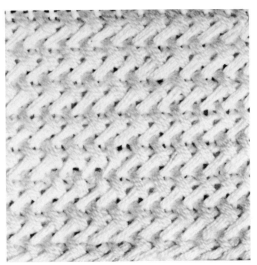

STITCH: *HERRINGBONE GROUND 1 *(Plaited-Interlaced)*
A variation of the Victoria and Albert Herringbone
Stitch. *See* preceding diagrams.

DIAGRAM 162

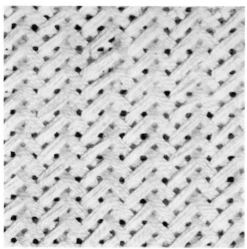

STITCH: Herringbone Ground 2 *(Plaited-Interlaced)*
This Herringbone encroaching ground requires the needle to be snugged under. This sometimes affects the neatness of its appearance for an inexperienced worker. Avoid multistranded yarn when learning. Shaded toning works well in this stitch.

DIAGRAM 163

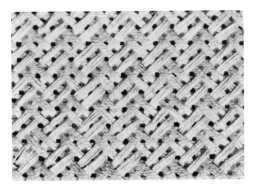

STITCH: ROUND-TRIP HERRINGBONE,
ENCROACHED *(Plaited-Interlaced)*
Generally called Herringbone Gone-Wrong. Round-
Trip seems more relevant to structure.

DIAGRAM 164

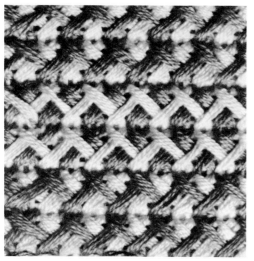

STITCH: * OPTICAL HERRINGBONE *(Plaited-Interlaced)*

DESIGN: Many interesting patterns may be formed by simple color changes and upside-down line reversals in Herringbone. This design is the result of reversing (upside down) every other line.

DIAGRAM 165

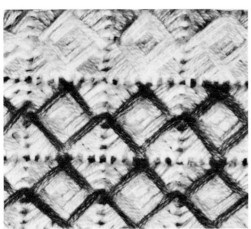

STITCH: Waffle *(Plaited-Interlaced)*
Rescale by increasing or decreasing the length and number of stitches used. The sampler shows one possibility for color variation; many others are possible. It also illustrates the stitch worked in monotone. The stitch may be employed for grounding or for spot ornamentation. If you prefer, the last stitch may be woven under (14).

DIAGRAM 166

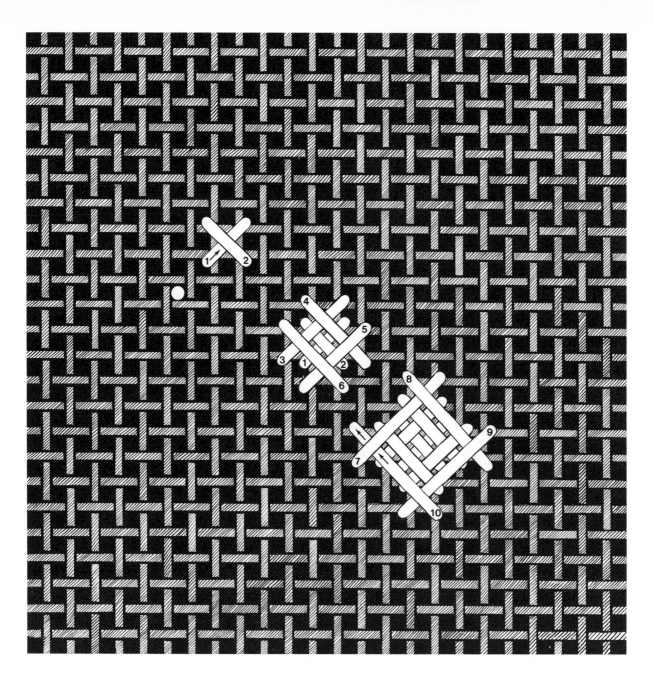

STITCH: * LAYERED DIAMOND *(Plaited-Interlaced)* and FLAT *(Flat)*

DESIGN: * The basic pattern is from medieval white-work embroideries, but the main stitch is changed from Flat to Herringbone Diamond.
The gold metallic yarn used for the interlacing is especially effective combined with white silk.

CAVALIER OF HEARTS   Enlargements of two sections from the *Playing Card* hanging.

KNAVE OF DIAMONDS   KNAVE OF SPADES

PLATE 11

Playing Card hanging (in work).

CAVALIER OF HEARTS

QUEEN OF DIAMONDS

KNAVE OF CLUBS

KNAVE OF CLUBS

PLATE 12

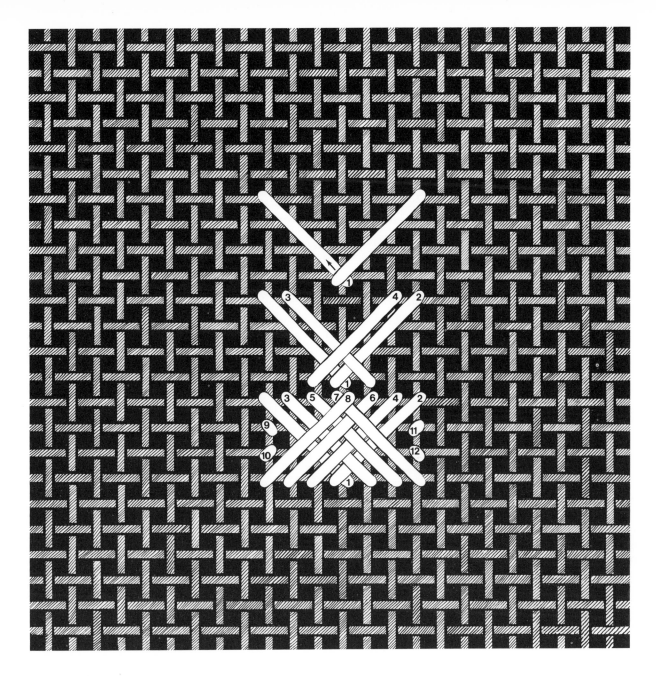

STITCH: * RAISED HERRINGBONE DIAMONDS *(Plaited-Interlaced)*

The Diamonds may be turned into Triangles by working every other horizontal row in a contrasting shade.

DIAGRAM 168

STITCH: HERRINGBONE SQUARE *(Plaited-Interlaced)*.
FILLER: FLAT, BRICK *(Flat)*

DESIGN: * From an Indonesian bag. It is very similar to the American patchwork-quilt pattern called Indiana Puzzle. It is frequently called Hounds' Tooth in textile design. I have seen this pattern in medieval Islamic tiles.

DIAGRAM 169

STITCH: GERMAN INTERLACE *(Plaited-Interlaced)*.
FILLER: BUTTONHOLE *(Loop, Tied)*

The Herringbone foundation is worked differently from conventional Herringbone. Follow the interlacement instruction carefully. Arrows show where the needle must weave *under* the previously worked stitch.

DESIGN: * In the past, German artisans employed this stitch for many complex designs. It is very decorative and can be used for special but simpler effects, less demanding for the modern worker. Other fillers, including Tent and Slanted Gobelin, are suitable.

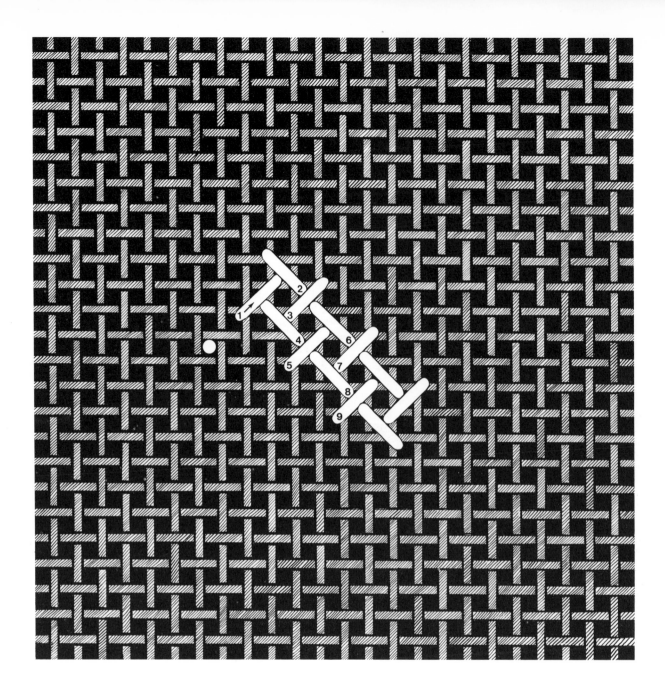

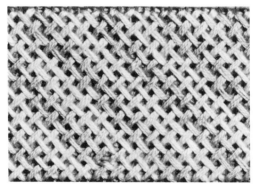

STITCH: SMALL DIAGONAL PLAIT *(Plaited-Interlaced)*
From a Metropolitan Museum of Art sampler, German, 19th century. In this sampler, the diagonal rows were worked in strongly contrasting colors.

DIAGRAM 171

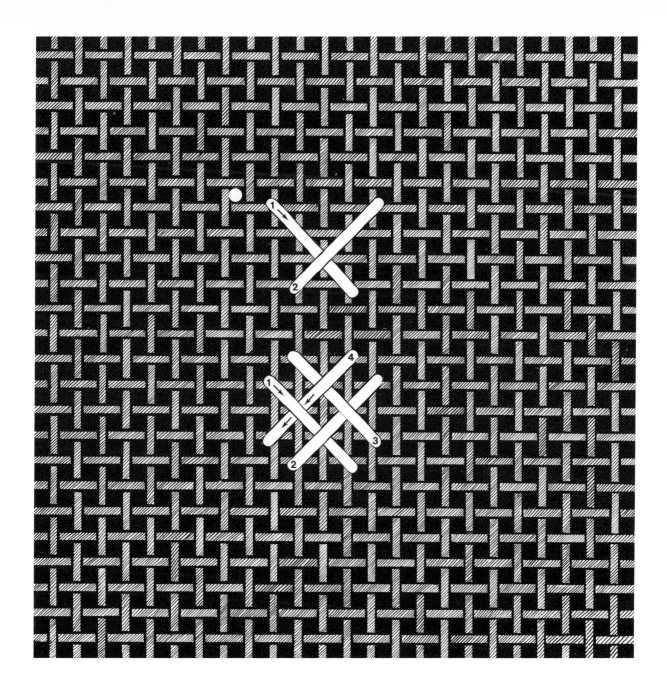

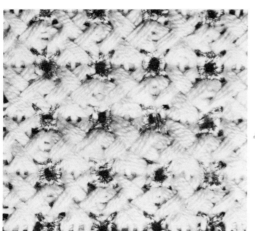

STITCH: * STRAP 1 *(Plaited-Interlaced)*. FILLER: EYE
(Pulled Yarn)
Strap is an invented stitch, and one I have found particularly useful.

DIAGRAM 172

STITCH: * STRAP 2 *(Plaited-Interlaced)*. FILLER: FLAT *(Flat)*

This is the same stitch as in the preceding diagram, but here the Flat Filler (instead of Eye Stitch) has been worked in the same shade as the Strap Stitch.

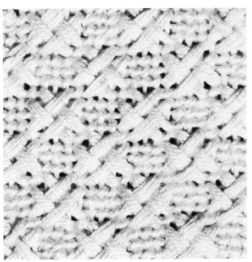

STITCH: * STRAP 3, VARIATION *(Plaited-Interlaced)*.
FILLER: TENT STITCH *(Flat)*
Strap is here used checkerboard-fashion with Tent
Stitch; the contrast between the two stitches produces
an interesting surface.

DIAGRAM 174

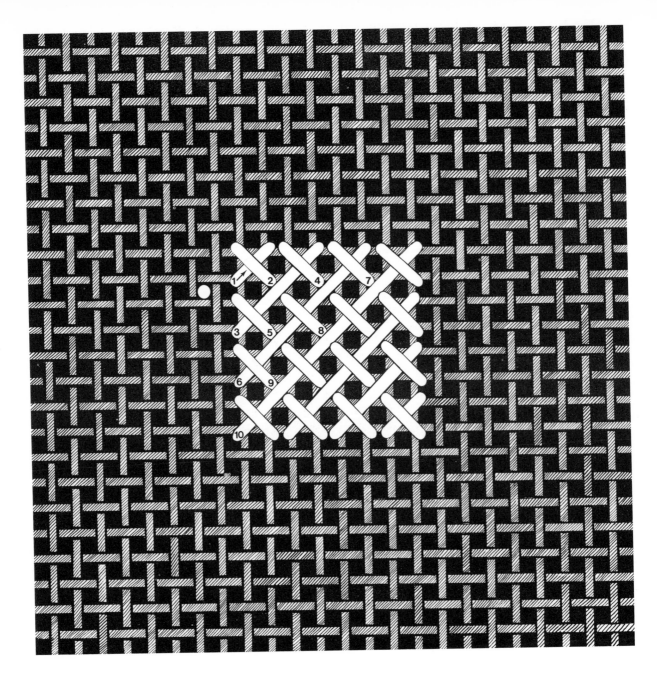

STITCH:[†] WEB *(Plaited-Interlaced)*
This stitch is always shown in a smaller version, one that I found too minute for the canvas; therefore I rescaled it.

DIAGRAM 175

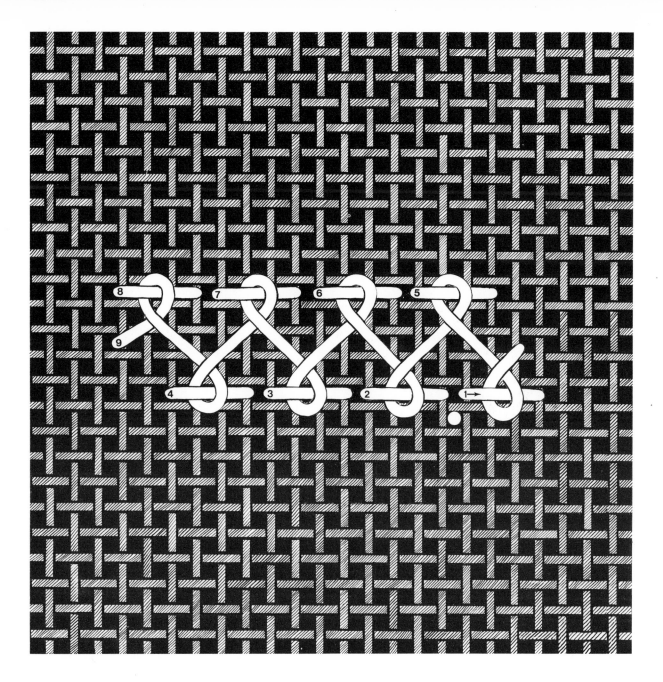

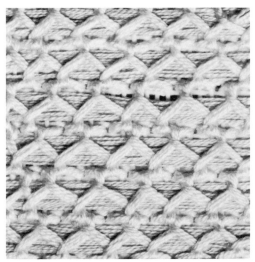

STITCH:[†] INTERLACED BAND, over LAID GROUND
(Plaited-Interlaced)
A conventional embroidery line or border stitch,
adapted for canvas by using Laid Stitches and super-
imposing the Interlaced band, thereby forming a
grounding. The textural effect is especially interesting,
and the stitch meshes well.

LOOP, TIED

Loop, Tied, stitches are self-descriptive. If you will refer to some of the names listed under this category and then look at the diagrams and sampler squares, I think you will be able to form a clear idea of their specific nature. Boundaries are unclear in this group and many stitches placed within it might reasonably find room in other categories. Many others, situated elsewhere, might logically be placed here—such as Crossed Corners, which is really a Tie Down Stitch. Knotted Stitches might claim squatter's rights because they are most frequently formed by a Buttonhole kind of looping and tying. But their bumpy surface has given them a separate grouping.

Buttonhole stitching is important in this group. It is of great age and has not been put to canvas use very much. I like it for its singular texture and versatility, and have given it broad coverage and exploration in my samplers.

Always select the simplest diagram within a type for learning. Once you have been introduced, meeting the rest of the family becomes easier.

All yarns may be used.

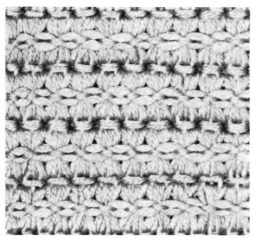

STITCH: SHELL *(Loop, Tied)*
Keep the last stitch (4) in each group loose so that the
needle can fit under the tie (5). After entry is made
at 5, tighten 4, then finish the tie (5). This suggestion
applies to all Shell- or Sheaf-type structures.

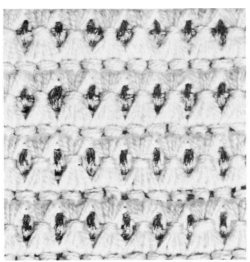

STITCH:[†] SHEAF *(Loop, Tied)*. FILLER: UPRIGHT CROSS *(Cross)*, BACK *(Flat)*

The Shell Stitch with the last looping step omitted, and Cross filler added.

DIAGRAM 178

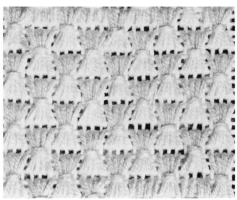

stitch: * Stepped Sheaf Ground *(Loop, Tied)*
Although I have not seen this stitch used this way
before, I think it provides a very effective texture for
a ground. It may be rescaled easily by adding to the
number of vertical stitches before tying them, or by
making the stitches themselves longer or shorter.
Color experiment would be interesting for geometric
patterning.

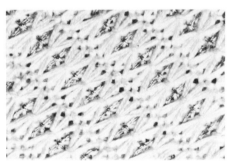

STITCH: * DIAGONAL SHEAF GROUND (*Loop, Tied*)
This stitch is conventionally shown in horizontal rows, but it is set diagonally here; it makes an interesting ground. The stitches in the second row start from the center stitch of the previous row.

DIAGRAM 180

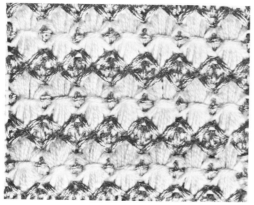

STITCH: * STEEPLED SHEAF *(Loop, Tied)*. FILLER: CROSS *(Cross)*, BACK *(Flat)*

DIAGRAM 181

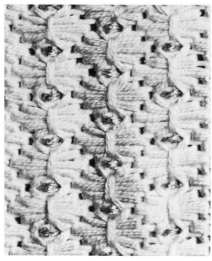

STITCH: * STEEPLED SHEAF, HALF-DROPPED *(Loop, Tied)*

The long stitches may be worked vertically, or horizontally as in this sampler square.

DIAGRAM 182

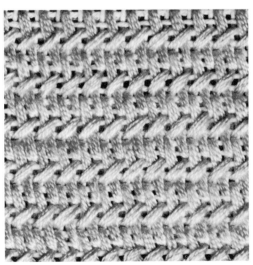

STITCH: ROUMANIAN *(Loop, Tied)*
This simple stitch has acquired many names: Roman, Renaissance, Oriental, Roumanian. The last appears most frequently. The scale may be altered.

DIAGRAM 183

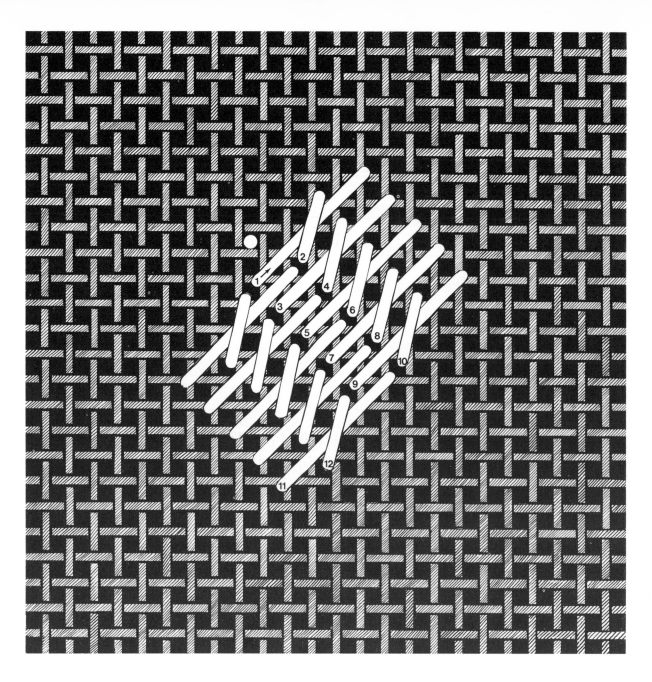

STITCH: ROUMANIAN DIAGONAL *(Loop, Tied)*
The scale may be altered.

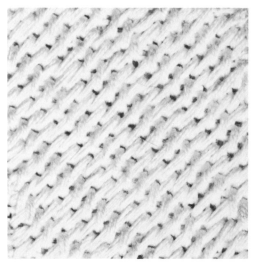

DIAGRAM 184

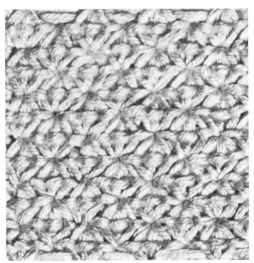

STITCH: RENAISSANCE *(Loop, Tied)*
A very old embroidery stitch, workable and interesting on needlepoint canvas.

DIAGRAM 185

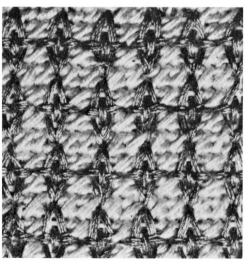

STITCH: * RENAISSANCE, VARIATION *(Loop, Tied)*.
FILLER: SQUARE MOSAIC *(Flat)*

Metallic yarn was used in this variation of Renaissance Stitch. Unfortunately, gold and silver yarn are not photogenic, but they are very handsome.

DIAGRAM 186

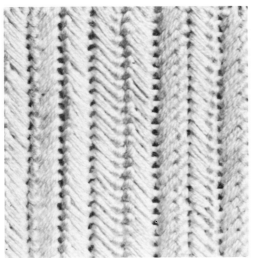

STITCH: FISHBONE *(Loop, Tied)*
Fishbone frequently looks a bit sloppy because it is often worked in a structural sequence that requires the snugging under of the needle. That is, the needle must return to space already occupied by a stitch. The numbering in the diagram prevents this. May easily be rescaled.

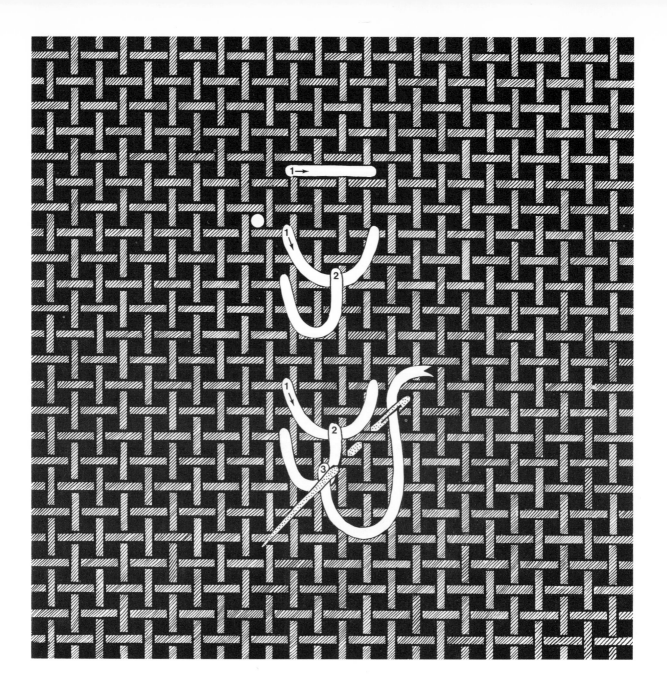

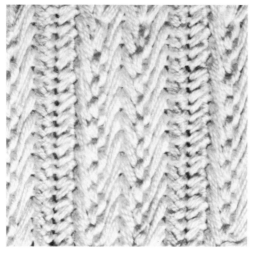

STITCH: CRETAN (*Loop, Tied*). FILLER: FISHBONE (*Loop, Tied*)

The Cretan Stitch is a conventional embroidery stitch. In adapting it for needlepoint canvas I felt this scale showed the pattern most effectively. Work the stitch from side to side in identical fashion. Only the direction changes: from left to right and from right to left.

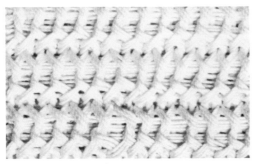

STITCH: BRETON *(Loop, Tied)* over LAID GROUND
A cloth ground embroidery stitch, it has an interesting
texture for canvas work.

DIAGRAM 189

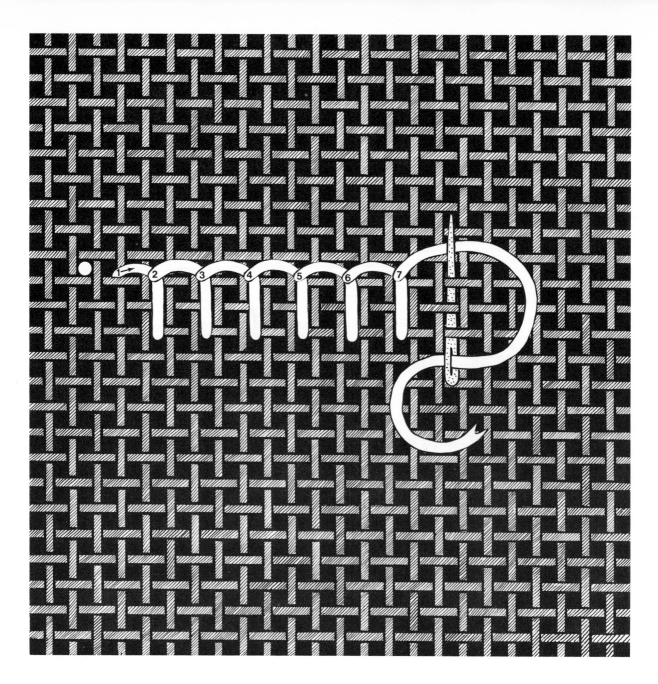

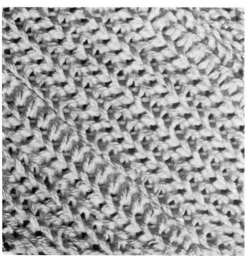

STITCH: BUTTONHOLE *(Loop, Tied)*
The diagram shows Buttonholes worked horizontally.
The photograph shows Buttonholes worked diagonally, with loops left free. The following diagram
shows Buttonholes worked *over* loops.

DIAGRAM 190

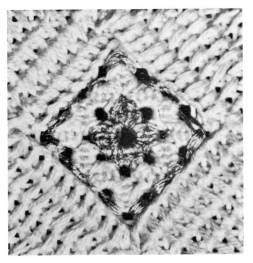

STITCH: BUTTONHOLE IN DIAGONAL ROWS *(Loop, Tied)*, CENTER FILLER: ROCOCO *(Loop, Tied)*

DESIGN:* The frame of this square was stitched in diagonal rows of Buttonhole stitching *over* the loops of the preceding lines *(see* previous diagram). The center is composed of Right-Angled Rococo Stitch, which has then been Back-Stitched in gold metallic yarn *(see* Diagram 202 for Right-Angled Rococo).

DIAGRAM 191

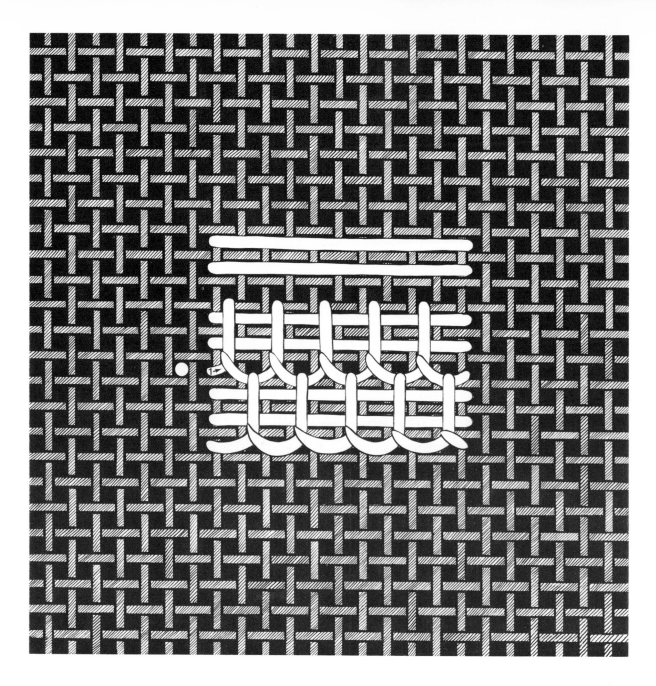

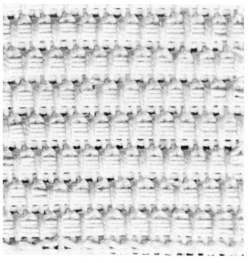

STITCH: BUTTONHOLE OVER LAID GROUND 1 *(Loop, Tied)*
Worked *over* loops , this method of Buttonholing comes from French 18th-century lace techniques.

DIAGRAM 192

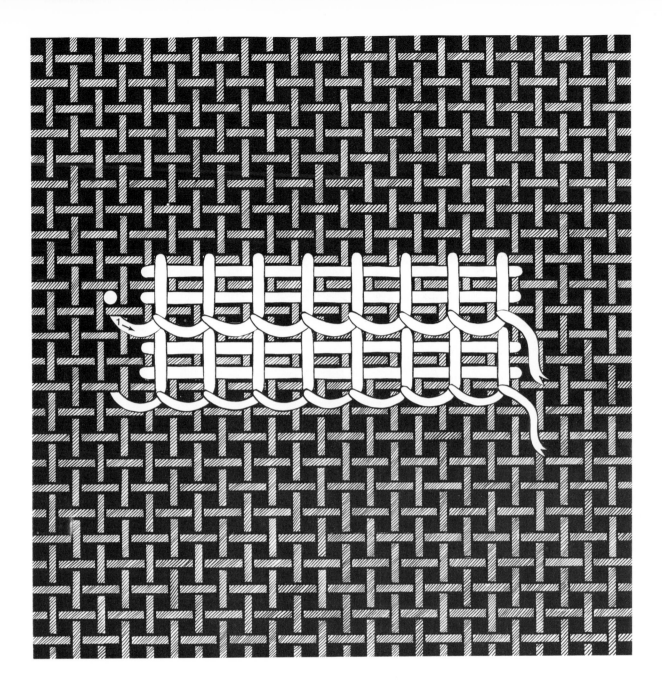

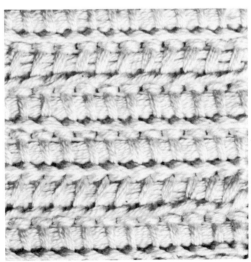

STITCH: BUTTONHOLE OVER LAID GROUND 2 *(Loop, Tied)*

In this square the Buttonhole was worked *without* using the loop of the previous row. The stitched example shows every other row worked upside down.

DIAGRAM 193

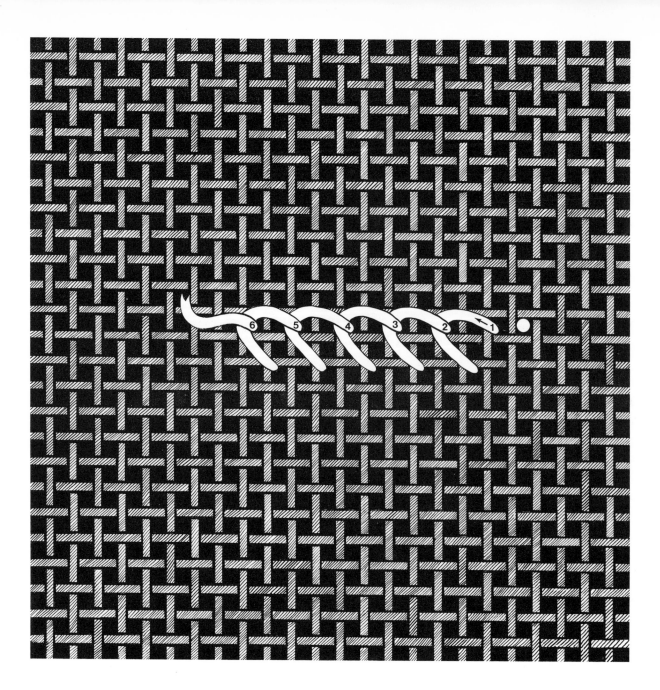

STITCH: SLANTED BUTTONHOLE *(Loop, Tied)*
The stitched example shows two directions and upside-down use of the stitch. Buttonhole is rarely used for canvas work. I find it handsome and versatile. It is most commonly found in French lace work. Once the placement of needle in relation to yarn is understood, Buttonhole and variations are simple and worthwhile.

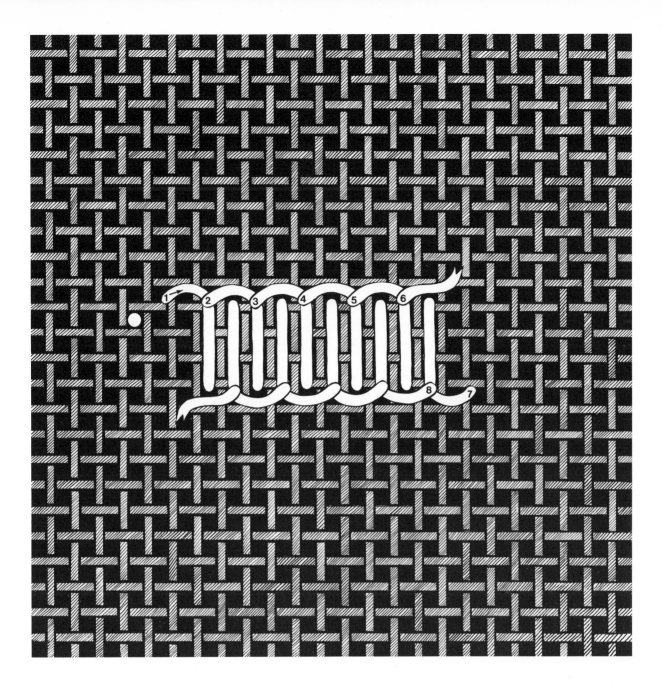

STITCH: BUTTONHOLE BARS *(Loop, Tied)*
The frame of this square is made up of Buttonhole Bars. The horizontal frames are worked over every other canvas row; the vertical frames are worked over every row. The diagram shows Buttonhole Bars worked over every row. The inside grounds are composed of Buttonhole Stitches in various scales.

DIAGRAM 195

STITCH: Buttonhole Circles *(Loop, Tied)*. FILLER: Rococo *(Loop, Tied)*

DESIGN: * Circle grounding is quite simple once you have mastered the Buttonhole Circle. Spaces may be filled with stitches other than Rococo, such as Flat or Tent.

NOTE: The dots above the circle show the entrance points for your needle when you work the Buttonhole Stitch. They are *not* stitches but a guide to the correct placement.

DIAGRAM 196

STITCH: * Buttonhole Half Moons *(Loop, Tied)*.
FILLER: Flat *(Flat)*

Toning or color contrast may be used. This may be done diagonally or horizontally.

NOTE: The group of dots above the Half Moons simply indicate the correct holes for your needle to enter when working the Buttonhole Stitch. They are points of reference, not stitches.

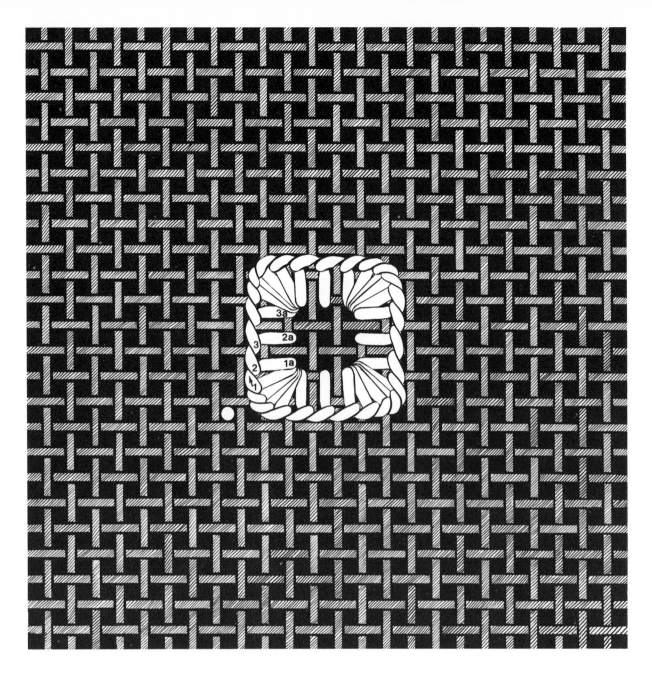

STITCH: * BUTTONHOLE SQUARES *(Loop, Tied)*. FILLER: EYE *(Pulled Yarn)*, SINGLE LEVIATHAN *(Cross)*

While experimenting with these Buttonhole Squares, I discovered that the corners warped and pulled the Square out of line. This may be prevented by using two Buttonhole Stitches in each corner rather than one. The Square will then remain intact.

302

DIAGRAM 198

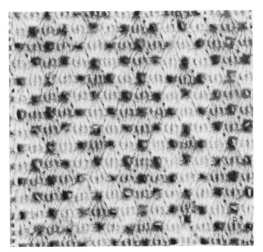

STITCH: ROCOCO *(Loop, Tied)*

My method of working Rococo is unconventional.
I have found this system more efficient because it
stabilizes and increases the pull. The pull is an essential
element in Rococo because the perforation that results
from it (often seen in 16th- and 17th-century geometric pattern work) is one of its principal charms.
This method may, in fact, be a lost technique. It is kin
to Buttonhole. When you move from 2 (up) to 2a
(down) be sure to pull. It is this motion that creates
the form and produces the holes. The usual construction is a long stitch first and then the tie-down.
Rococo must be worked in diagonal lines whichever
plan you follow.

DIAGRAM 199

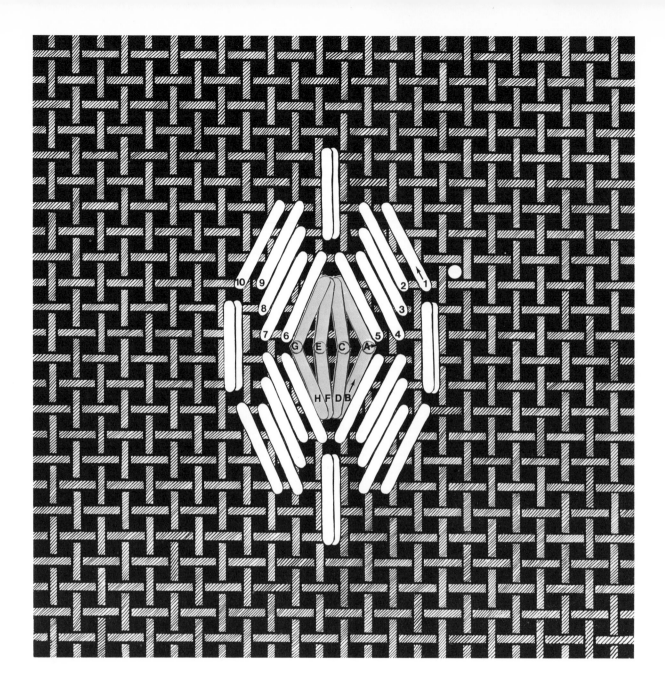

STITCH: FLAT *(Flat)*. FILLER: ROCOCO *(Loop, Tied)*

DESIGN: * Ribboned Diamonds. Follow guidance of Rococo (Diagram 199).

DIAGRAM 200

STITCH: To and Fro Buttonhole *(Loop, Tied)* Brick *(Flat)*

DESIGN: * Hour-Glass. Follow Rococo instructions for basic system (Diagram 199).

STITCH: * RIGHT-ANGLED ROCOCO *(Loop, Tied)*
If you place the Rococo stitches at right angles to one another they will form this interesting square pattern. Experiment for color variations. Please *see* Diagram 199 (Rococo) for instructions.

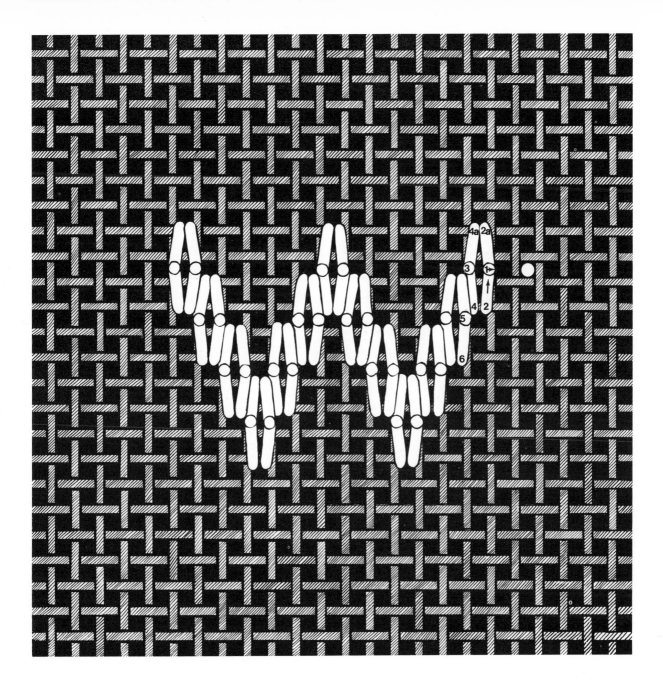

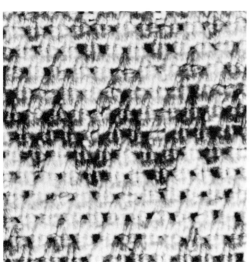

STITCH: FRENCH *(Loop, Tied)*

This is formed exactly like the Rococo (in a Button-hole fashion) but with two vertical stitches instead of four. It must be worked in diagonal lines and is useful for many geometric diaper patterns. It is also very hardy and may be employed for articles that will have to endure hard wear. *See* Rococo (Diagram 199).

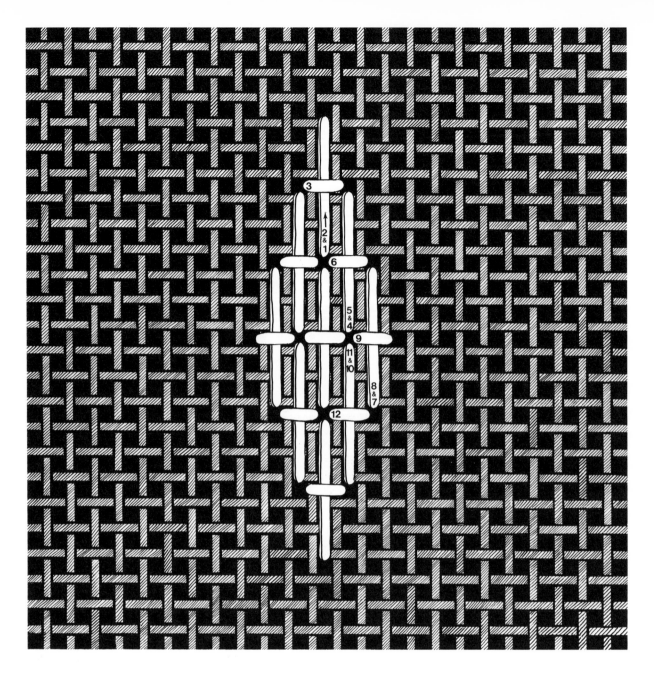

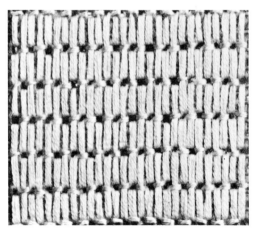

STITCH: FRENCH DOUBLE TIE OVER SIX *(Loop, Tied)*
Although this stitch may look similar to Upright Cross (Diagram 118) it has a different method of construction. The vertical stitch (in this case over six canvas threads) is worked *twice* and then tied down by a stitch worked over two threads. The perforation, which is desirable, is achieved by the double stitching and by the sequence of moves. The stitch must be worked in diagonal rows. It may be rescaled. Just make certain that the thread count of the vertical stitch is evenly divisible by a center bar.

DIAGRAM 204

CHAIN

The chain formation is one of the oldest. It is infrequently used in canvas work. There is no reason for its state of unemployment for it covers well, behaves properly, has a unique texture and rhythm, and is not difficult to work. The beginner should avoid multistranded yarn. Silk and metallic thread are especially effective but more difficult than wool. Take care to pull with even tension so that your chains remain reasonably uniform. They do not have to be mechanically identical. Slight irregularities testify to the presence of the hand and add interest. The Chain Stitch is very versatile, the chess queen of the needle, because it moves in so many directions with ease. When you wish to make rounded forms, it is the most obliging.

All yarns may be used. Gold and silver are especially good in chain stitch because the links cause shadows; these cut the glare of modern metallic thread.

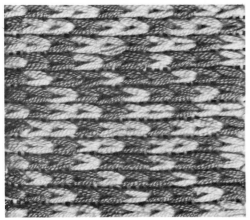

STITCH: Basic Chain, top; Magic Chain, bottom
Sometimes called Chequer Chain

DESIGN: * The Magic Chain pattern is worked in back-and-forth horizontal rows. The needle is threaded with two tones of yarn. While making the chain, allow one shade to drop behind the needle and keep one shade on top. When the needle is pulled through, only one color will be visible on the surface in each chain. This stitch is much easier to do than to explain verbally. Use one-ply, single-strand yarns when learning. Multistranded yarns are more difficult to control.

DIAGRAM 205

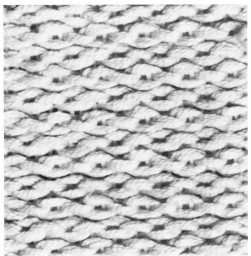

STITCH: CABLE CHAIN *(Chain)*

This ground was arranged so that the loop of the second row touches the cable of the first row; the cable of the second row touches the loop of the first row. Follow this system throughout so that the lines mesh. Cable Chain is worth learning because it has an individual and handsome texture. Do not use metallic yarn for Cable Chaining; the yarn does not glide well enough for smooth work.

DIAGRAM 206

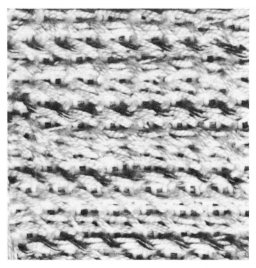

STITCH: WHIPPED CHAIN *(Chain)*
Whipping is, as the name indicates, a system of over-stitching after a stitch line, or lines, has been completed. Whipping may be applied to many stitches, such as Herringbone, Flat Stitch Blocks, among others.

DIAGRAM 207

STITCH: DETACHED CHAIN (*Chain*)
Sometimes called Lazy Daisy.

DESIGN:[†] I have seen variations of this pattern from the 1st century onward. If the center Cross is stitched in the dark tone of the Diamond, the effect will be quite different.
This particular pattern was adapted from a medieval Bulgarian mosaic pavement.

DIAGRAM 208

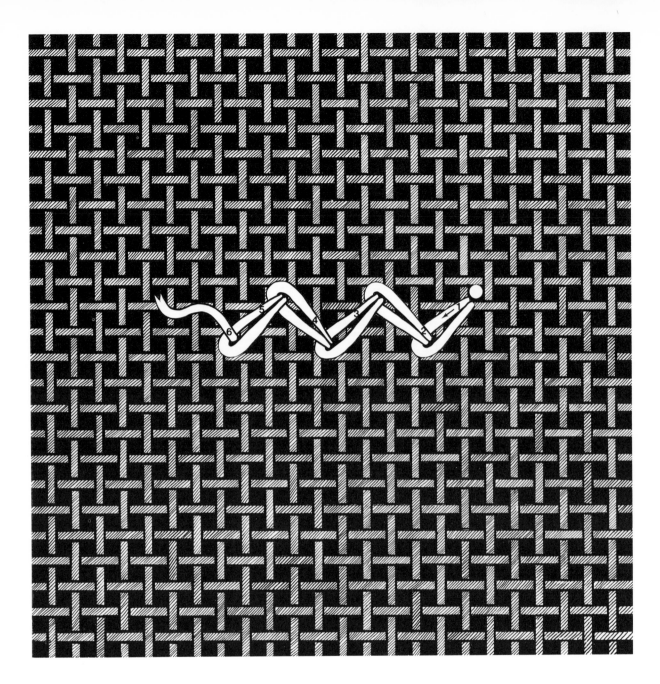

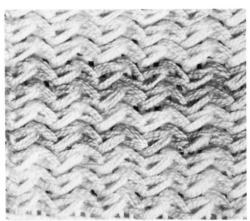

STITCH: † ZIG ZAG CHAIN GROUND *(Chain)*
Conventionally this chain formation is used as a single-line border decoration. In the Sampler square it is stitched as a ground. It is obviously a good texture for water. May also be worked in monotone. Rescaling is simple.

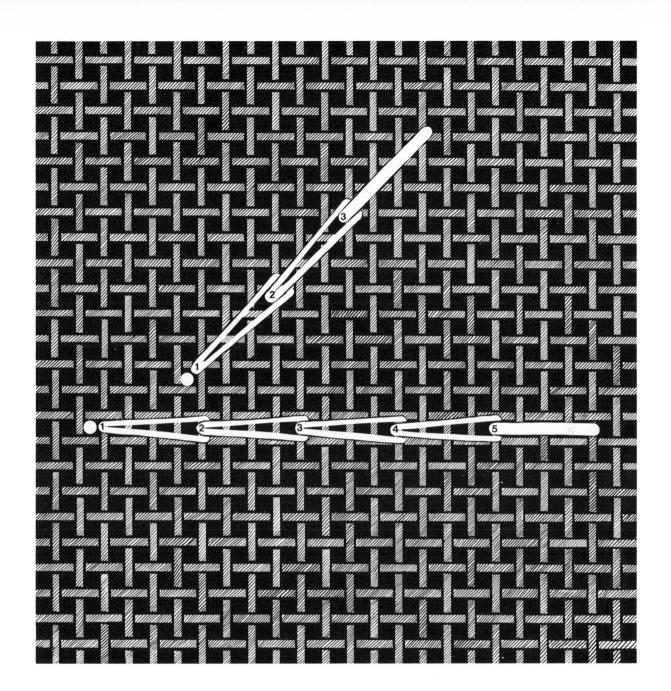

STITCH: SPLIT (*Chain*)

A popular medieval ecclesiastical stitch. The undersides of antique fragments all used frugal, small pick-
up stitches. Though difficult to show in diagram, the
second stitch always splits the yarn very near the tip
end of the previous stitch: the needle enters the canvas
at 1 but its point must halve the yarn as close to 2
as possible. Use an even strand count of yarn so that it
can be divided equally by the needle. The surface
looks like Chain Stitching. Worked in any direction—
horizontal, vertical, diagonal, random, etc., and in
various scales.

DIAGRAM 210

KNOTTED

These stitches give high relief pattern whether used for detail or overall pattern or ground. Although usually formed in the Loop-and-Tie method, they merit a separate treatment because they have a special texture, peculiar to them alone. It is not an architecturally separate group, but one that is set apart visually. The stitches are not difficult to understand, but they may appear so initially. Having once conquered one, you will be enabled to move easily through the others. Steady tension for drawing through the yarn is vital. Avoid multistranded yarn if possible. Metallic yarns are resistant to smooth slide-through and should be used sparingly.

Many Middle Eastern and Sicilian designs were worked entirely in one knotted stitch. Chinese embroiderers also made deft use of them. Chinese embroiderers made deft use of everything. I have not referred to their work because their accomplishments span so many dynasties, cultures, and techniques. A brief look would be presumptuous and unsatisfactory to all of us.

All yarns but discretionary use of gold and silver.

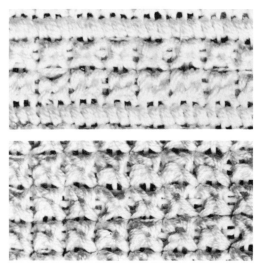

STITCH: SORBELLO KNOT *(Knotted)*, left. FILLER: SLANTED GOBELIN *(Flat)*

This stitch is very popular in Sicilian and Neapolitan embroidery where workers use it on its own to carry out complete designs. Southern Italy still shows pronounced Arabic influence and the Sorbello Knot is placed here with the Egyptian Knot so that the relationship may be seen.

STITCH: EGYPTIAN KNOT *(Knotted)* right

Called Egyptian because it appeared on some garments discovered in ancient tombs, or so it has been claimed. These two Knots form squares and fit into geometric patterning very comfortably.

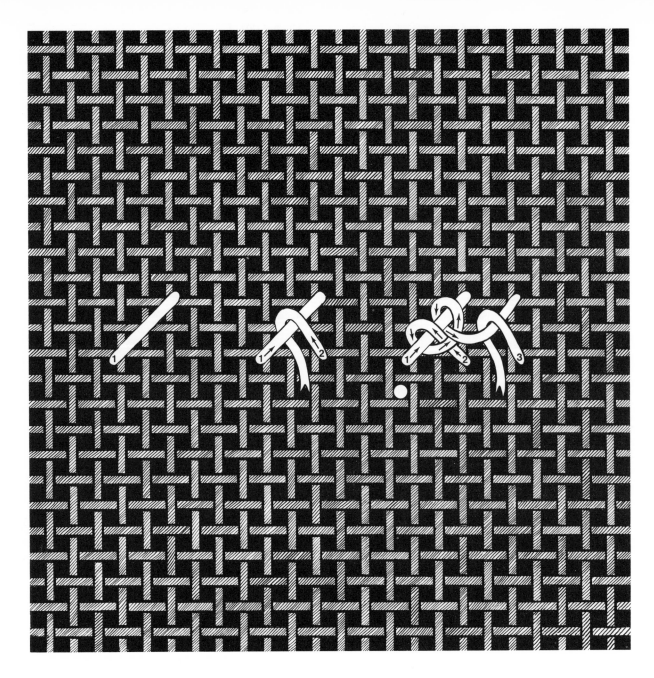

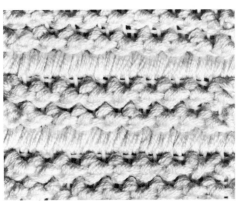

STITCH: Palestrina Knot *(Knotted)*. FILLER: Gobelin *(Flat)*

This embroidery stitch, not usually suggested for canvas work, is useful, stable, handsome, and easy to work.

DIAGRAM 212

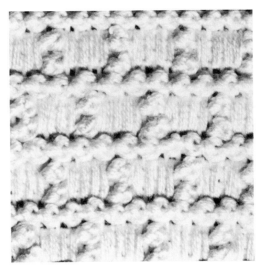

STITCH: REVERSE PALESTRINA KNOT *(Knotted)*.
FILLER: FLAT *(Flat)*
This Knot, like the first Palestrina Knot (preceding diagram) is easy to work, beautiful, and very well-suited to canvas work.

DESIGN:[†] From an embroidered altar curtain, brick wall pattern, St. George and the Dragon, c. 1460, Catalonia, Spain, now in Barcelona.

DIAGRAM 213

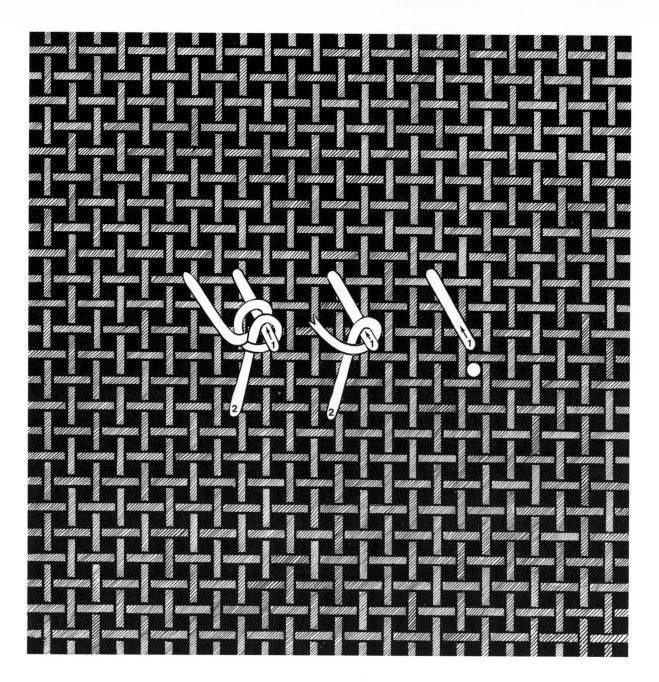

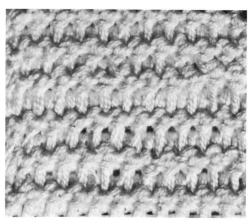

STITCH:[†] LOOP STITCH, VARIATION (*Knotted*)
Worked with a double, rather than the conventional single Knot. The Knot formation is similar to that of Reverse Palestrina Knot. In order to make it into a ground stitch, every other line was stitched and the second line was placed between the stitches of the upper line. This arrangement is attractive in contrasting colors. It may also be worked so the stitches are placed next to one another with no spaces between. In this case, the lines would not encroach.

320   DIAGRAM 214

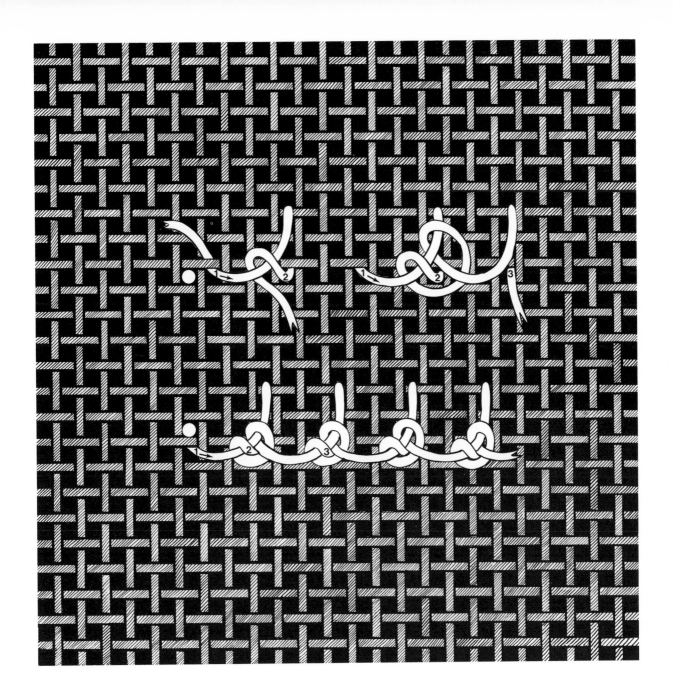

STITCH:[†] Scroll Ground *(Knotted)*

In order to convert this stitch, usually used for embroidery line decoration, into a ground, each line is begun one hole further in so that the loops mesh and leave no canvas exposed.

DIAGRAM 215

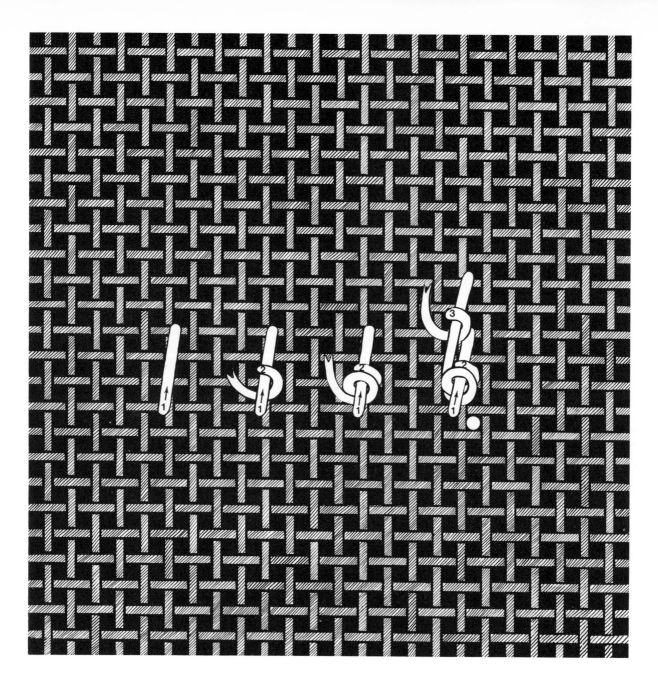

STITCH: KNOTTED PORTUGUESE STEM (*Knotted*)
A conventional embroidery stitch which can provide
an interesting and stable texture on needlepoint canvas.

DIAGRAM 216

LAID AND COUCHED, WOVEN

Laid and Couched work was put to superlative use in medieval ecclesiastical embroideries of France, Flanders, England, Spain, and Germany. Much of their gold and silver work was carried out in this technique.

It requires the laying down of yarn on canvas (*see* Diagram 217 for frugal method) in straight, parallel lines. After these are set down smoothly, you couch (tie) them down with smaller stitches, sometimes slanted and sometimes at right angles to the line. This depends on the method in use.

You may use this technique for special effects, but the hard, clearly defined canvas does not receive this stitch with much hospitality. Your ground is covered by the laid yarn and somehow your needle must find its way back into the obscured hole. Obviously, a soft ground is the fabric of choice, because it will receive the couching stitches wherever you place your needle. You may use laid stitches to form a ground for many decorative stitches like Herringbone, Buttonhole, Cross.

Woven patterns are worked over and under Laid yarn.

All yarns may be used.

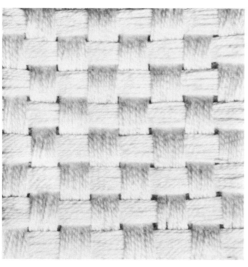

STITCH: WEAVING (*Couched and Laid, Woven*)
Weaving is surface work and not integral to the canvas warp and woof. It is harder to work than it may appear. The in-and-out threading needs careful handling in direction and tension. Multi-stranded yarn is easily twisted. The arrows indicate weaving without entering canvas. To save yarn, start 2, 4, 6, etc., at the bottom line, being very careful to keep the previous line in place.

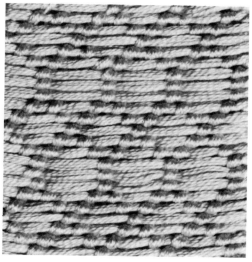

STITCH: COUCHING PATTERN *(Couched and Laid, Woven)*

Difficult to do on canvas, but it forms a very attractive surface. Make the small stitches in thinner yarn to achieve the quilted effect.

DESIGN: * Two colors may be used. Many other geometric patterns are made possible by tying down the Laid Yarn at different intervals. It is more economical to lay the yarn in the manner shown in the preceding diagram, but I do not advise this method here because the nature of the Tent Stitch arrangement would displace the Laid lines.

DIAGRAM 218

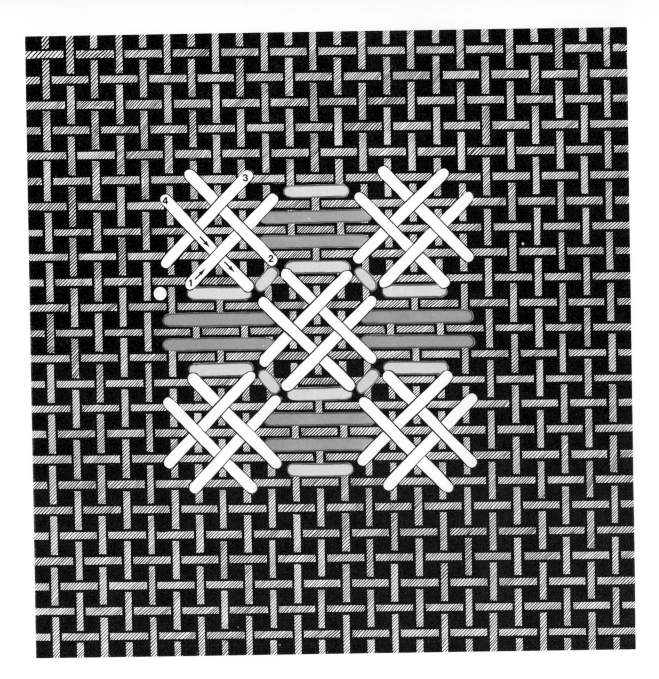

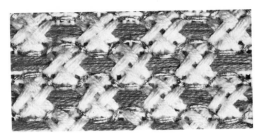

STITCH: * STRAP (*Interlaced*) over LAID GROUND (*Couch and Laid, Woven*)

The diagram shows individual Flat Stitches filling the areas between the Strap Stitches. In the sampler square below, the Strap Stitches are worked over Laid yarn. *See* Diagram 217 for Laid Yarn method.

DESIGN: [†] From a medieval wall mosaic, Siena Cathedral.

DIAGRAM 219

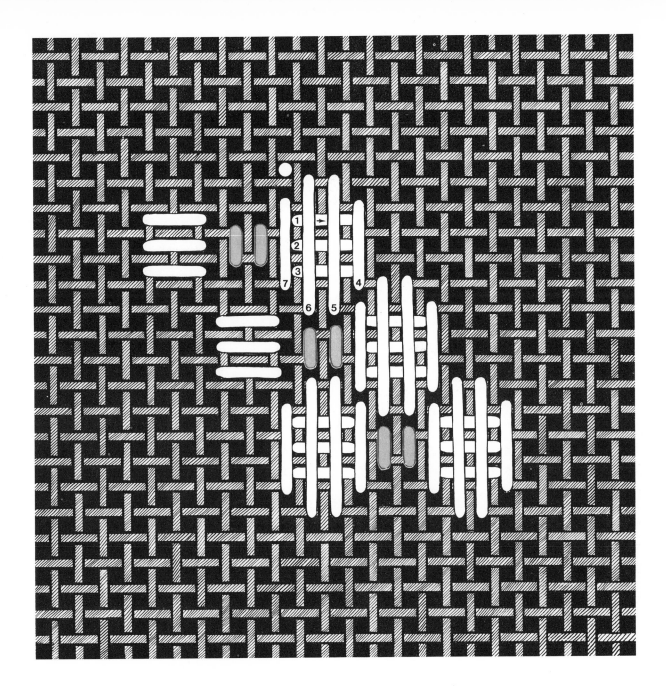

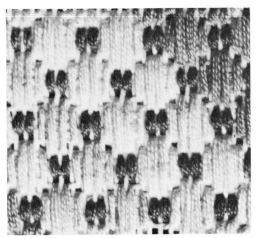

STITCH: FLAT, CUSHIONED *(Couched and Laid, Woven)*

DESIGN: Typical pattern of 19th-century samplers. The color tones varied in each sampler I saw, producing different geometric forms. This one is arranged in diagonal color rows. This pattern may be worked without the Laid understitches. The term cushion is used when ground is Laid and then covered over. This plumps up the stitch.

DIAGRAM 220

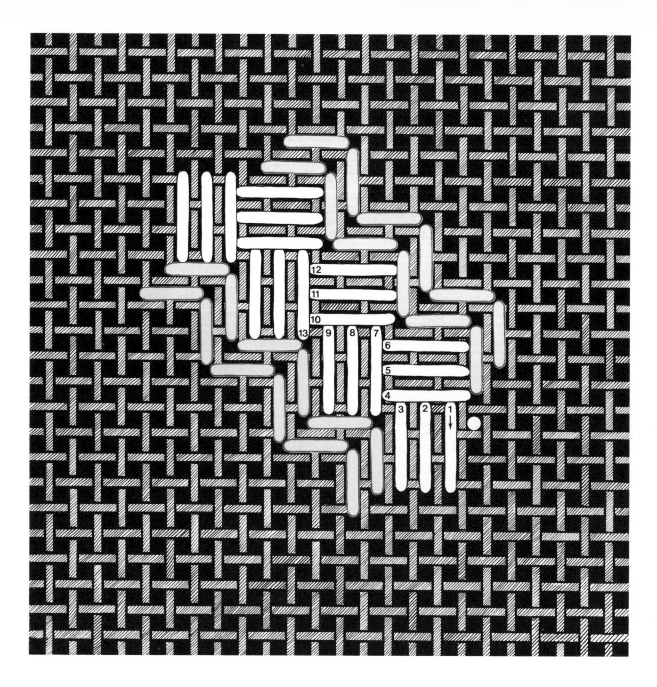

STITCH:* DIAGONAL BRAID *(Couched and Laid, Woven)*

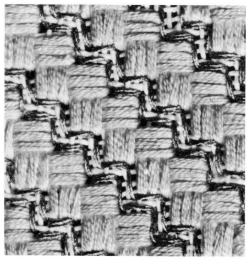

DIAGRAM 221

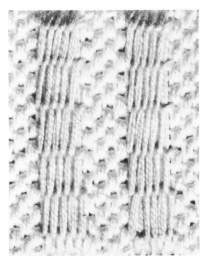

STITCH: RAISED STEM *(Couch and Laid, Woven).*
FILLER: BRICK *(Flat)*

A conventional embroidery stitch not usually suggested for canvas work. I think its texture and stability have something to offer needlepoint canvas, and therefore have included it. It is combined here with simple Brick Stitch (Flat). Lay the long vertical stitches first (1, 2, etc.), then start each successive stem line at the base (no. 8 line).

DIAGRAM 222

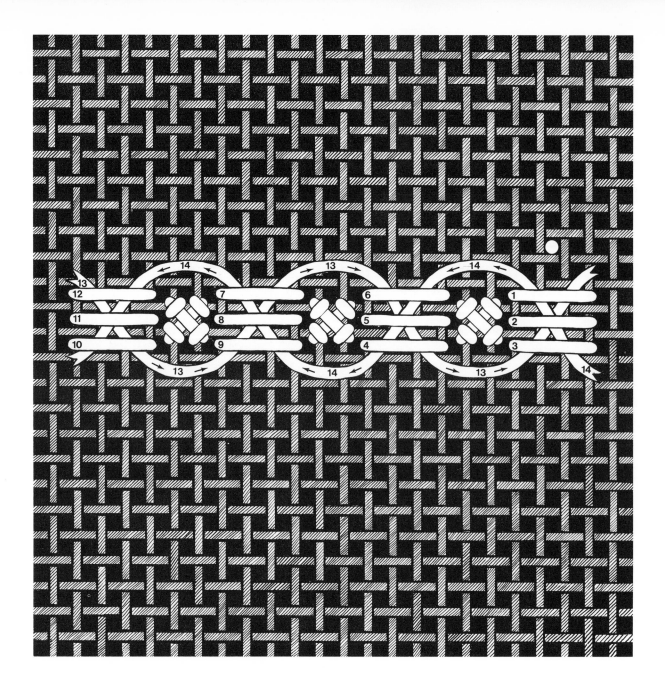

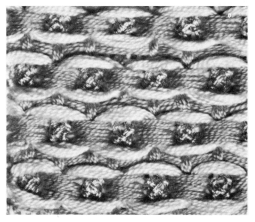

STITCH:[+] Guilloche Ground (*Couched and Laid, Woven*). FILLER: Crossed Corners (*Cross*) Upright Cross (*Cross*) laid horizontally under Guilloche

DESIGN: A conventional embroidery stitch converted to canvas. Only for special effects; the surface is not really stable. Scale may be changed easily.

DIAGRAM 223

STITCH:[†] PEKINESE GROUND *(Couched and Laid, Woven)*
A Chinese embroidery stitch usually employed for line ornamentation, here turned into a ground pattern.

DIAGRAM 224

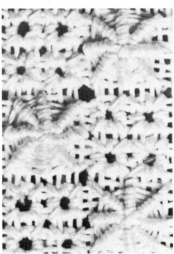

STITCH: RIBBED WHEELS *(Couched and Laid, Woven)*, EYE *(Pulled Yarn)*

Wheels look delicate and complicated. They are neither; they are quite simple to work and offer a strong stable surface. The size of the Wheels may be varied by changing the size of the foundation Cross to suit your needs. Here the Wheels are placed in a checkerboard arrangement with Eyes, but they may be used alone for a ground, or singly for spot ornamentation, or combined with numerous other stitches such as Raised Square, Leviathans, Sorbello, Brick, Tent, etc.

STITCH: RIBBED WHEELS, REVERSED (*Couched and Laid, Woven*). FILLER: SMALL WHEELS

The Wheels in this square are the reverse of the previous stitch. Where the outside spokes meet, smaller Wheels have been interlaced. Other fillers may be used. When working the foundation for these Wheels, stitches may be extended from corner to corner and from top to bottom and side to side, eliminating the central hole. The needle would emerge from the same area (center) for the weaving. The stitched square shows this method.

DIAGRAM 226

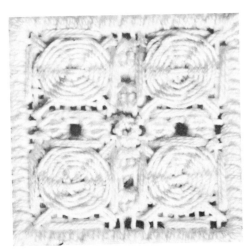

STITCH: SPIDER WEB WHEELS (*Couched and Laid, Woven*). FILLER: RIGHT-ANGLED ROCOCO (*Loop, Tied*). SMALL FILLER: BUTTONHOLE (*Loop, Tied*)

Concentrate on the Wheels in this pattern. Use Diagram 202 for Right-Angled Rococo instructions and Diagram 190 for Buttonhole instructions or use simpler filler. Spider Web Wheels may be rescaled but the foundation must always be woven through an *odd* number of spokes. The essential point to remember is the *odd*-number foundation lines (they do not have to be equidistant). The stitch is simple to work and may be rescaled easily.

DIAGRAM 227

Ladies Playing Double Sixes.

Swan and Cygnets.

PLATE 13

Snow at Dusk.

PLATE 14

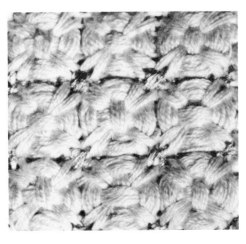

STITCH:[†] LACE WHEELS *(Couched and Laid, Woven)*
This stitch was adapted from French lacework construction and can be recommended for its sturdiness. It is uncomplicated to work. You may fill the small spaces with Flat Stitches, Crosses, or Knots.

DIAGRAM 228

STITCH:[†] LACE WHEELS, REVERSED *(Couched and Laid, Woven)*
The same as the preceding diagram, but the understructure is reversed and rescaled.

DIAGRAM 229

FLAT

Flat stitches are self-descriptive. They may be made in any direction but they lie flat without ties, crossovers, interlacing. If they are formed in the medieval manner with a light tension, they will show small perforations which, to my way of thinking, enhance and emphasize the pattern. They are usually simple to work out because they offer no structural complexity. Some of them are fairly long and you must take special care to try to keep your yarn flat and untwisted. It is very difficult to do this with multistranded silk but you must make every effort. They are not meant for hard wear, unless they are very small because they will dislodge too easily to function well on frequently used articles.

These are the stitches used for what is called Florentine or Flame Stitch work. They are very responsive to shading and geometric form. Florentine work is not, in fact, a special stitch. It is simply a method of using *ombré*-toned flat stitches in steeple, diamond, or other mathematical formations. This applies as well to Hungarian Point, which I have treated separately.

Silk, wool, and linen yarns are best.

STITCH: TENT, HORIZONTAL *(Flat)*

This stitch is sometimes called Continental. Tent Stitch is almost synonymous with "needlepoint." It is this stitch that is most frequently employed in tapestry-like designs. It adapts to any canvas, coarse or fine, with simple yarn adjustment; it is perfect for geometric or representational composition; it covers the reverse side sturdily which makes it exceptionally hardy; it is pleasant to work and enduringly pleasing to the eye. In my opinion, Tent Stitch (along with Brick Stitch and Hungarian Point) merges with the canvas square particularly well and produces a most satisfying, always interesting, textural pattern. Almost all the geometric patterns

adapted for this book can be transformed with ease to Tent Stitch construction. Therefore, the designs may be used without learning a broad stitch vocabulary. Horizontal or vertical structuring tends to distort the canvas more severely than diagonal formation (*see* the following diagram) and necessitates the turning of the canvas for successive lines. Diagonal and horizontal are indistinguishable on the surface. Their undersides will reveal which technique was used. Horizontal may be simpler for the beginner. Most experienced workers in the United States prefer the diagonal. Of course, *single-line* outlining (vertical and horizontal) is structured as shown.

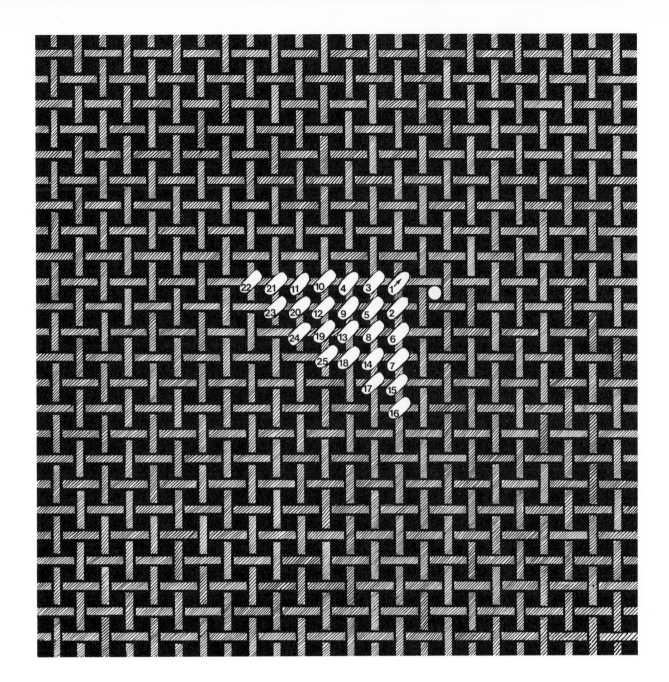

stitch: TENT, DIAGONAL *(Flat)*

The diagonal method distorts canvas less dramatically than horizontal Tent Stitch method. Another advantage enjoyed by the diagonal worker is the elimination of the need to turn the canvas after every row—an irksome procedure even on a fairly small piece. Obviously, when shades, designs or outlines are stitched in one line only, this system is not applicable—unless the single slant line coincides with the slant of diagonal Tent. The reverse side of the canvas shows a basketlike interweave. This has led to the use of the name Basket Weave Stitch in the United States.

When starting or finishing a length of yarn, run the reverse side stitches along a *horizontal* or *vertical* line to prevent ridges. When leaving off work it is wise to stop in the middle of a row, thus preventing the error of two successive rows being worked in the same direction again, to prevent ridges. *See* Color Plates 6 (St. George and the Dragon pillow), 7, and 9, and sampler square photograph with Diagram 174 for Tent Stitch examples.

DIAGRAM 231

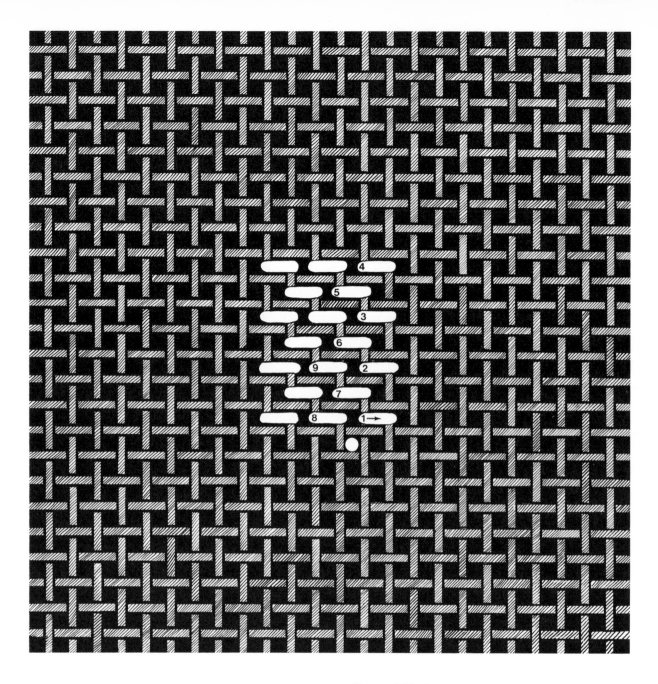

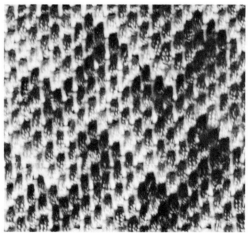

STITCH: BRICK *(Flat)*

This stitch is second only to Tent Stitch in popularity and usefulness. Excellent for geometric design. Its texture is exceptionally beautiful and useful for grounds. The sampler square shows Brick Stitch used for patterning. In this case, the structuring follows the dictates of the design. *See* sampler square photographs with Diagrams 67 and 222 for Brick monotone textures.

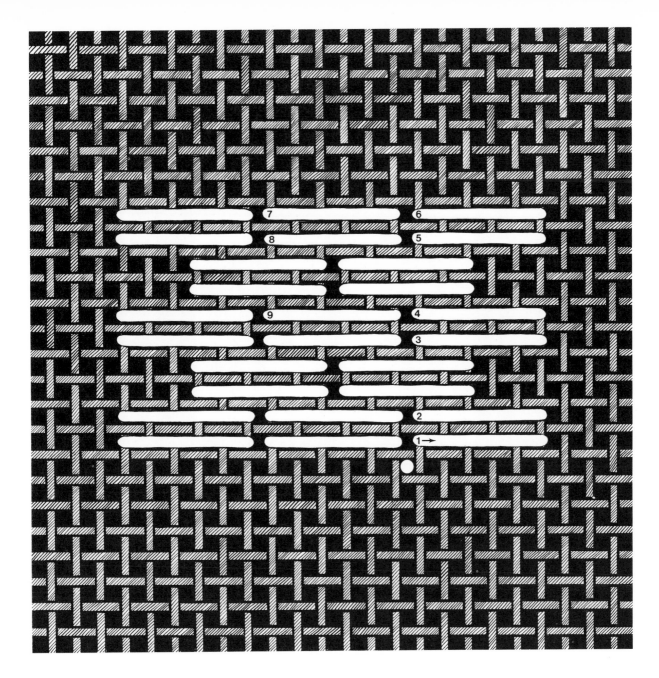

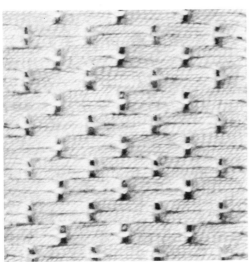

STITCH: BRICK, VARIATION 1 *(Flat)*

These simple and effective bricklike formations are to be seen frequently in medieval whitework embroidery. They may be made any length or height as long as they are divisible in the center so that the following line can be placed properly. A number of variations are to be seen in the diagrams following.

DIAGRAM 233

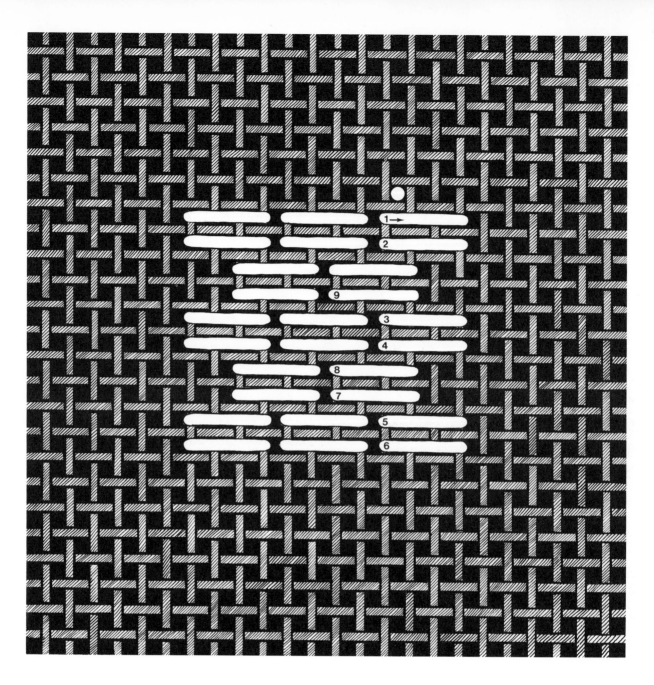

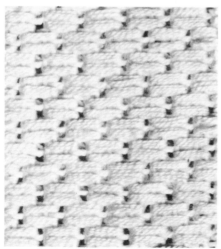

STITCH: BRICK, VARIATION 2 *(Flat)*
Note the importance of clean perforations in all Brick construction. All Brick Stitches may be worked horizontally or vertically.

DIAGRAM 234

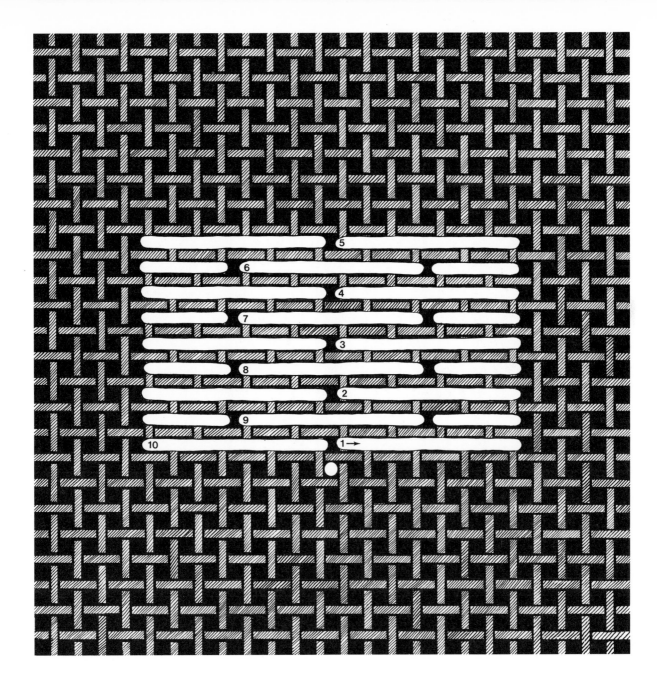

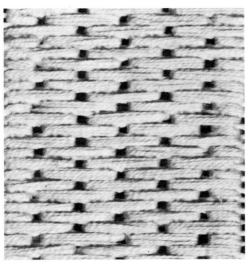

STITCH: BRICK, VARIATION 3 *(Flat)*

DESIGN:† Basket weave (wall pattern) in a Persian miniature painting, Nizami's Khamsa by Bihzad, c. 1494.

DIAGRAM 235

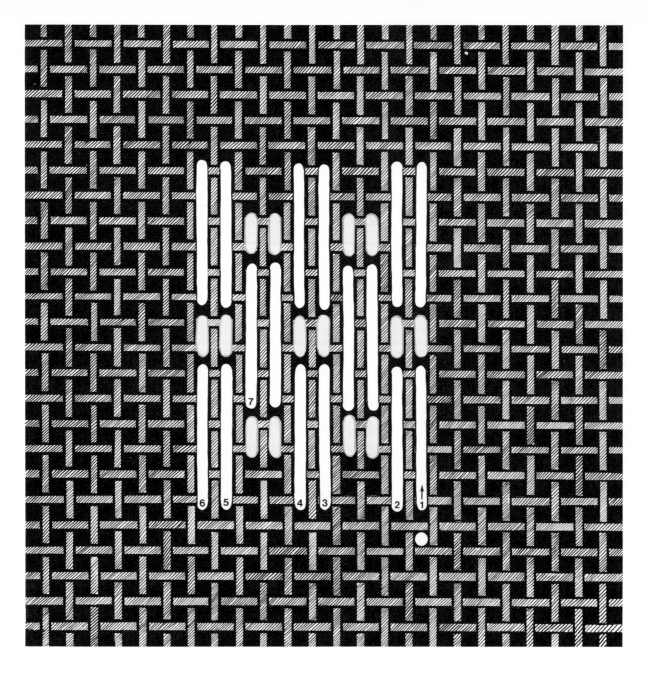

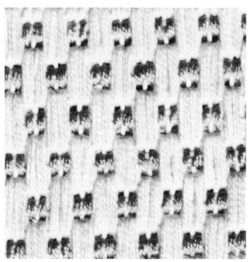

STITCH: OLD FLORENTINE *(Flat)*
Good bricklike pattern. Excellent in both mono and double tones.

DIAGRAM 236

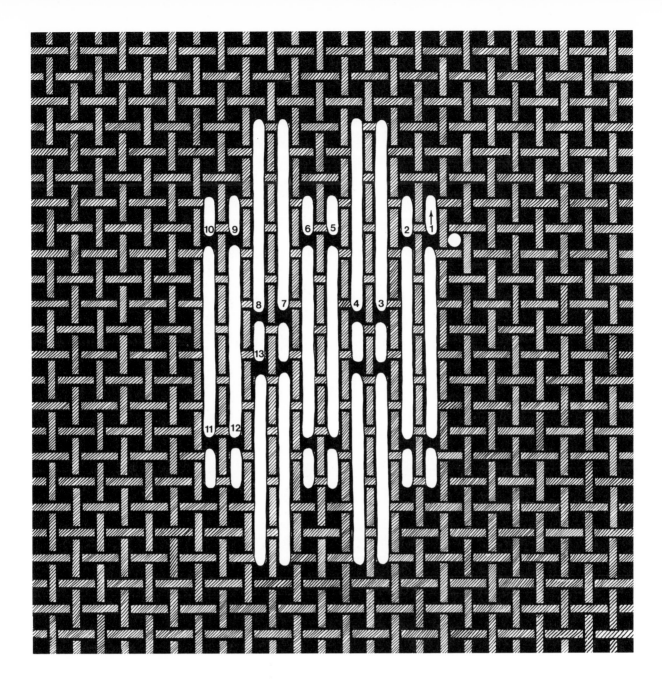

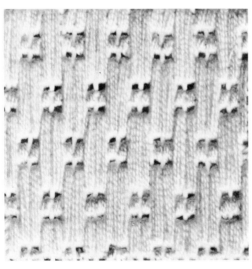

STITCH: OLD FLORENTINE VARIATION *(Flat)*

DESIGN: This variation is taken from an 18th-century Swedish-Lace Filling embroidery. It is another bricking structure. It may be used vertically or horizontally, mono or double-toned.

DIAGRAM 237

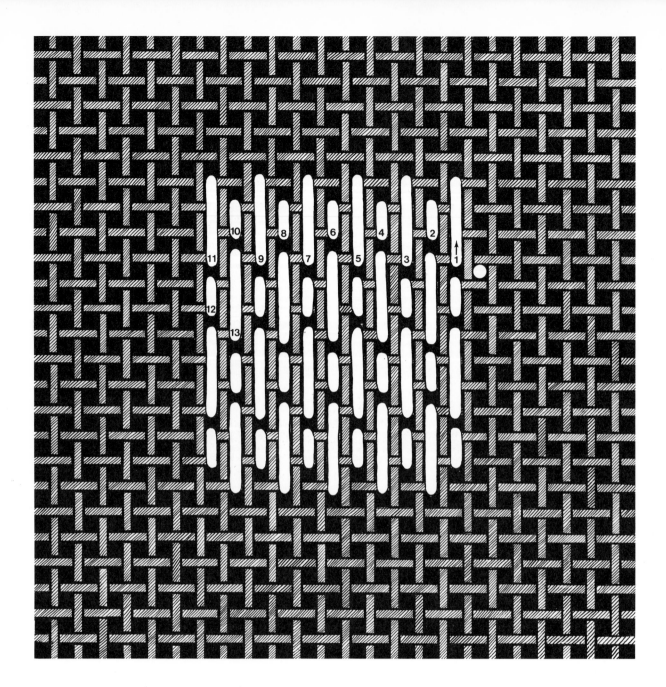

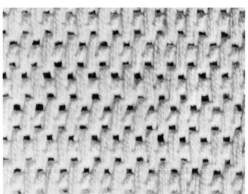

STITCH: Old Parisian *(Flat)*

DESIGN: A cousin of Old Florentine, and also related to Brick patterning. Use either horizontally or vertically.

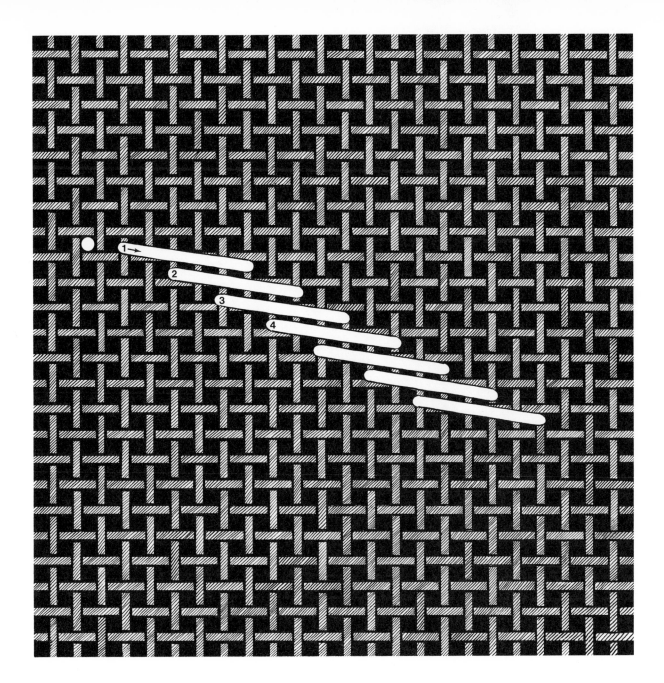

STITCH: DIAGONAL GROUND *(Flat)*
The diagram shows a diagonal structure. It is also possible to work the stitch horizontally (as I did for the sampler square). The surface effect is the same.

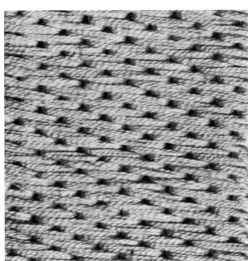

DIAGRAM 239

STITCH: DIAGONAL MOSAIC *(Flat)*
See Diagram 69 for Square Mosaic Stitch.

STITCH: CASHMERE DIAGONAL *(Flat)*
This stitch distorts canvas, so work with lightened tension.

DIAGRAM 241

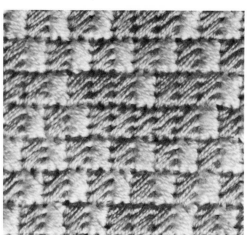

STITCH: CASHMERE BLOCKS *(Flat)*
This stitch distorts, therefore dark and light blocks
have been worked in opposite directions. The blocks
may be worked in horizontal or vertical sequence if
preferred, and in one direction only.

DIAGRAM 242

STITCH: CHEQUER *(Flat)*
Scottish Stitch is a variation of Chequer. *See* page 489.

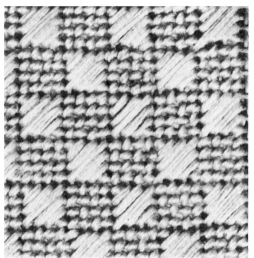

351

DIAGRAM 243

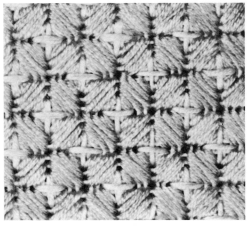

STITCH: * FLAT GROUND PATTERN *(Flat)*. FILLER:
UPRIGHT CROSS *(Cross)*
The Cross was stitched in a different tone in the
stitched square.

DIAGRAM 244

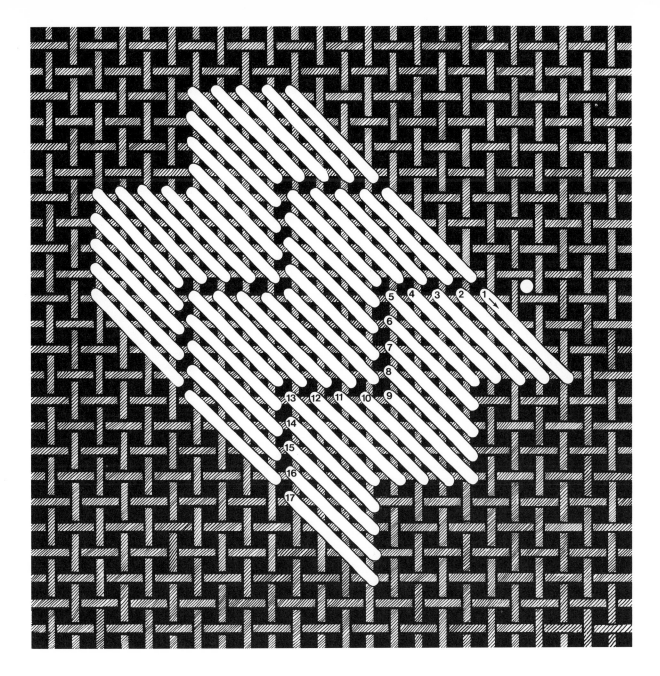

STITCH: BYZANTINE *(Flat)*
This stitch distorts the canvas which will thus need careful blocking.

DIAGRAM 245

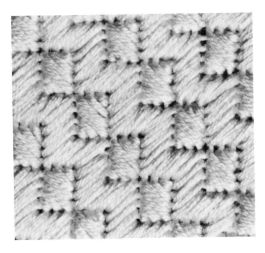

STITCH: BYZANTINE VARIATION *(Flat)*
The Step Stitch and Blocks are made in reverse directions to counterbalance distortion of canvas.

DIAGRAM 246

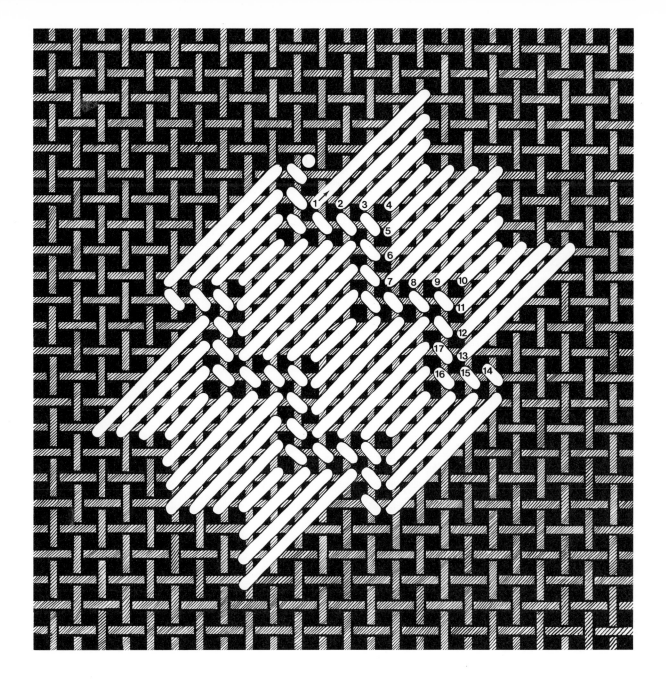

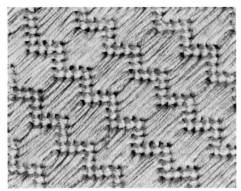

STITCH: MOORISH (*Flat*)

The Tent Stitch is worked in opposite direction from the Flat to inhibit distortion of canvas. This is not traditional however. One of many "composite" stitches that by traditional marriage has developed its own name. You can see (in the photograph) that the final Tent Stitch tends to displace the long strands. Therefore, it may be advisable to work Tent first in stitches of this kind.

DIAGRAM 247

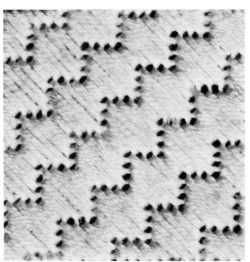

stitch: Diagonal *(Flat)*
Very attractive ground, but the slant of the stitch
warps the canvas.

DIAGRAM 248

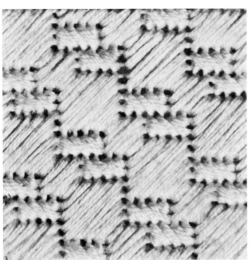

STITCH: * DIAGONAL , VARIATION *(Flat)*
Finding that the Diagonal Stitch distorts the canvas
too radically for practical use, I developed this pattern
which employs reverse-direction fillers.

DIAGRAM 249

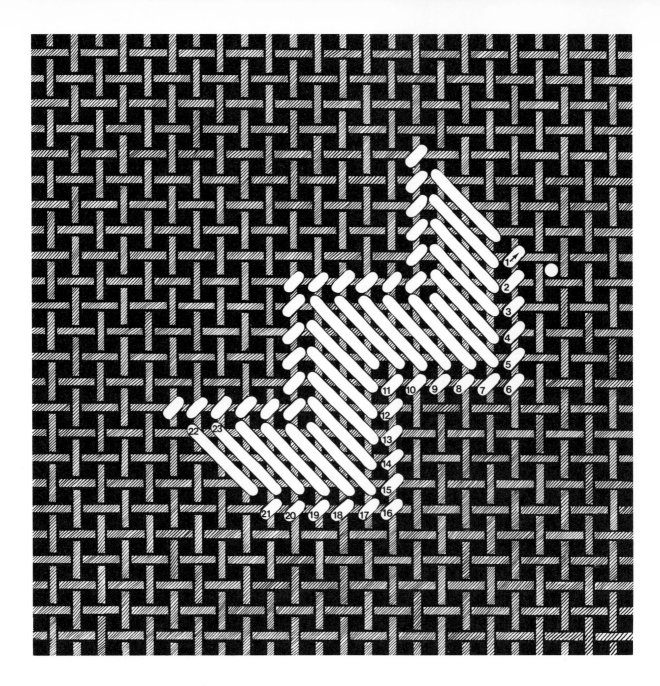

STITCH: JACQUARD *(Flat)*

This may be constructed in monotone or in a variety of colors. It consists of both long diagonal and short diagonal stitches (Tent Stitch).

Conventionally all the stitches slant in one direction only. They are used here in counterbalance pull. Can be rescaled.

STITCH:* JACQUARD, VARIATION *(Flat)*

DIAGRAM 251

STITCH: MILANESE *(Flat)*
Distorts canvas.

DIAGRAM 252

STITCH: ORIENTAL *(Flat)*
Distorts canvas.

DIAGRAM 253

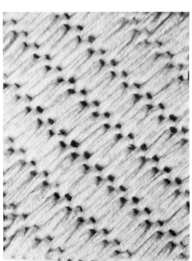

STITCH: ZIG ZAG *(Flat)* over two
May be worked as in the diagram or re-scaled to go
over 3 threads as in the photograph.

DIAGRAM 254

STITCH: MITRED FISHBONE *(Flat)*
A conventional embroidery stitch.

DIAGRAM 255

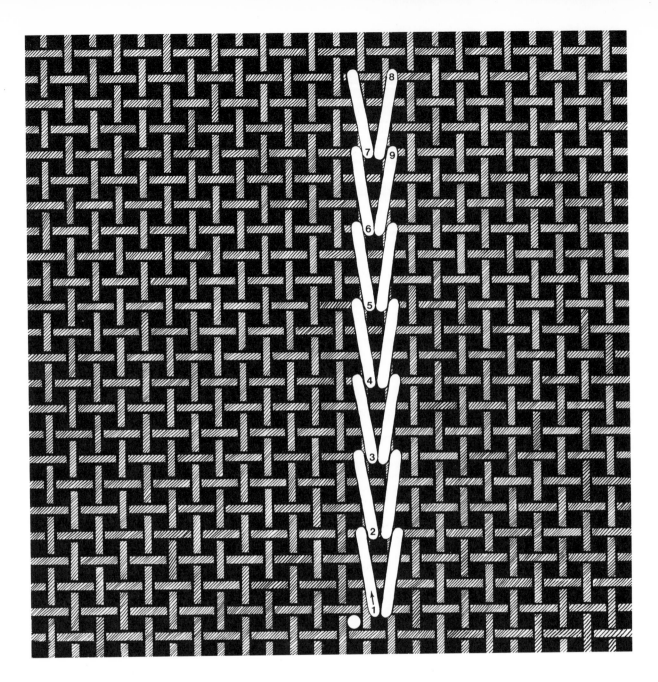

STITCH: Knitting *(Flat)*
Interesting shading can be worked in this stitch.

DIAGRAM 256

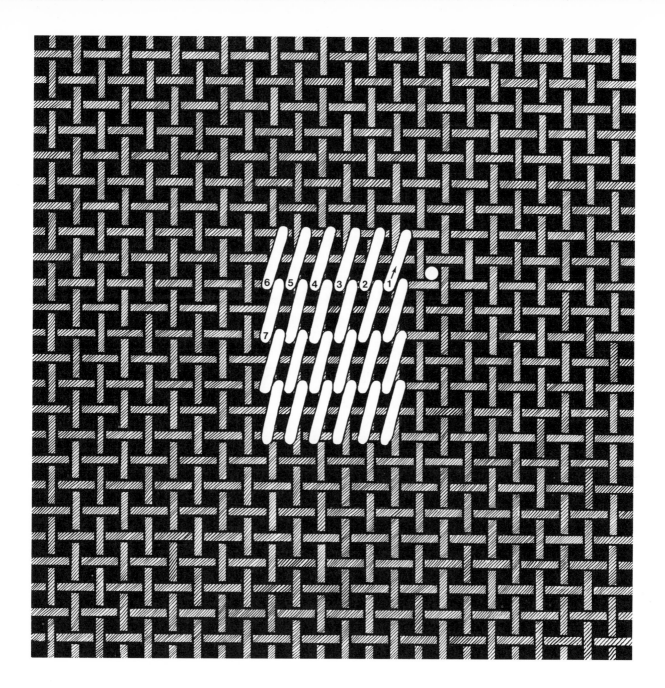

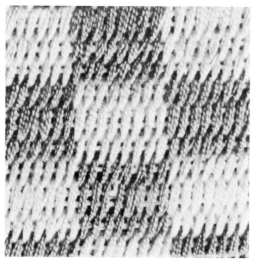

STITCH: ENCROACHING GOBELIN *(Flat)*

The length of the stitch may be changed as desired—just alter the thickness of the yarn to accommodate the length of the stitch for coverage. It gives a good firm woven texture. It is used here in a checkerboard arrangement, but many patterns may be formed with it. Basic Gobelin uses the same slant but the second row starts one square lower and does not encroach. *See* Diagram 258.

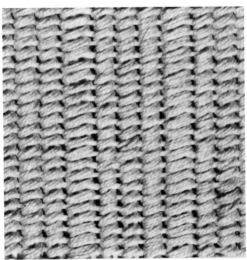

STITCH: SLANTED GOBELIN *(Flat)*
When Gobelin is used in this fashion, it is sometimes called Rep Stitch because of its ribbed appearance. The scale may be altered and it may be worked vertically.

DIAGRAM 258

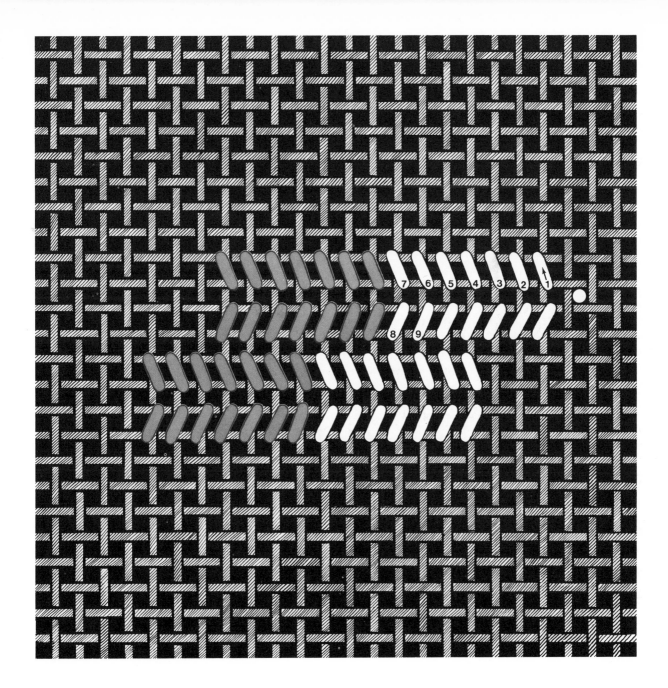

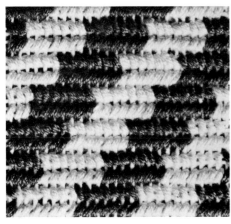

STITCH: REVERSED GOBELIN *(Flat)*

DESIGN: * This design is known as Streak o' Lightnin' in American patchwork quilting.

DIAGRAM 259

STITCH: GOBELIN, TENT *(Flat)*

DESIGN: * Vertical and horizontal Gobelin Stitches in a basketry ground arrangement.

DIAGRAM 260

STITCH: STRAIGHT GOBELIN *(Flat)*. FILLER: CROSS *(Cross)*

DESIGN: * Square Meander.
This design may be worked in any number of stitches:
Cross, Upright Cross, Leviathan, Mosaic Squares,
Tent, and many others.

STITCH: Oblique Slav Horizontal *(Flat)*

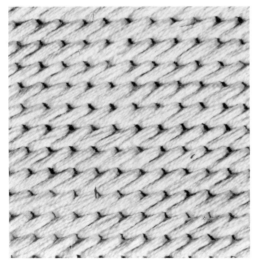

DIAGRAM 262

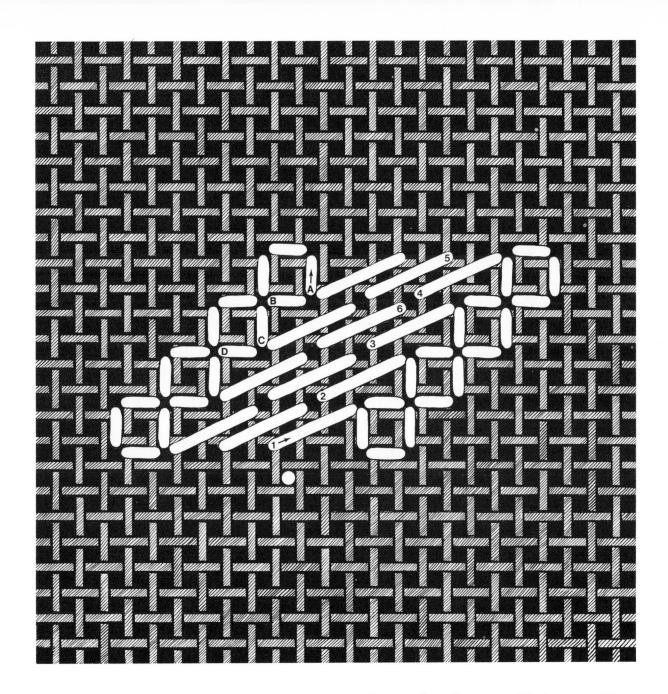

STITCH: OBLIQUE SLAV DIAGONAL *(Flat)*. FILLER: FLAT
(Flat)

DIAGRAM 263

STITCH: Leaf *(Flat)*

Worked, Victorian-style, with a stitch covering the perforations. The last vertical stitch may be omitted from the leaf, in which case perforation will contribute to the pattern. When worked the A, B, C method the rows should be worked from the bottom up.

STITCH: DIAMOND LEAF *(Flat)*

May be rescaled by adding or subtracting the number of stitches. The stitch forms a perfect Diamond square and may be used in monotone or the colors may be varied for geometric patterning.

DESIGN: * Leaf Lattice.

DIAGRAM 265

STITCH: DIAGONAL LEAF *(Flat)*. FILLER: UPRIGHT CROSS *(Cross)*

DESIGN: * Strewn Leaves, Victorian-Sampler fashion.

STITCH: * RIGHT-ANGLED LEAF GROUND (*Flat*)
An interesting ground, but it requires great care in stitching or it will distort the canvas.

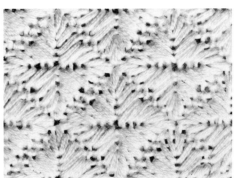

DIAGRAM 267

STITCH: DIAGONAL, DIAMOND RAY *(Flat)*

DESIGN:[†] An 18th- and 19-century sampler pattern. In the square the Ray Stitch (Filler) has been worked both horizontally and vertically, but only one form should be used. Diamond Ray Stitch may be used on its own for a monotone ground, or in tones for geometric patterning.

STITCH: Diagonal Leaf Borders, Back *(Flat)*

DESIGN: * Meandering Borders.
These borders may be kept intact or the motif may be continued as a ground pattern, filling in spaces with small Flat Stitches when necessary.

DIAGRAM 269

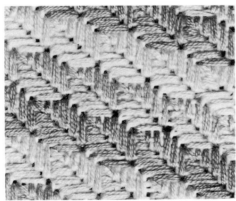

STITCH: DIAGONAL LEAF *(Flat)*

DESIGN: * For this pattern the leaves have been stepped and shaded. Many other designs may be created by altering the color distribution. It is essential to start this pattern at the bottom right.

378   DIAGRAM 270

STITCH: SQUARE RAY *(Flat)*
The direction of this stitch may be alternated every
other row. Easily rescaled.

DIAGRAM 271

STITCH: FLAT WITH SQUARE RAY *(Flat)*

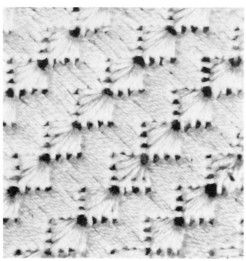

DIAGRAM 272

STITCH: DIAMOND RAY, RIGHT-ANGLED *(Flat)*. FILLER: SMALL FLAT STITCH *(Flat)*

DIAGRAM 273

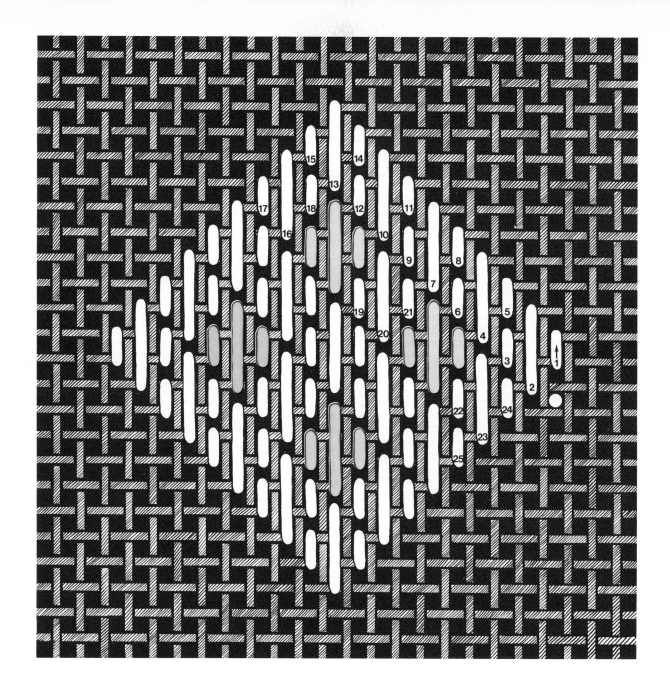

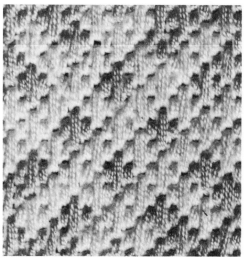

STITCH: HUNGARIAN STITCH *(Flat)*

DESIGN:[†] A typical Islamic motif. I have seen it in Turcoman saddlebags, Syrian textiles, Seljuk brickwork of the 13th century, Venetian and French lace pattern books of the 16th century. It is very simple, and is included as an easy learning example for Hungarian Stitch.

DIAGRAM 274

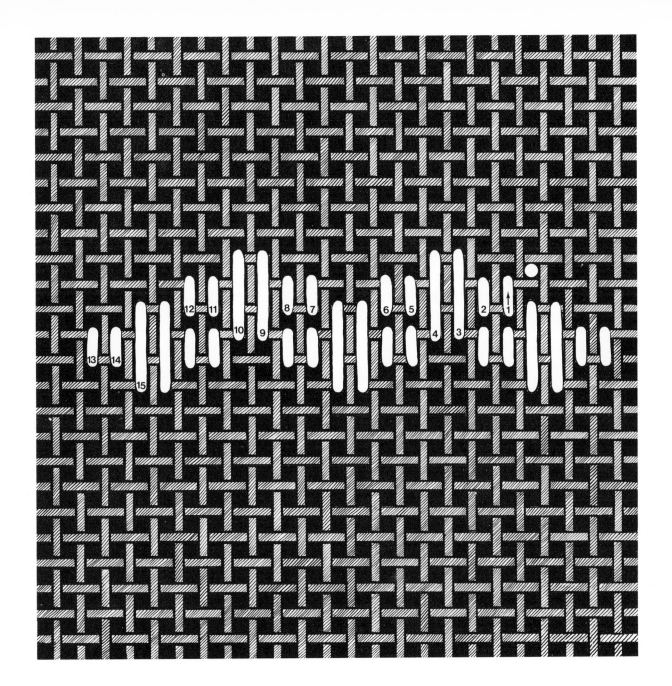

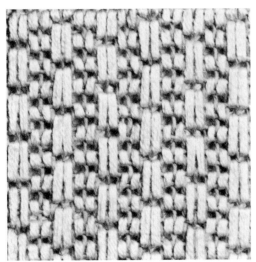

STITCH: DOUBLE HUNGARIAN STITCH *(Flat)*
Stitches may be worked over four and eight canvas threads.

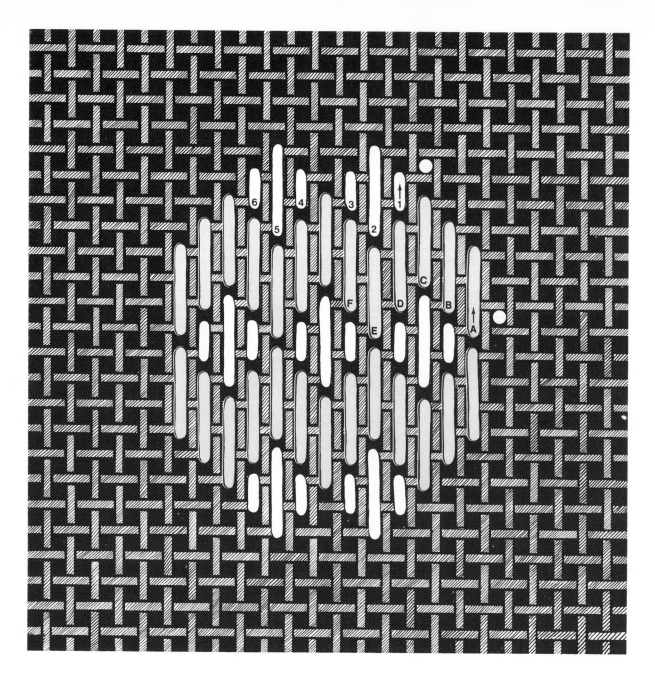

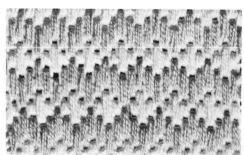

STITCH: HUNGARIAN GROUND *(Flat)*
This stitch is excellent in monotone, because of its pronounced perforations; color variations are also interesting in this structure. It is a medieval geometric ground.

DIAGRAM 276

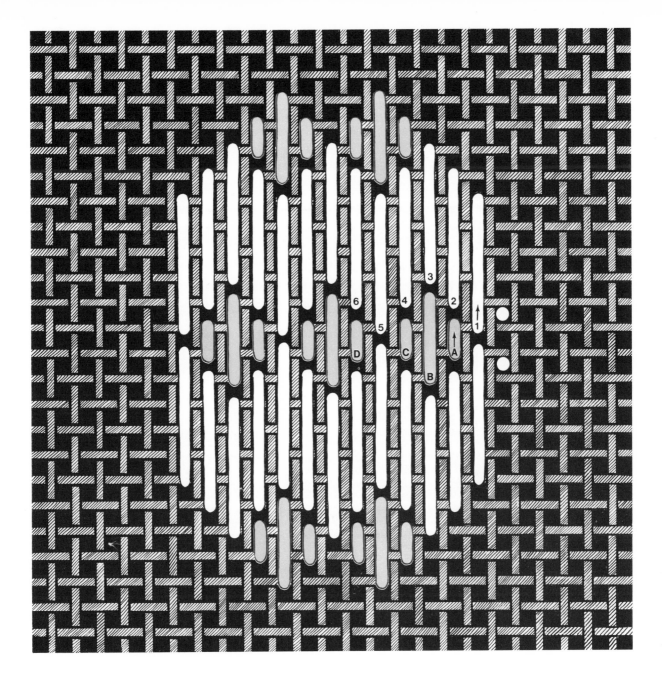

STITCH: * Hungarian Ground, Variation *(Flat)*

DIAGRAM 277

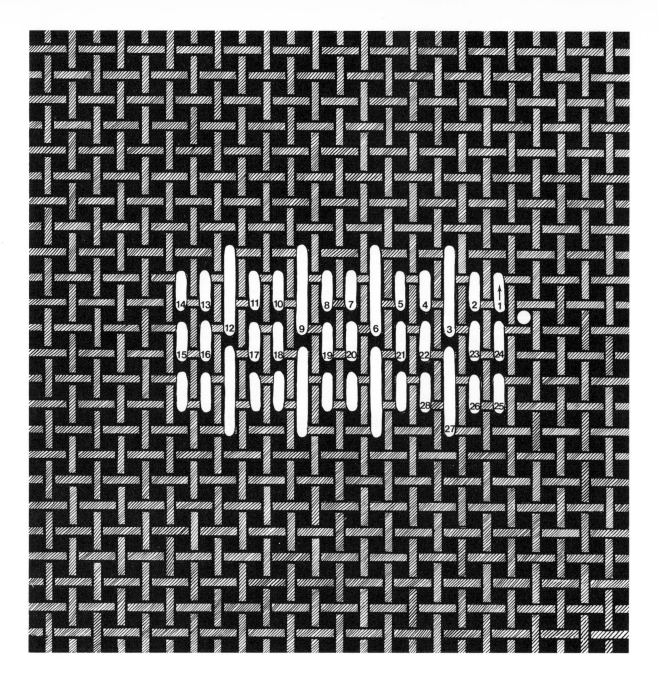

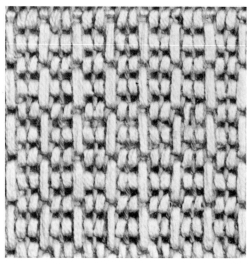

STITCH: * SMALL GROUND PATTERN 1 *(Flat)*

DESIGN: This pattern (and the two that follow) were arranged as alternatives to Tent or Brick Stitches when a small-scale ground is desired. The numbers on the diagrams are arranged to allow for maximum perforation in these patterns.

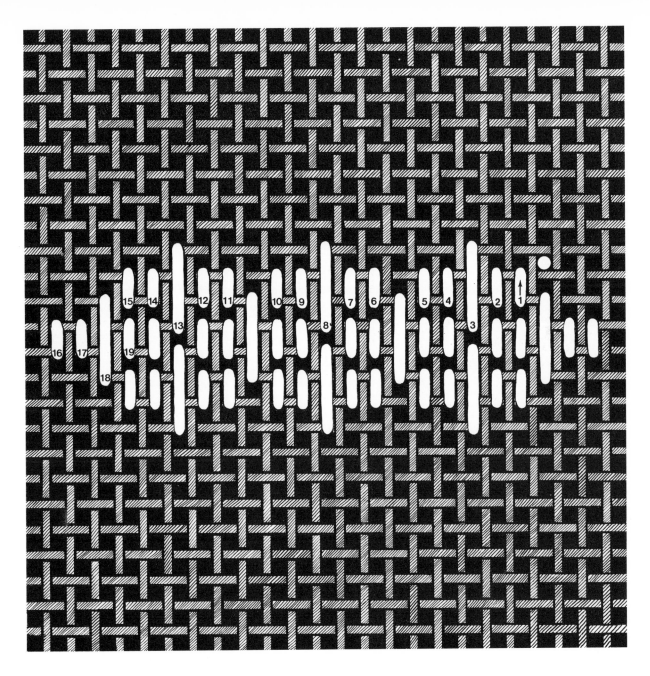

STITCH: * SMALL GROUND PATTERN 2 *(Flat)*

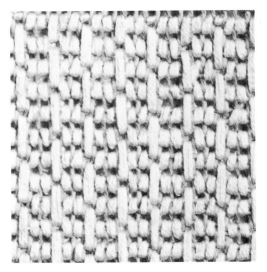

DIAGRAM 279

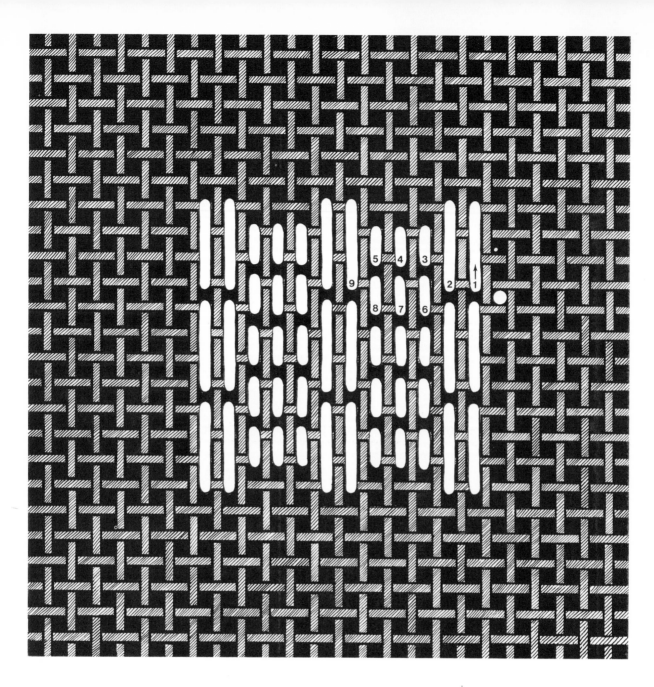

STITCH: * SMALL GROUND PATTERN 3 *(Flat)*

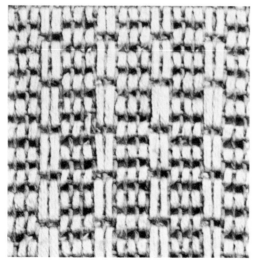

DIAGRAM 280

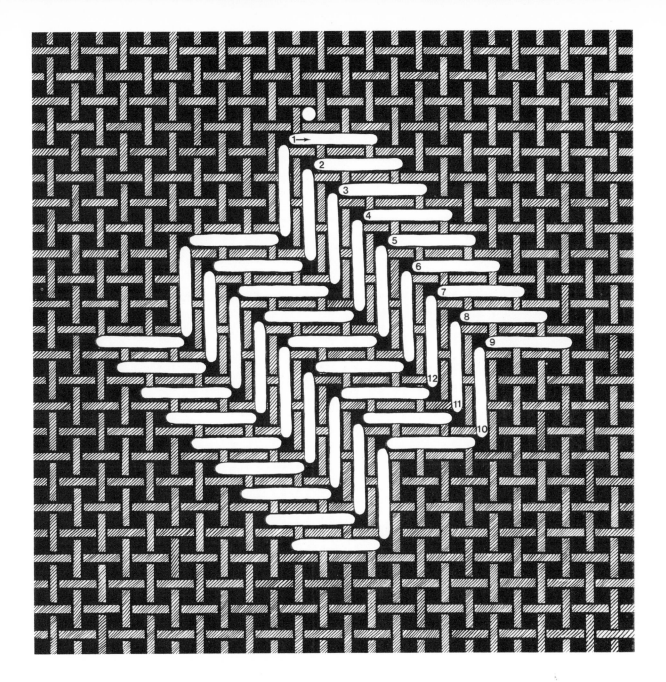

STITCH: DAMASK DARN *(Flat)*

The length of the vertical or horizontal stitches, or both, can be rescaled. Contrasting tones can be used. This is traditionally called Damask Darn but, as it does not expose the canvas threads as part of the design, it is placed here in Flat instead of the Darning group.

DIAGRAM 281

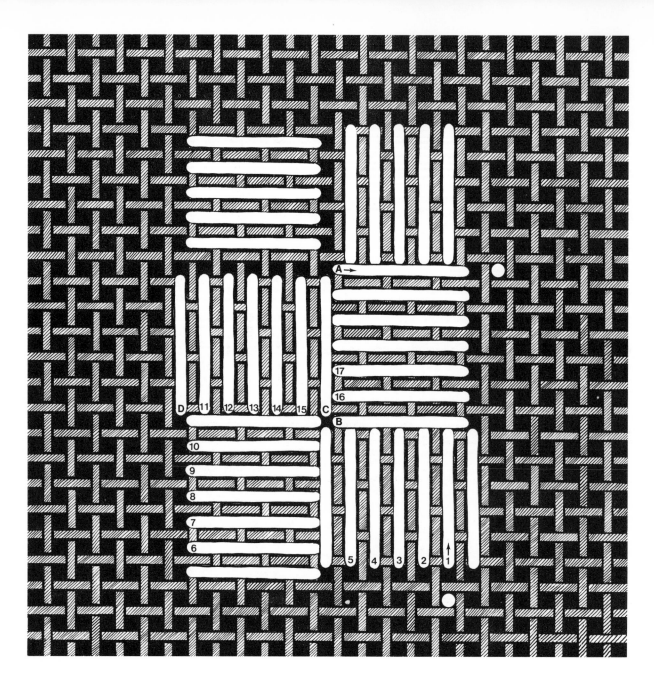

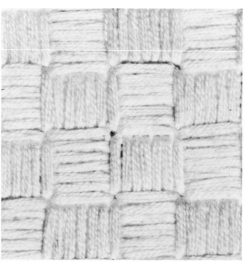

STITCH: * MEDIEVAL BASKETRY GROUND *(Flat)*
I have always liked this typical medieval basket pattern, but found it difficult to work out on canvas because of the overlap of the stitches. I then discovered it was possible to do all the center stitches first, both vertical and horizontal, leaving the outside border stitches (A, B, C, etc.) to the very last.

DESIGN: In the 13th and 14th centuries, this pattern is frequently shown in paintings, very often in sharply contrasting lines of color—black and white or brown and white. Its presence almost always indicates a real basket.

DIAGRAM 282

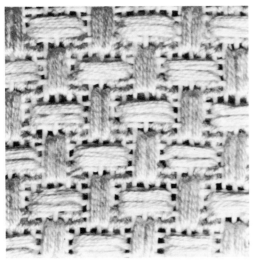

stitch: * Basketry 1 *(Flat)*
The little squares left by this design may be filled in or
left open.

DIAGRAM 283

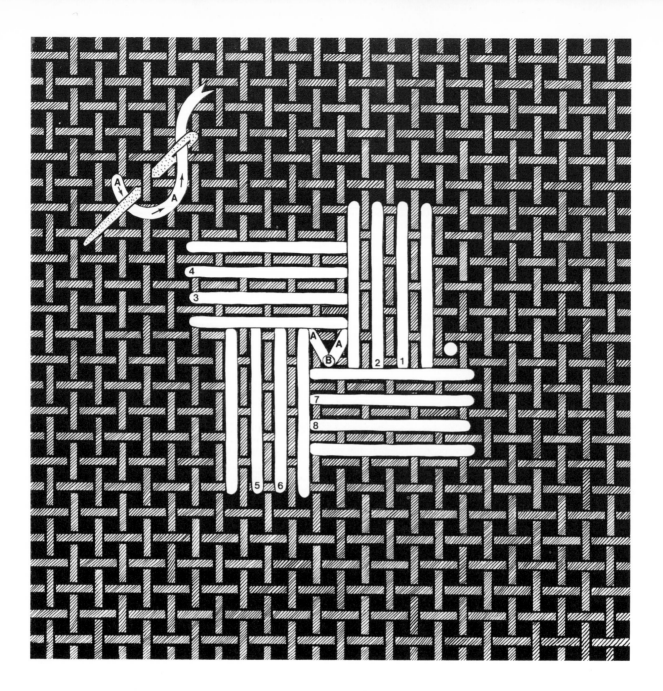

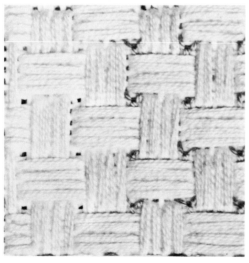

STITCH: * BASKETRY 2 *(Flat)*. FILLER: FLY STITCH
(Loop, Tied)
Another version of basketlike patterning. The two
center stitches—horizontal and vertical—are made
first, the outside stitches last. Fill the small area space or
not. Fly Stitch may also be used on its own in line or
ground formation.

DIAGRAM 284

FLAT–DARNING

These patterns are always geometric and use the canvas as part of their design. This interruption by canvas thread is the particular feature of this stitching. If you find canvas unsightly, skip over this group. It is always formed of running stitches that break at different intervals to make pattern. For instance, the first line may have the yarn crossing over five threads, under one, over five, while the second is set up in a different sequence. This is what sets the pattern. The stitch is always the same —flat—and can be made in a vertical, horizontal, or oblique line. I have found that the rough edges of the canvas often fray the yarn when it is plied in Darning (running) Stitch. Unless your yarn is unusually resistant to friction, I think it may be better, though technically incorrect, to form the stitches by the ordinary Flat Stitch method.

Darning does not give a strong surface and is best used for hangings because it permits fast patterning over large areas on articles that will not be subjected to hard wear.

For wool, silk, and linen yarns.

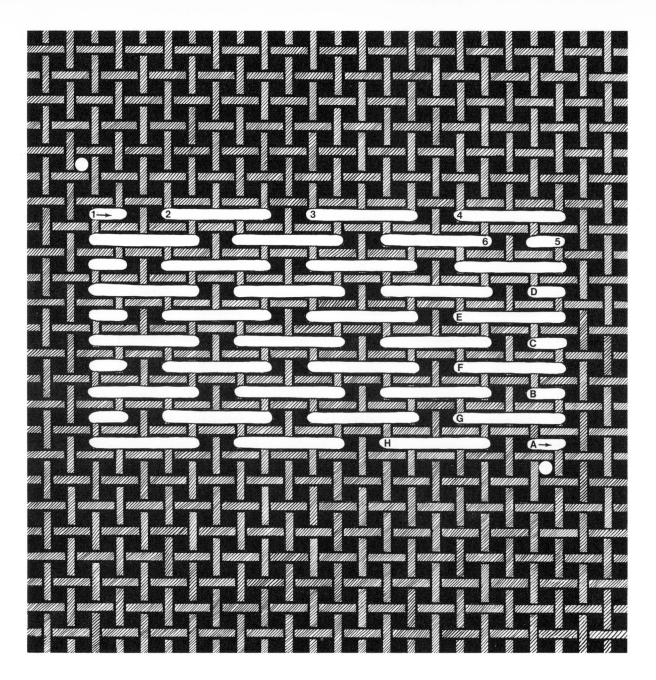

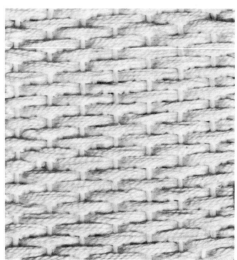

STITCH: DARNING PATTERNING 1 *(Flat)*

Darning Patterning makes use of the canvas thread as part of the design. Traditionally, it is worked by running the yarn in and out as shown in the diagram (1, 2, 3, etc.). It may, however, be worked in the conventional canvas Flat Stitch method. (A, B, C, etc., show conventional canvas system.) The yarn is easier to control on hard canvas if the latter technique is employed. Many of the patterns in the Playing Card hanging Knave of Clubs (Color Plate 12) are formed in this method.

See also Mrs. Lane's background for Ladies Playing Double Sixes, Color Plate 13.

DIAGRAM 285

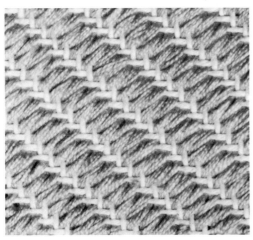

STITCH: DARNING PATTERNING 2 *(Flat)*
In the diagram, 1, 2, 3, etc., show the canvas method;
A, B, the Darning method.

DIAGRAM 286

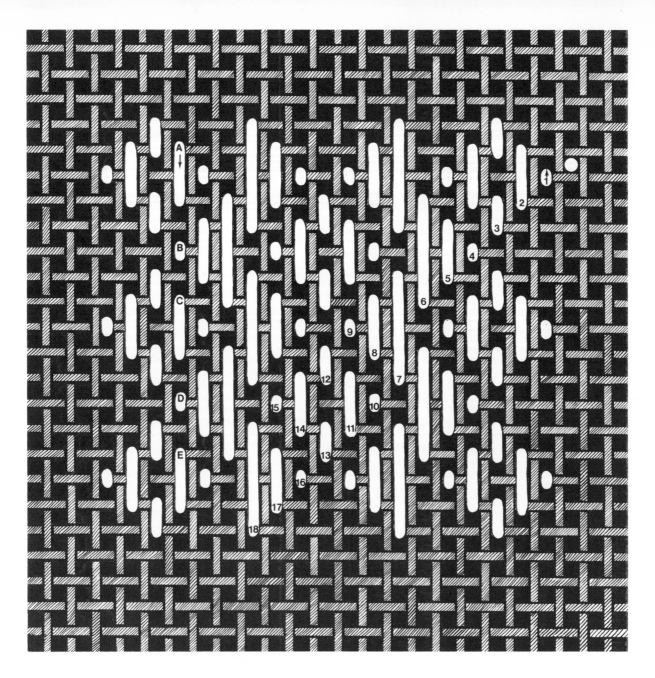

STITCH: * DARNING PATTERNING 3 (Flat)
A, B, C, Darning method. The sampler square was
worked in the Darning method—this produces a
slightly different texture; 1, 2, 3 shows canvas method.

DIAGRAM 287

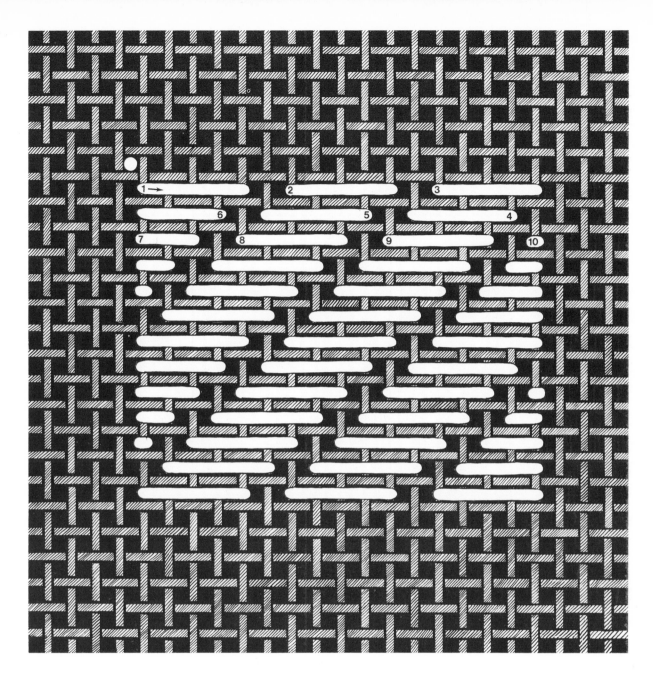

STITCH: DARNING PATTERNING 4 *(Flat)*

DIAGRAM 288

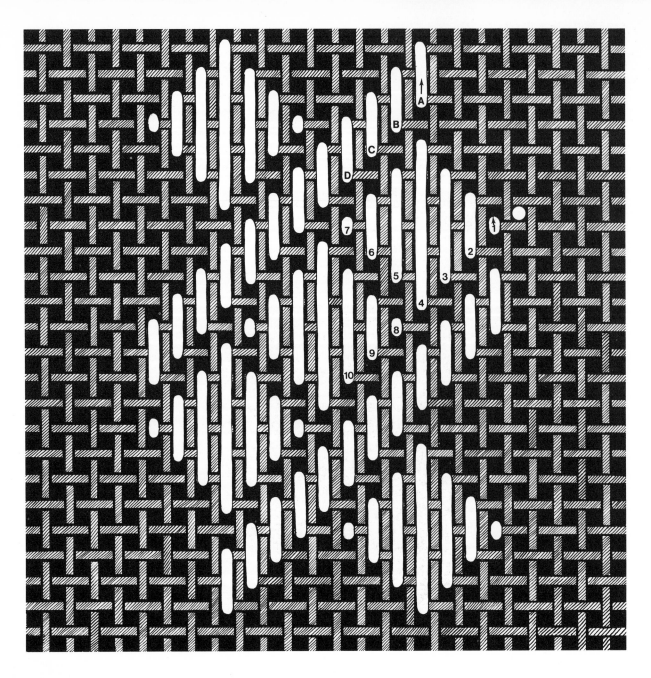

STITCH: * DARNING PATTERNING 5 *(Flat)*

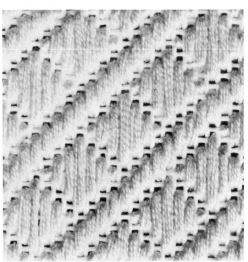

DIAGRAM 289

The Scholar's Table.

A Flower Basket.

PLATE 15

A Warrior's Farewell (in work).

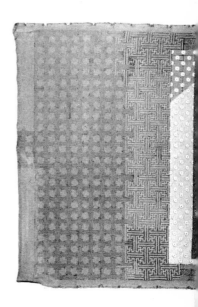

PLATE 16

FLAT—HUNGARIAN POINT

This is a form of straight stitching with unique architecture (*see* Chapter 6, Hungarian Point). The first line, which establishes the design, must be fastidiously counted. If you do not establish this correctly, you will face a hopeless tangle. After this, it is pleasant to work, especially when you are familiar with its special rhythm. There is one pitfall that requires caution and concentration in the *free-standing* peaks (the stitches you make on *top* of or *below* the peaks, rather than within them). You must attend to your mathematical count for these throughout the work. I have introduced many friends to Hungarian Point and they encountered few problems after rehearsing with a practice piece. Although each line is not duplicated by the following one, it does act as a guide for your needle and you will find your hand propelled to the right place after a while.

Linear design is limited in this work. Most of your effects will be determined by how, when, and where you use shading and change of color. Color intensifies dramatically and often disturbingly in Hungarian Point, so begin with muted or neutral tones. In the eighteenth and nineteenth centuries woolen yarn was frequently used for the deeper shades and silk for the pastels. Red affects everything around it and visually bleeds into its surroundings. I think it should almost never be employed for this stitch.

The finished effect is more like a remarkably textured woven fabric than embroidery. This makes it particularly handsome for walls and upholstery, although the length of the long stitches decreases durability to a degree. It is not for those who dream of presents for posterity.

The tonal repeats, when worked with interesting variations, are usually very distant from one another. If you wish to use this work for small-scale objects, select a fine canvas—eighteen threads to the inch or more. For large-scale work, I have always used twelve threads to the inch and a

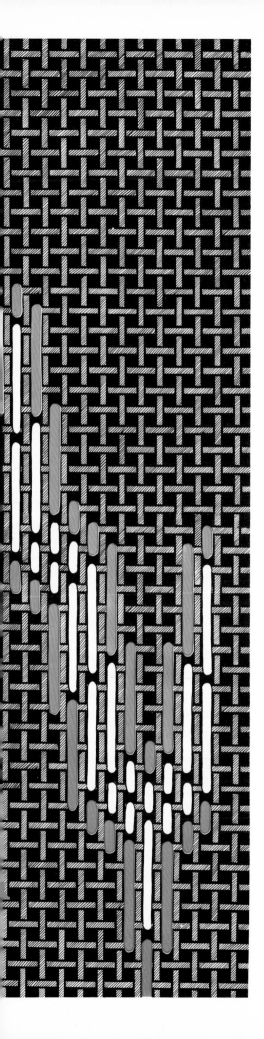

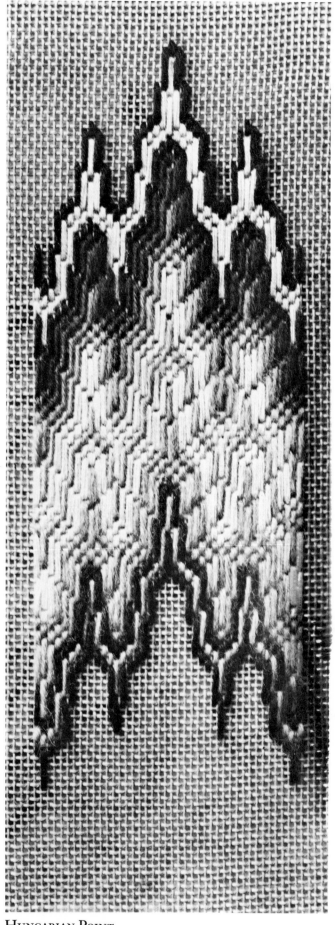

HUNGARIAN POINT

401

DIAGRAM 290

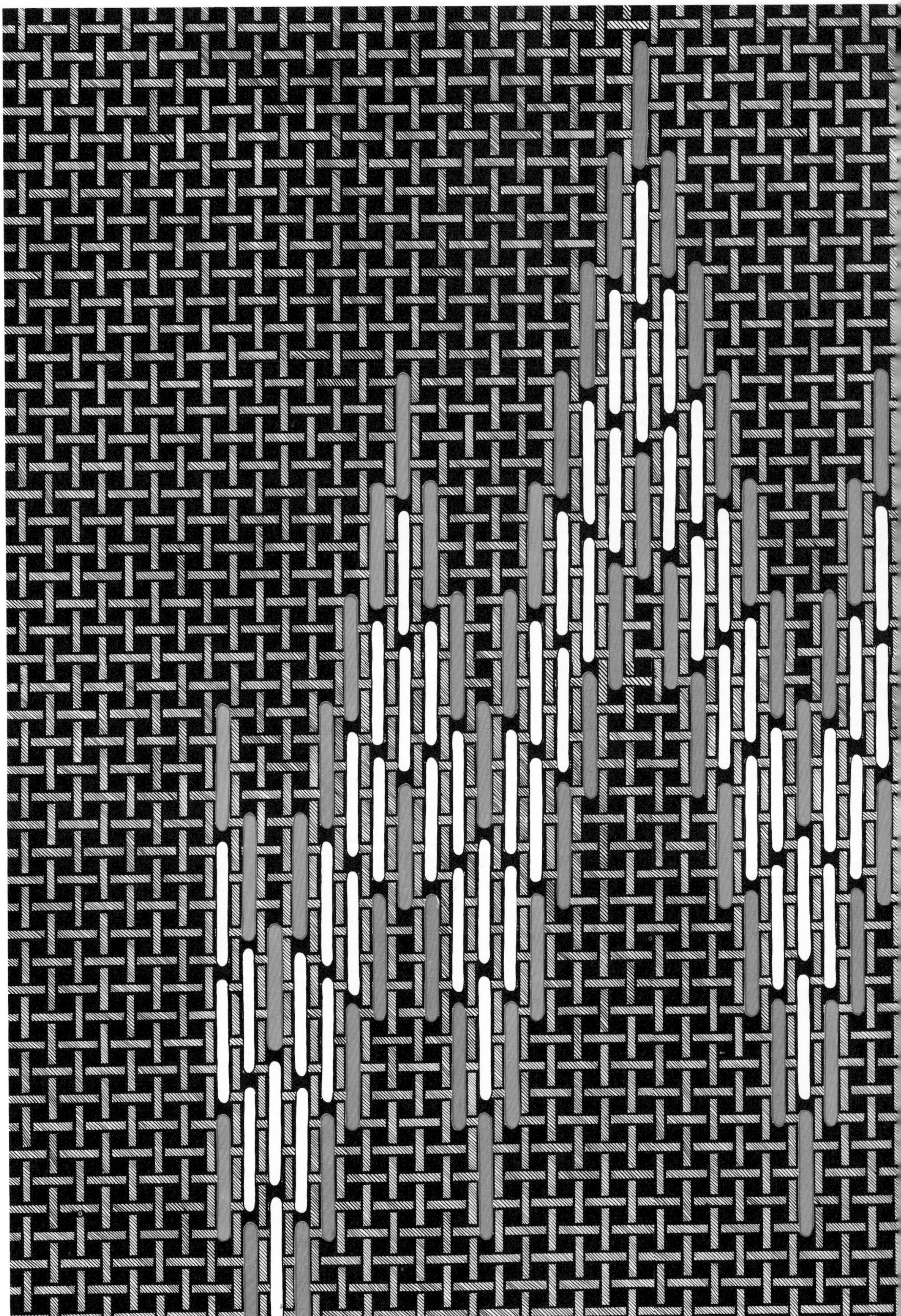

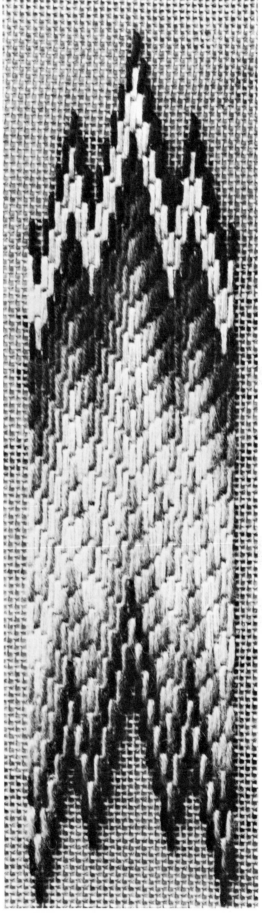

FLORENTINE STITCH

403   DIAGRAM 291

full strand of Persian three-ply yarn or its equivalent in crewel or tapestry wool.

Until you get to know the wonderful possibilities of the secondary textural surface and what you can do with the fascinating color interruptions or mergers, it is hard to make full use of the unique properties of this stitch pattern. So start with a limited ambition and range of tones. You can get more adventurous when you have a more intimate acquaintance with the nature of its structure. A diagram for Florentine stitch is also included here. Please refer to Chapter 6 for further information.

Silk and wool yarns.

PULLED YARN

Except for the Eye Stitch, this group is rarely recommended for canvas work because the ground is not always fully covered. I happen to like the appearance of canvas and see no reason for its being snubbed as a design element.

Pulled Yarn stitches partner very well with more conventional types because they usually have an equilateral pull that minimizes distortion. This pull also prevents them from shrinking the space they occupy. They work up quickly because they do not require full ground coverage. I have stitched one Pulled Yarn sampler on fourteen mono canvas. I have also used Pulled Yarn, with conventional stitches for neighbors, in the master sampler to show their commendable adaptability. They form a hard, stable surface, although they look delicate. Obviously, the exposed canvas makes them unsuitable for carpets and upholstery. If you dislike the idea of showing your canvas, pass on by.

Their construction is of utmost importance because the tension or pull creates the pattern. The yarn becomes secondary. They may be worked in wool, cotton, linen, or silk to equal advantage. Very frail yarn would break under the stress essential to this work. The yarns, whatever their composition, should be kept pale to emphasize the play of light and dark made by stitch (light) and perforation (dark). The thinner the yarn, the larger the hole. The placement of these holes gives this work its geometric design and interest.

Many pieces of medieval embroidery show flat stitches worked with sufficient tension to create small but defined holes. These are really a cross between conventional stitching and Pulled work. Perhaps the embroiderer was pleased by the small perforations and was thus encouraged to experiment with still larger ones. Pulled work may have originated this way. The German nuns of this period were particularly skilled in this Flat-stitch work. The most thrilling and satisfying realization of the endless variety within severe constriction may be seen in their pieces known to the world as White Work. Limited to one color, white, for yarn and ground, these remarkable women adorned their material with the shimmer and twinkle of ever-changing geometric forms. These White Works dance with pattern. This fireworks display of versatility was produced with quite ordinary white fabric and yarn, usually linen; in fact it was made necessary by this limitation. Had they had access to a broad range of colors, velvets, gold and silver, they most likely would have neglected the lure of their geometric adventures for that of sumptuous materials and colors.

In the past, this work has been variously called "Lace Filling," "Drawn Fabric Work," or "Pulled Work." There is an embroidery technique, not covered by this book, called "Pulled Thread" or "Drawn Thread Work." This work requires the extracting (pulling out or drawing out) of *canvas* threads. In other words, different lengths of warp or weft are pulled or drawn *out* to create an open-work ground before stitching. There is inevitable confusion among all these names. I hope to bring some order by referring to our group as "Pulled Yarn." Certainly the word *yarn* cannot be misinterpreted. I think no one can possibly imagine that it refers to the thread of the canvas or cloth.

Do remember, the character and visual appeal of this work depend entirely on your construction. You must follow directions with attention. If you don't adhere to numerical order, your pattern will show alarming changes and your perforations will not be uniform. Exceptional care must be taken to prevent reverse-side stitching from crossing behind the holes. You may easily invent new patterns by combining or rescaling stitches.

All pale yarns may be used. You may wish to dye yarn and canvas in pastel tones, or match pastel yarns by painting over the canvas. Make certain that dyes and paints are permanent. Ordinary thin string is most effective for pillows and wall hangings. Use larger gauge canvas for larger pieces.

406

Pulled Yarn sampler pillow. Although this surface appears delicate and lacy, it is actually extremely hardy. Most of the squares have been diagrammed in the following pages along with many more that were stitched in the Master Sampler. A brown cotton cover was used for the down casing so that the holes of the patterns would be clearly delineated. Because much of the canvas is left exposed (the threads become a design element) this sort of pillow can be worked very swiftly.

CANVAS: 14 mono, white.   STITCHES: Pulled yarn, varied.
YARN: Off-white (shade: Mode) French silk.
Designed and worked by S. Lantz.

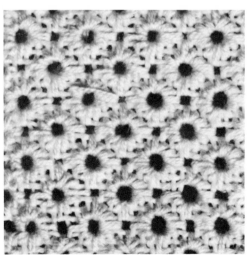

STITCH: DIAMOND EYE *(Pulled Yarn)*
The diagram has been numbered in the most logical
sequence (half-diamonds). It is usually worked by
completing each diamond as a unit, but the relationship of diamond-to-diamond does not work out in
proper stitch sequence this way. This stitch is also
good for conventional canvaswork, as are most Eye
structures.

DIAGRAM 292

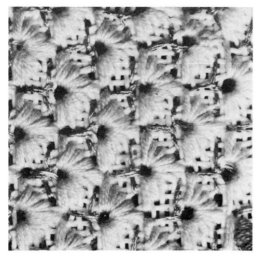

STITCH: HALF DIAMOND EYE GROUND and UNEVEN GREEK CROSS *(Pulled Yarn)*

DESIGN:* This ground was designed by using a Half Diamond Eye Stitch and a Greek Cross over an uneven thread count (6 horizontal threads and 4 vertical threads). The diagram leaves the Greek Cross area empty; the Half Diamond may be used on its own. *See* Diagram 325 for basic Greek Cross one arm, the right horizontal, was omitted for this pattern.

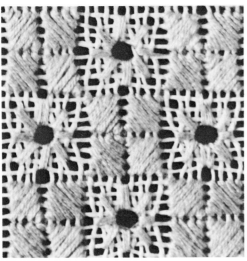

STITCH: LACE FILLING 1, FRENCH *(Pulled Yarn)*
May be rescaled.

DIAGRAM 294

STITCH: LACE FILLING 2, FRENCH *(Pulled Yarn)*

DESIGN: The pattern is taken from French lace work. This checkerboard is effective on a larger field. May be rescaled.

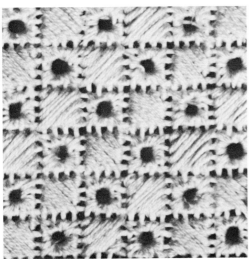

DIAGRAM 295

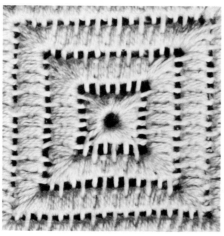

STITCH: * SQUARES WITHIN SQUARES *(Pulled Yarn)*
May be rescaled.

DIAGRAM 296

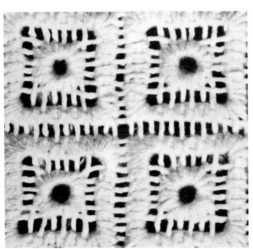

STITCH: * CIRCLE IN THE SQUARE *(Pulled Yarn)*
Circle Eye Stitches outlined by frames. May be re-scaled.

DIAGRAM 297

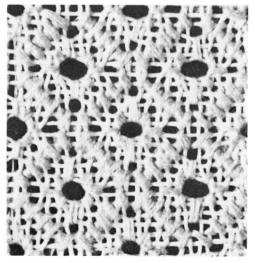

STITCH: Diagonal Overcast Ground, Diamond Eye
(Pulled Yarn)

DIAGRAM 298

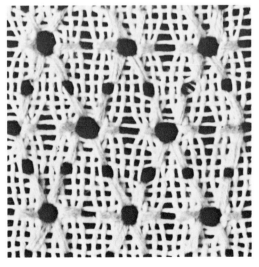

STITCH: Oblique Filling *(Pulled Yarn)*

DIAGRAM 299

STITCH: Eye Filling *(Pulled Yarn)*

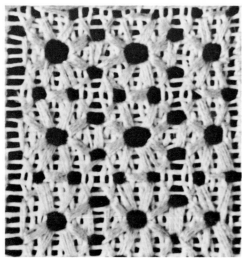

DIAGRAM 300

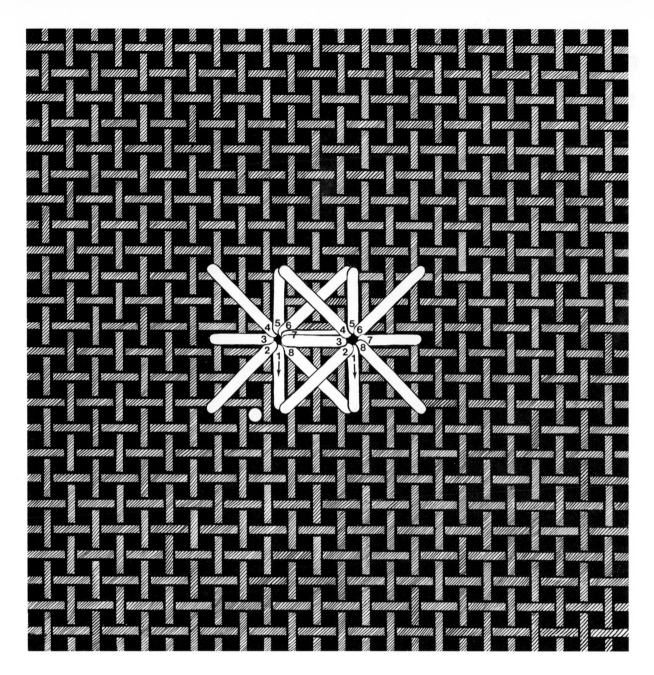

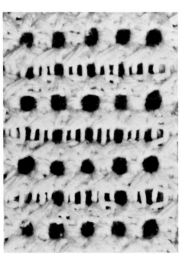

STITCH: ITALIAN EYE (*Pulled Yarn*)
The sides of Italian Eye Stitch overlap and form an interesting geometric pattern. May be used for conventional canvas work.

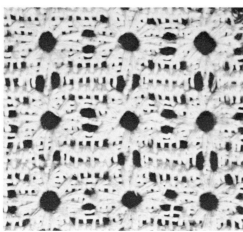

STITCH: * EYE, VARIATION 1 *(Pulled Yarn)* and FLAT STITCH GROUND *(Flat)*

The Flat Stitch filler bars are worked over two threads of the canvas. May be used for conventional canvas work if you decrease tension.

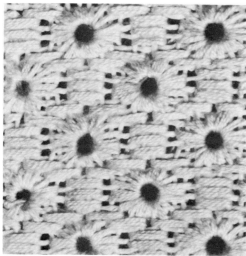

STITCH:* Eye, Variation 2 *(Pulled Yarn)* and Flat *(Flat)*

DESIGN:* Loosely based on Swedish 18th-century Needle Lace piece. May be used for conventional canvas work.

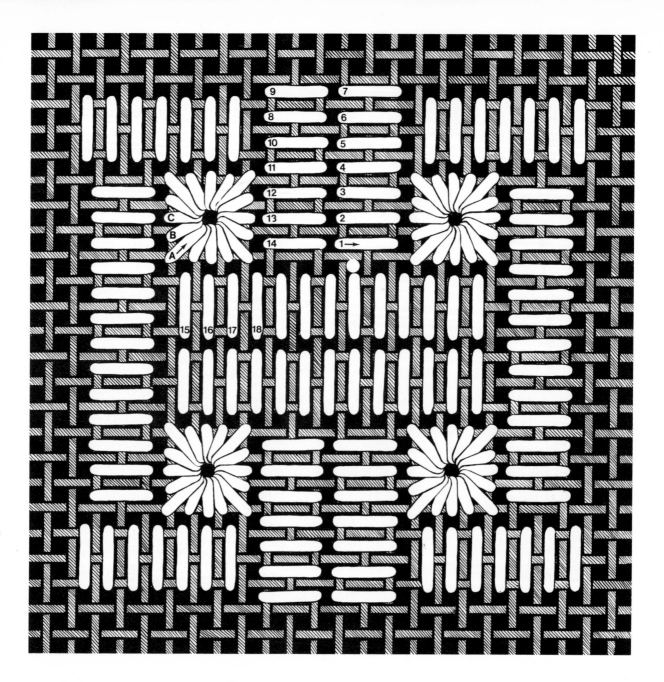

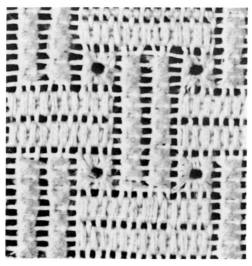

STITCH: FLAT and EYE GROUND (*Pulled Yarn*)

DESIGN: * Basket Ground.
May be rescaled.

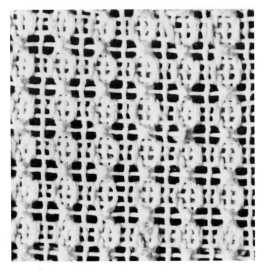

STITCH: FOUR-SIDED OVER THREE *(Pulled Yarn)* (in vertical rows)
The back will show Large X Cross Stitches.

DIAGRAM 305

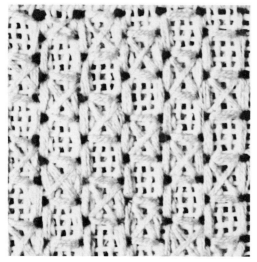

STITCH: FOUR-SIDED HALF-DROPPED *(Pulled Yarn)* over four, plus CROSS *(Pulled Yarn)*

DIAGRAM 306

STITCH: FOUR-SIDED WITH BLOCKS *(Pulled Yarn)*

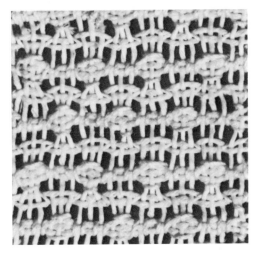

DIAGRAM 307

STITCH: FOUR-SIDED DIAMOND *(Pulled Yarn)*
May be rescaled.

DIAGRAM 308

STITCH: Three-Sided Over Four *(Pulled Yarn)*

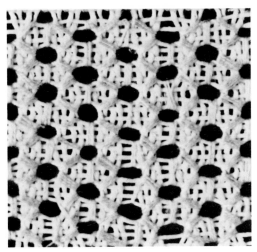

DIAGRAM 309

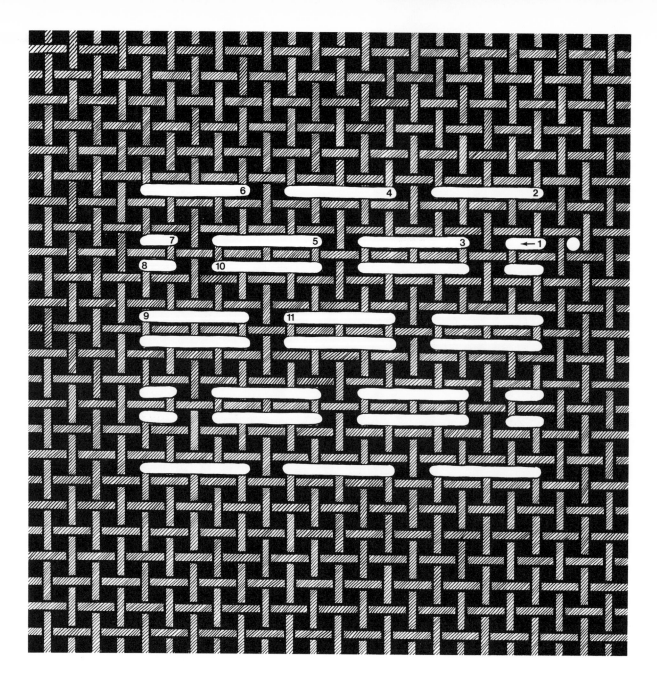

STITCH: DOUBLE *(Pulled Yarn)*

DIAGRAM 310

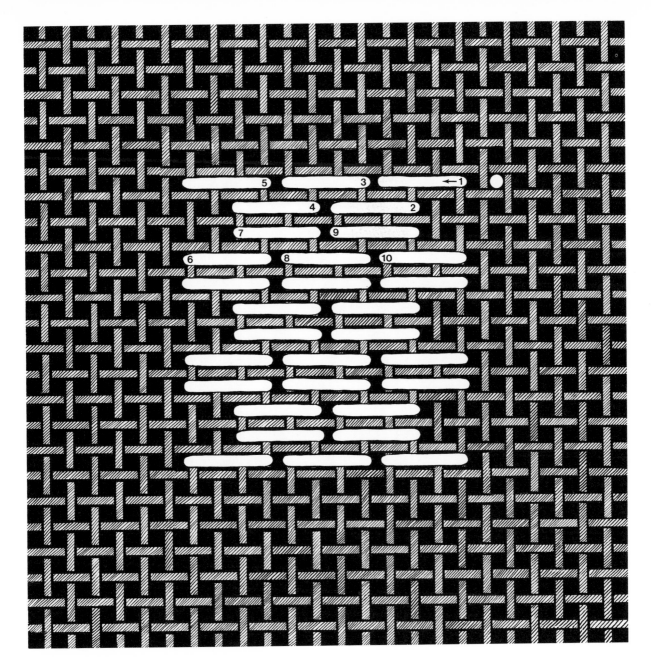

STITCH: * DOUBLE VARIATION OVER FOUR *(Pulled Yarn)*

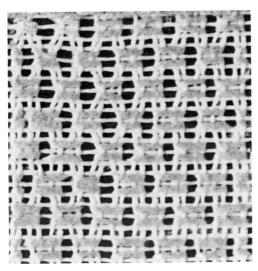

DIAGRAM 311

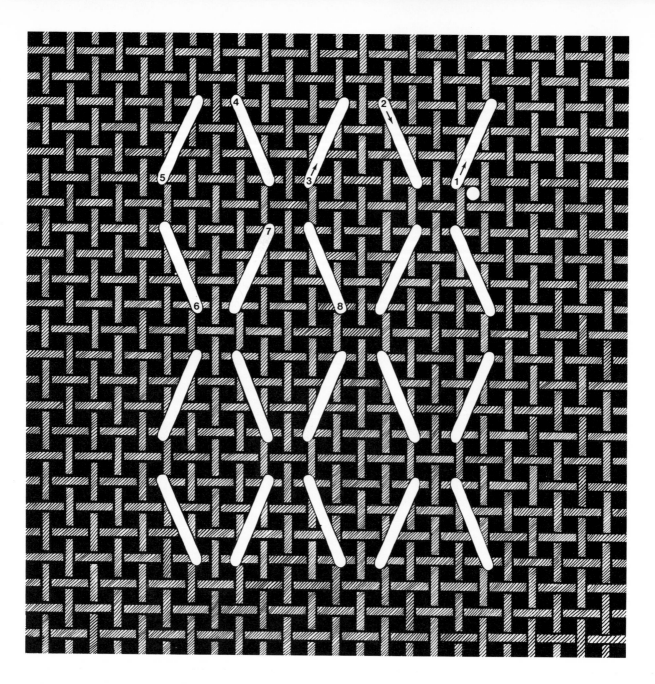

STITCH: WINDOW FILLING *(Pulled Yarn)*

DIAGRAM 312

STITCH: WAVE FILLING *(Pulled Yarn)*

DIAGRAM 313

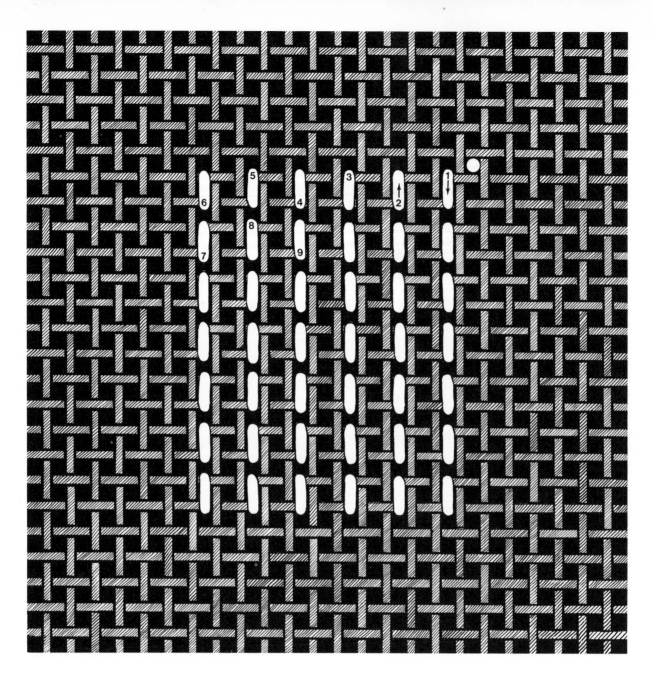

STITCH: Diagonal Darn Over Two *(Pulled Yarn)*
May be rescaled.

DIAGRAM 314

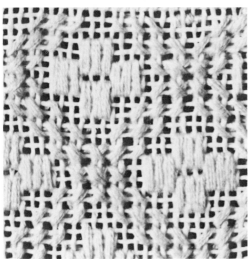

STITCH: STRAIGHT BLOCKS plus DIAGONAL CHAIN
(*Pulled Yarn*)

Note how the Chain Stitches (the slanted stitches) cross over one another. Turn canvas for A, B, C sequence after finishing the first row.

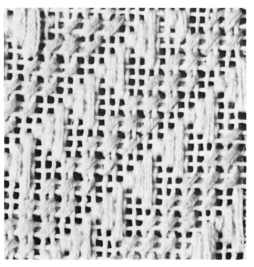

STITCH: DIAGONAL CHAIN and STRAIGHT *(Pulled Yarn)*
Pulled Yarn Chain pattern is not related to conventional canvas Chain Stitch. Diagonal Chain is a form of Reverse Faggot Stitch. It may be used to cover a ground completely.

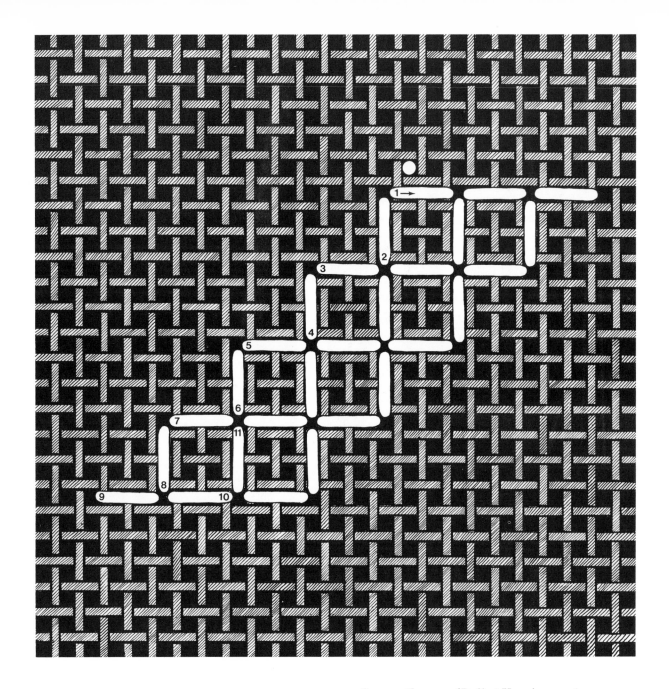

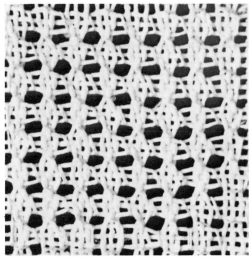

STITCH: Single Faggot (Pulled Yarn) over three
Turn canvas upside down for second row. May be
rescaled.

DIAGRAM 317

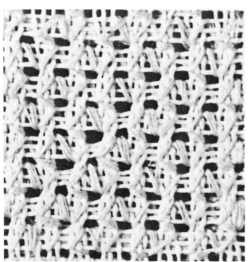

STITCH: DIAGONAL CHEVRON *(Pulled Yarn)*
Single Faggot Stitch, in diagonal rows, are worked
first. The oblique lines (Chevron) are worked last, as
the diagram shows.

434   DIAGRAM 318

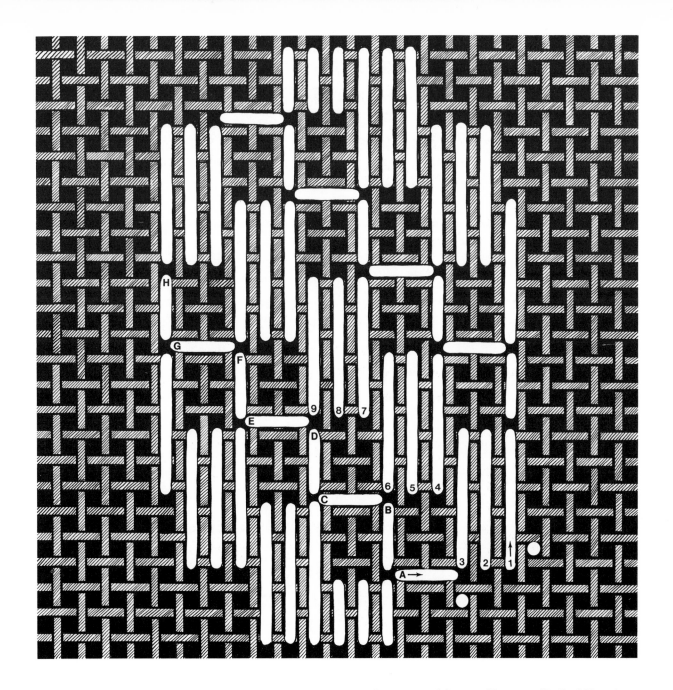

STITCH: * BLOCKS and SINGLE FAGGOT *(Pulled Yarn)*

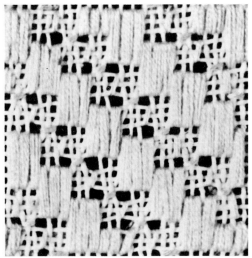

DIAGRAM 319

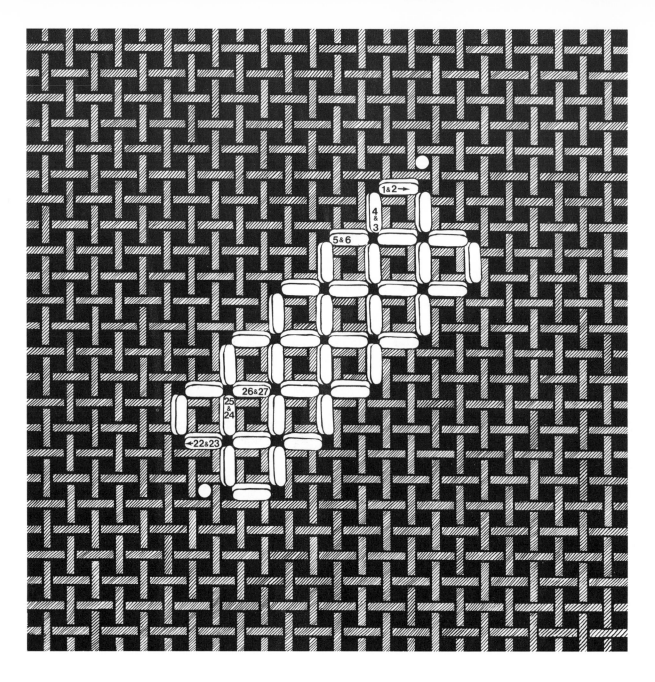

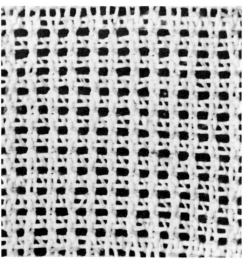

STITCH: DOUBLE FAGGOT, GROUND *(Pulled Yarn)*
May be rescaled.

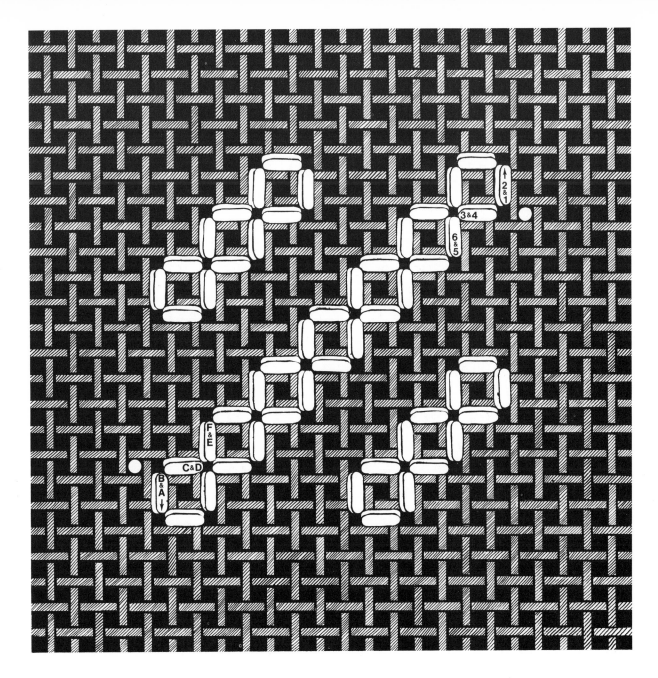

STITCH: DOUBLE FAGGOT (*Pulled Yarn*) in spaced
diagonal rows
Turn canvas upside down for A, B, C row.

DIAGRAM 321

STITCH: CROSS-CHEVRON *(Pulled Yarn)*
A composite of two rows of Reverse Faggot Stitch
and two rows of diagonal Cross Stitches.
The diagonal lines show how Reverse Faggot Stitch
(A, B, C, etc.) is constructed.

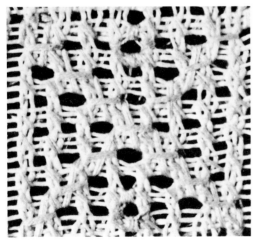

STITCH: CROSS FILLING OVER DIAGONAL GROUND
(Pulled Yarn)
First fill ground with Diagonal Stitches (A, B, C, etc.)
and then execute Crosses as shown (1, 2, etc.).

DIAGRAM 323

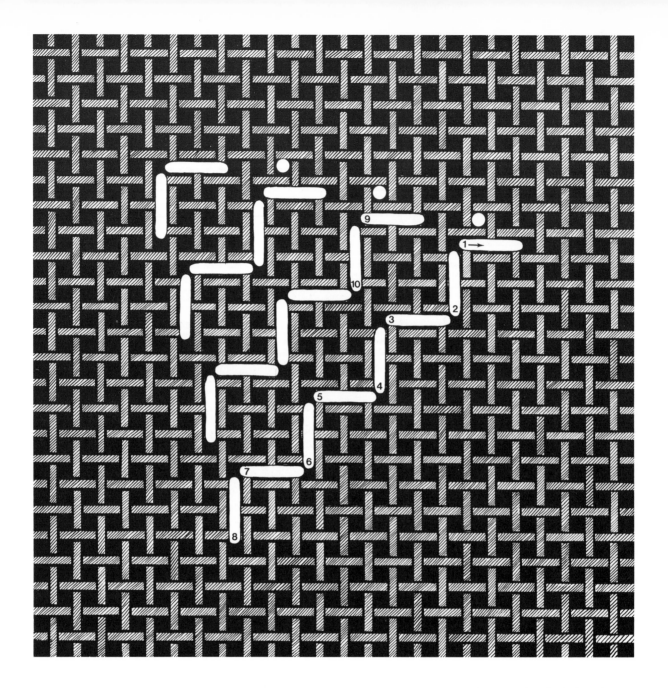

STITCH: DIAGONAL DRAWN FILLING *(Pulled Yarn)*
over three
Worked in Single Faggot Stitch. Each row is begun
one thread lower.

                                    DIAGRAM 324

STITCH: GREEK CROSS *(Pulled Yarn)*
The stitch is formed in a structure similar to Button-holeing. It gives an unusually interesting pattern when pulled tautly.

DIAGRAM 325

STITCH: GREEK CROSS *(Pulled Yarn)*

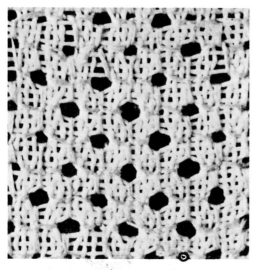

DIAGRAM 326

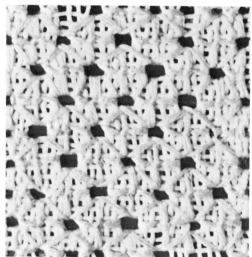

STITCH: * GREEK CROSS over three with CHEVRON
(Pulled Yarn)
Work Greek Cross Stitch first. Form the Chevron
Stitch horizontally, as shown in diagram (1, 2, 3, 4).

443

DIAGRAM 327

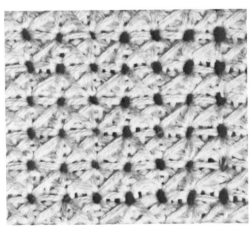

STITCH: ITALIAN CROSS *(Pulled Yarn)*

May be used for canvas or Pulled Yarn work. Slacken the tension slightly for ordinary canvas work. There are two methods:

A. The final cross line is formed on the return journey.
B. The Cross is formed as a complete unit with the frame.

DIAGRAM 328

STITCH: Ridge Filling *(Pulled Yarn)*

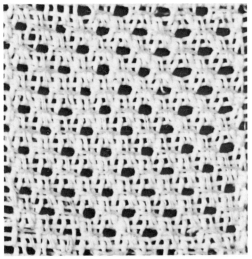

DIAGRAM 329

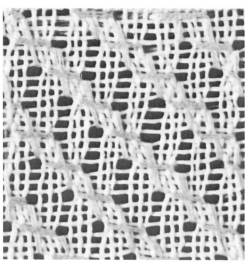

STITCH: DIAGONAL RAISED BAR *(Pulled Yarn)*
The diagram shows the Cross bars used as a ground filling; the sampler square shows the bars worked as single diagonal rows spaced 3 rows apart from one another.

DIAGRAM 330

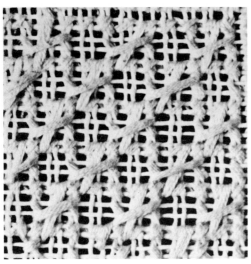

STITCH: SQUARES and CROSS *(Pulled Yarn)*
Follow sequence carefully—1, 2, 3, etc. (vertical), are
formed first; A, B, C, etc. (horizontal), are formed
second; a, b, c, etc. (large Crosses), are formed last.

DIAGRAM 331

STITCH: CHEQUER FILLING *(Pulled Yarn)* over three
Cover your ground with Crosses in one direction only.
Then work Crosses in the opposite direction. You may
rescale.

DIAGRAM 332

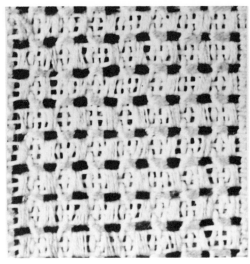

STITCH: PUNCH *(Pulled Yarn)* over three
Cover ground with vertical stitches (1, 2, 3) first.
Turn canvas halfway round and cover the ground
with the next sequence of stitches (A, B, C).

DIAGRAM 333

STITCH: COBBLER *(Pulled Yarn)*

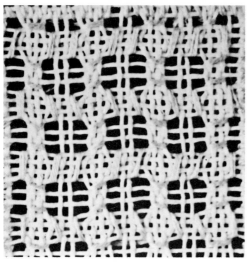

DIAGRAM 334

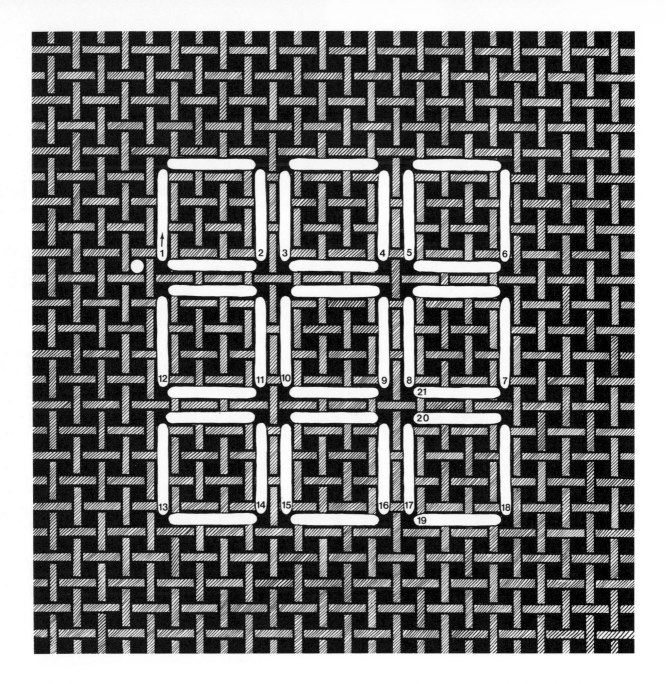

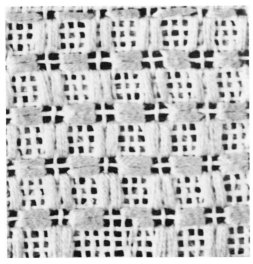

STITCH: FRAMED CROSS FILLING *(Pulled Yarn)*
Turn canvas to the side after finishing Number 18.

STITCH: Honeycomb Filling *(Pulled Yarn)*
Horizontal stitches are single. Vertical stitches, except for beginning and ending rows, are double. Thread yarn back carefully on the underside, to the left, after 11, thread to the right, then emerge at A.

DIAGRAM 336

STITCH: Rosette Filling *(Pulled Yarn)*

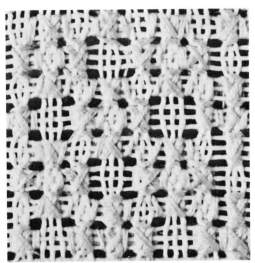

DIAGRAM 337

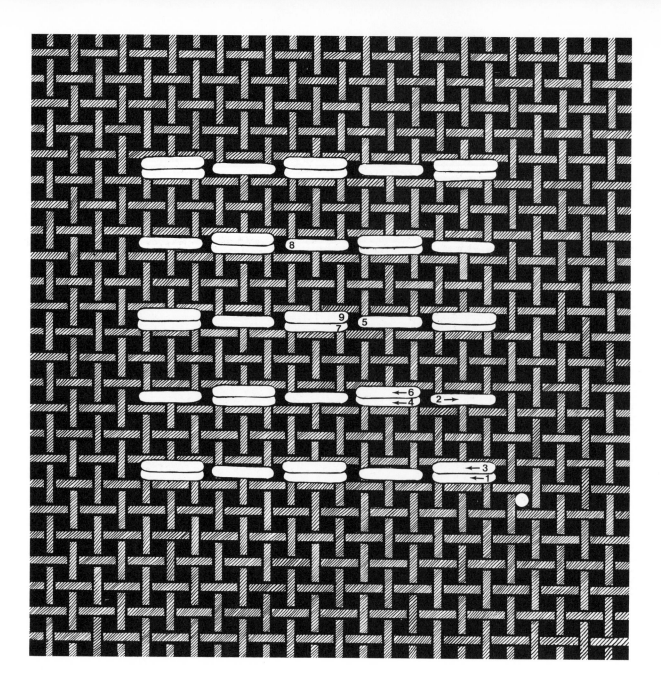

STITCH: Indian Drawn Ground (*Pulled Yarn*)

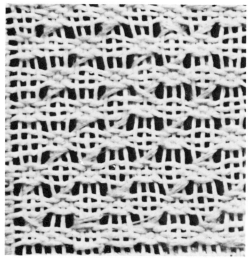

DIAGRAM 338

STITCH: Coil Filling *(Pulled Yarn)*

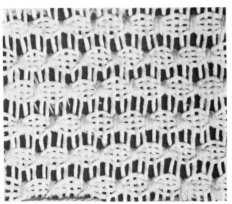

DIAGRAM 339

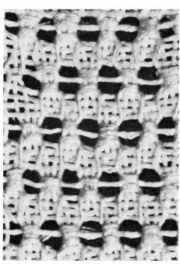

STITCH: * LONESOME BAR *(Pulled Yarn)*
It is not too difficult to invent Pulled Stitches. This stitch is one example I have worked. Before allowing creativity full rein, however, it is essential to master the basic concepts of Pulled Yarn structure. This ground resembles hexagonal caning, interspersed with a single thread.

DIAGRAM 340

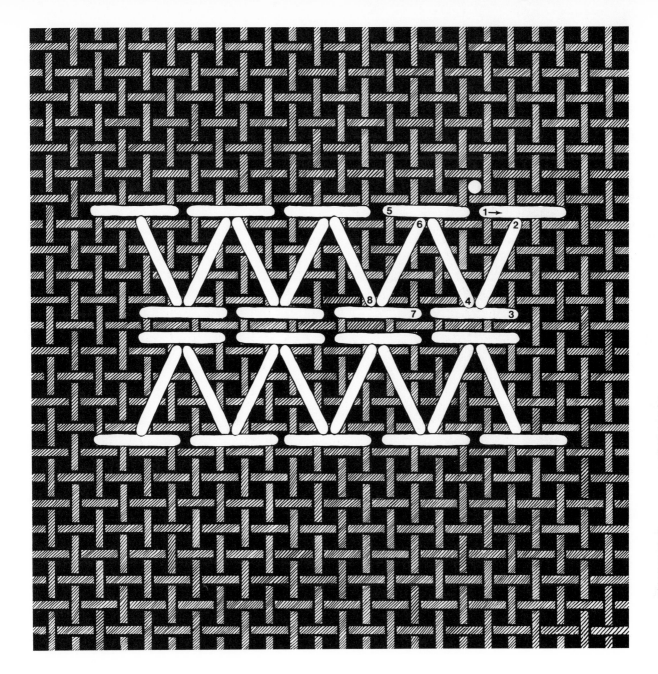

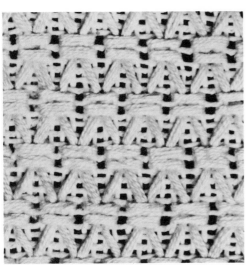

STITCH:* MEDIEVAL SMOCK *(Pulled Yarn)*
Adapted from medieval German whitework, Altenberg altar cloth, Metropolitan Museum of Art, New York (*see* page 10). I haven't seen the original, which is in storage, therefore, the technique may not follow that of the medieval worker. I experimented with a number of methods and feel that the one worked in the sampler square is the most logical. The effect is that of smocking.

DIAGRAM 341

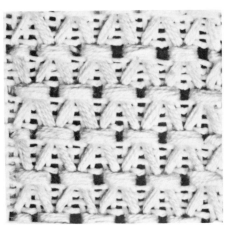

STITCH:* MEDIEVAL SMOCK VARIATION *(Pulled Yarn)*
This construction shows a single center bar. It is actually doubled, the same hole being entered twice for the center bar.

DIAGRAM 342

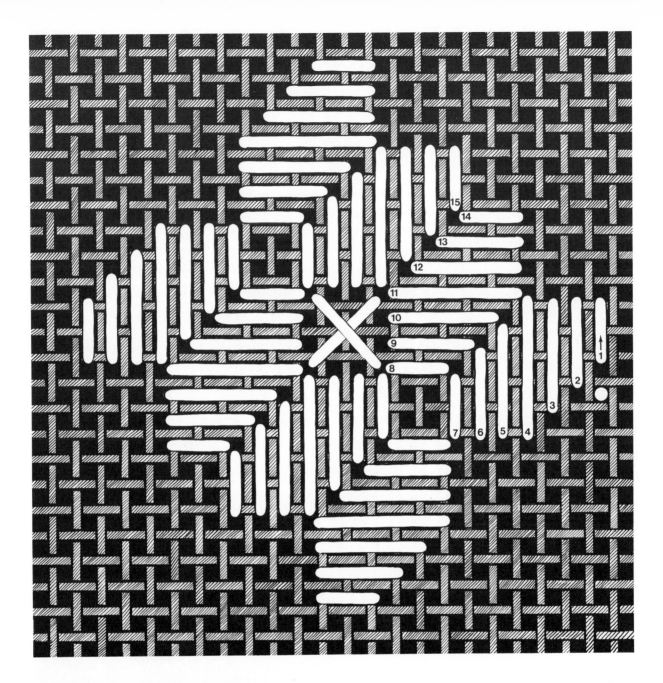

STITCH: FRENCH DAMASK plus CROSS *(Pulled Yarn)*

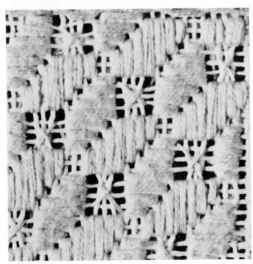

DIAGRAM 343

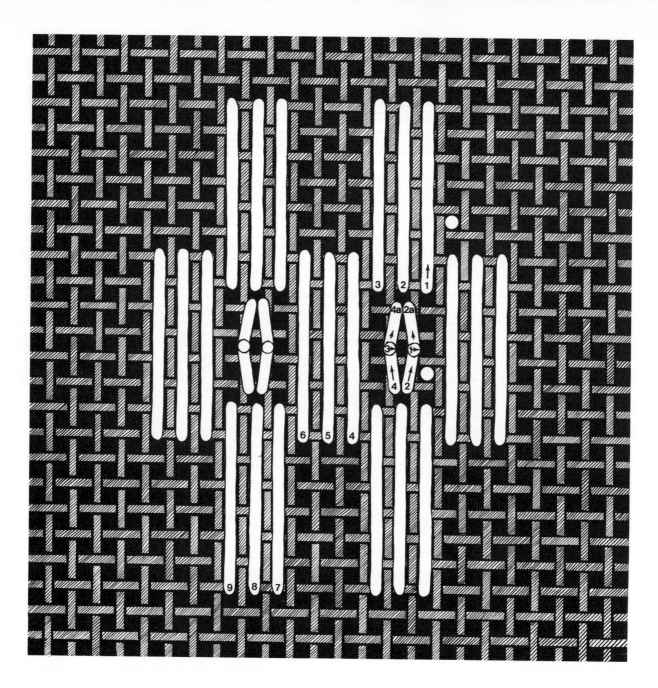

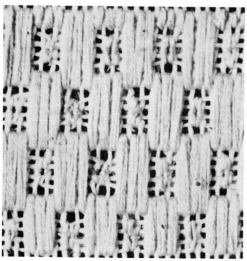

STITCH: FRENCH DAMASK *(Pulled Yarn)* and FRENCH *(Loop, Tied)*

For French Stitch construction, see Diagrams 203 and 199. Relax yarn tension for Flat Stitch bars; the pull should not be as strong as in other stitches.

DIAGRAM 344

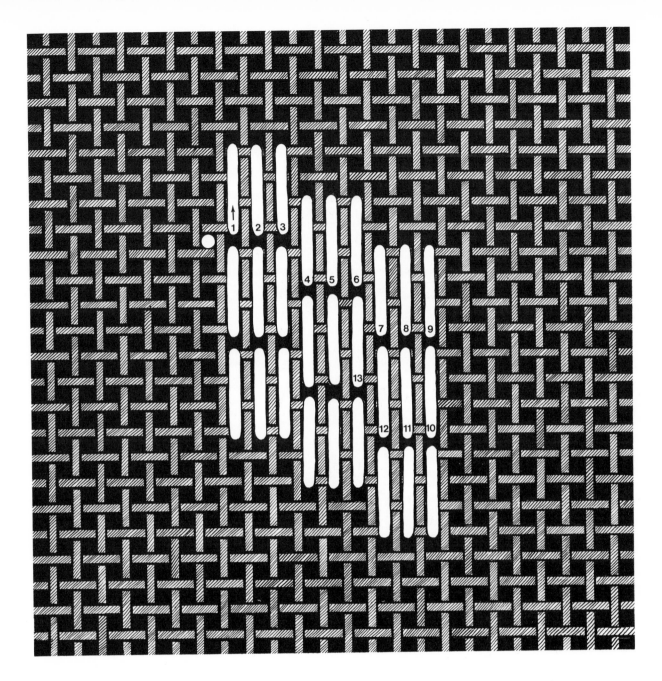

STITCH: ALGERIAN FILLING *(Pulled Yarn)*
May be rescaled. Relaxed or taut tension maybe used
for different effects.

DIAGRAM 345

STITCH: MOSAIC FILLING *(Pulled Yarn)*

DIAGRAM 346

STITCH: MALTESE FILLING *(Pulled Yarn)*
The center motif is Mosaic Filling. The frame is usually worked first and the center last, but you may reverse the order.

DIAGRAM 347

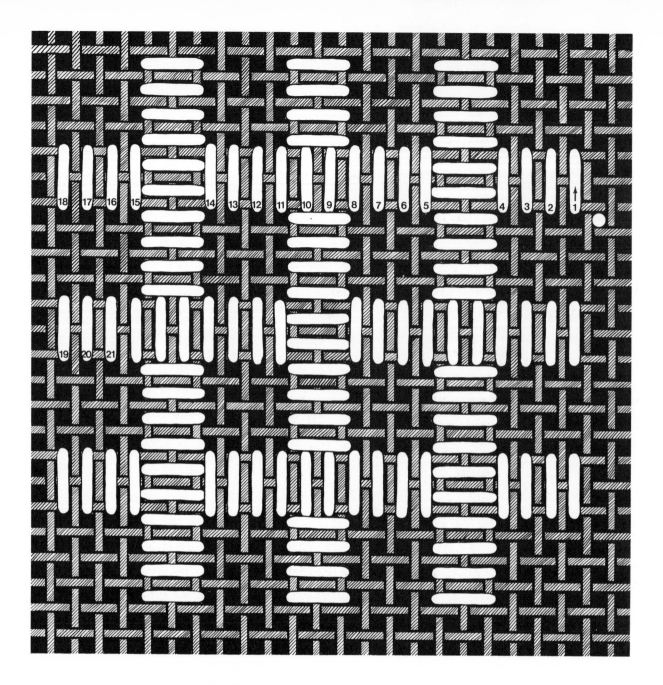

STITCH: OPEN BASKET FILLING *(Pulled Yarn)*
Work all horizontal rows first, then work vertical rows.

DIAGRAM 348

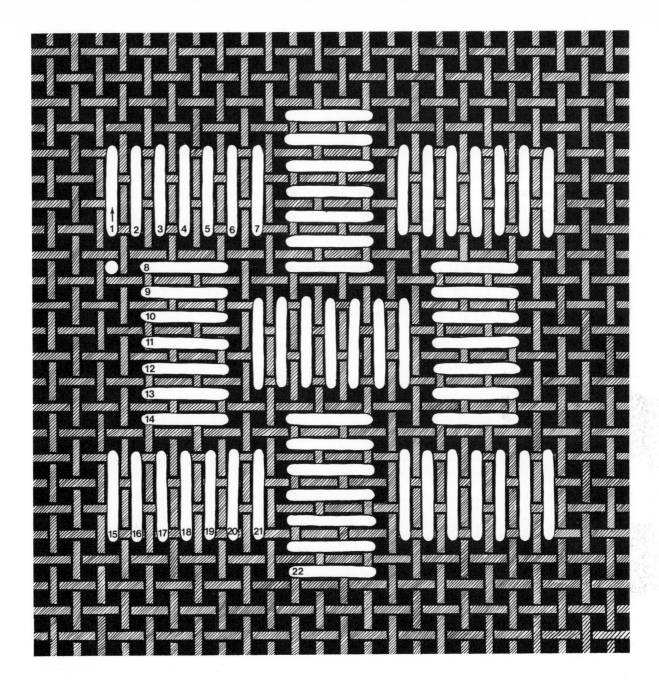

STITCH: * RIBBON INTERLACE GROUND *(Pulled Yarn)*

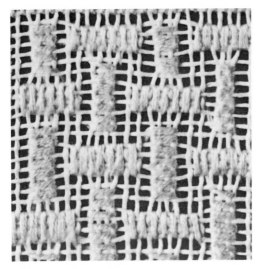

DIAGRAM 349

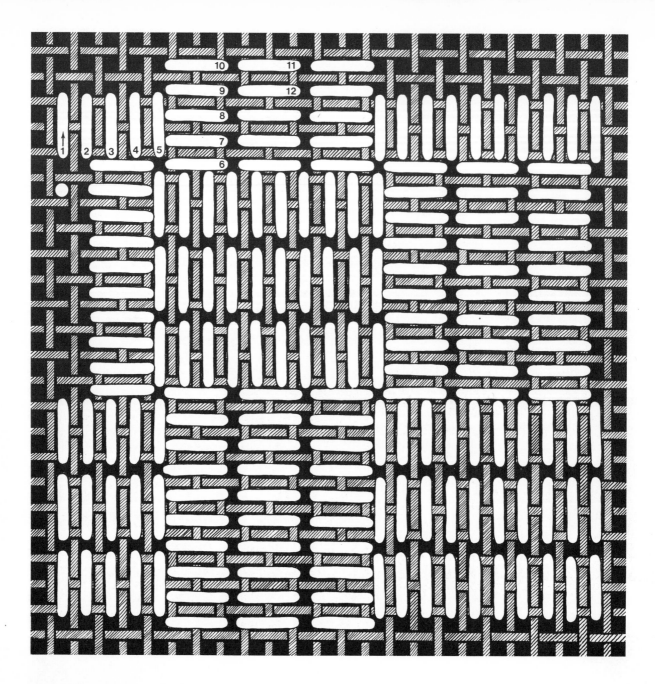

STITCH: CHESSBOARD FILLING *(Pulled Yarn)*

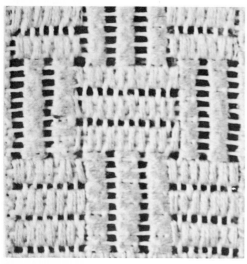

DIAGRAM 350

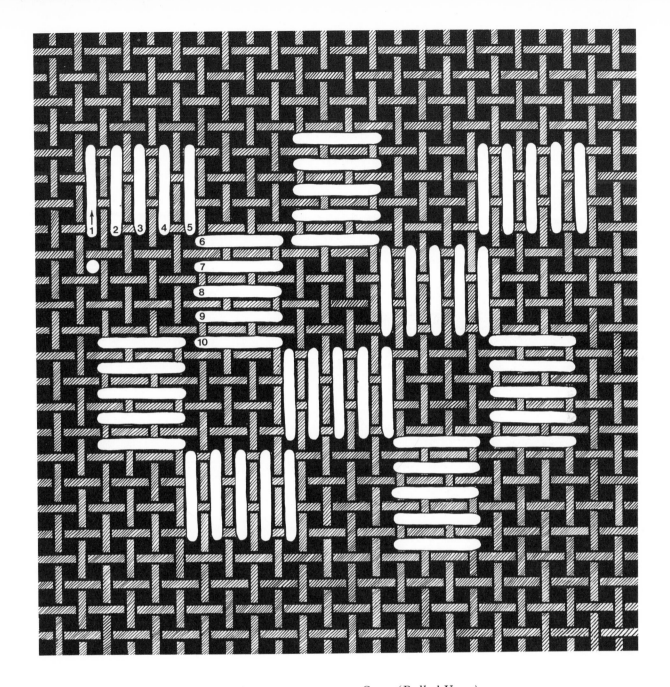

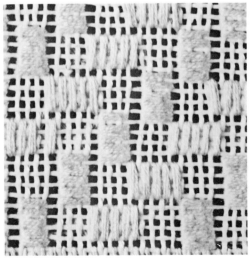

STITCH: STEP *(Pulled Yarn)*
Tension may be increased for a different effect.

467

DIAGRAM 351

UNDIAGRAMED PATTERNS AND
STITCH VARIATIONS

STITCH: FLAT, BACK *(Flat)*

DESIGN:[†] 1. A mosaic pavement pattern in the Casa Cinghiale, Pompeii, 1st century; 2. African ceremonial garment, probably late 18th century.

STITCH: FLAT *(Flat)*

DESIGN:[†] This hexagonal box is from a medieval mosaic pattern in the San Marco Cathedral, Venice. The small white stitch on the "lid" is worked last. The slanted stitches on either side of the square must be worked in a shade darker than the square, but lighter than the Lid. This is not clear in the photograph.

STITCH: FLAT *(Flat)*

DESIGN: * A diaper pattern known as Storm at Sea in American patchwork quilting. It appears very frequently in early mosaic pavement work. The Cologne Museum has a portion of Roman pavement that employs it, and Holbein has featured it in at least two paintings. In both, however, the squares and diamonds are intercepted with lines (border). It is unusually interesting and deserves a larger area than here given. The juxtaposition of the different angles of squares and long diamonds produces interesting geometric rhythms and strange curves.

STITCH: FLAT *(Flat)*

DESIGN: † St. Denis Cathedral, France, 12th century, window pattern. The triangle placement is similar to that in many American pieced patchwork quilts—for example, Birds in Air.
The large diamond formed by the light and dark triangles may be neighbored by monotone diamonds in contrasting color and stitch—such as Brick.

STITCH: FLAT *(Flat)*

DESIGN: † The St. Denis pattern on a smaller scale. Triangles may be made smaller or larger in most mosaic designs.

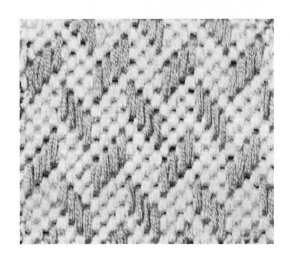

STITCH: Flat *(Flat)*
Color variation in two tones. *See* Diagram 48

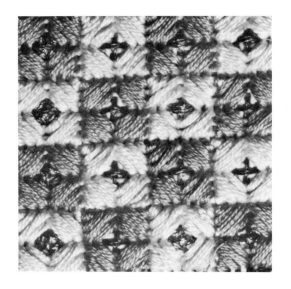

STITCH: Flat *(Flat)*. FILLER: Small Upright Cross *(Cross)*

DESIGN:[†] 1. Simple counterchange taken from a Roger Van der Weyden painting, medieval pavement design, 15th century. 2. 19th-century German sampler, Metropolitan Museum of Art, New York.

STITCH: Flat, Brick Background *(Flat)*

DESIGN: From a 13th-century embroidery border, Rupertsberg altar frontal, Rhineland, now in Musées Royaux d'Art et d'Histoire, Brussels. It is a typical Islamic pattern and another example of the transfer of design from East to West.

470

STITCH: FLAT *(Flat)*. FILLER: COUCHED CROSS *(Cross)*
BACK *(Flat)*

DESIGN:[†] A medieval pattern. 1. Swinburne Pyx, 1310,
rare medieval silver, background motif, Victoria and
Albert Museum catalogue; 2. Wilton Diptych, 1380,
background motif, National Gallery, London; 3. Illuminated manuscript, Bedford Trend, early 15th century, Biblioteca Reale, Turin.

STITCH: FLAT *(Flat)*

DESIGN:[†] From a Russian ecclesiastical costume 16th
century, *see* Diagram 21. This pattern is from the same
painting.

STITCH: FLAT *(Flat)*

DESIGN: Mosaic pavement pattern to be seen in embroidered mass vestments, The Golden Fleece, mid-
15th century, Brussels.

STITCH: FLAT *(Flat)*
Rescaled example of Diagram 30.

DESIGN:[†] St. Denis Cathedral pattern rescaled. Colors arranged as in patchwork quilt, Star of Bethlehem. *See* Chapter 5 for quilt pattern in photographic history.

STITCH: FLAT *(Flat)*. FILLER: CROSS *(Cross)*

DESIGN:[†] Taken from Venetian Lace "Esemplario" pattern books, 16th century. Requires more repeats for pattern to emerge. May be rescaled.

STITCH: FLAT *(Flat)*. FILLER: CROSS *(Cross)*

DESIGN:[†] From an Islamic brick pattern of the 12th century. Here it is shaded to show its resemblance to American Log Cabin patchwork-quilt patterns. American Log Cabin quilt designs like Straight Furrow, Barn Raising, Dark and Light, Courthouse Steps, are all to be found in medieval mosaic pavements. The Log Cabin is one of the most interesting of all patchwork designs. The patterns are constructed in large squares (formed by ribbonlike pieces in progressively increasing sizes). These squares are half light and half dark (as in the stitched example). The placement of these squares, and the many possible relationships of the dark and light areas, determine the field pattern. The composition of light and dark is like that of medieval pavement mosaics.

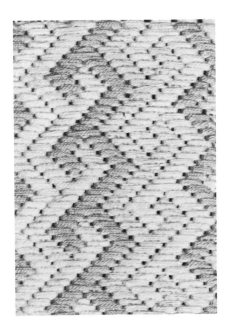

STITCH: FLAT *(Flat)*

DESIGN:[†] From a Russian-language study of Turcoman carpets. It may be used as a border or field pattern. Although few Turcoman carpets and saddlebags, etc., can be dated earlier than the 19th century, it can be assumed that the patterns have a much older history. These Turcoman nomads remained remote from the West much longer than other tribes noted for woven articles. Their designs, therefore, were not debased by accommodation to Western demands, nor did they have access to the inferior chemical dyes that were and are so destructive to the works of more accessible carpet-producing peoples. Their articles are unusually dignified and preserve geometric pattern and tones in pure, restrained, indigenous form.

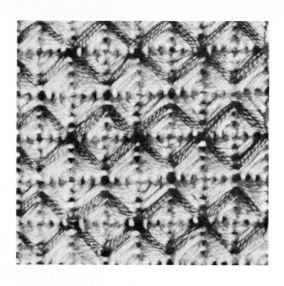

STITCH: FLAT *(Flat)*

DESIGN:† Simple Islamic tile pattern. Use this way or turn on side.

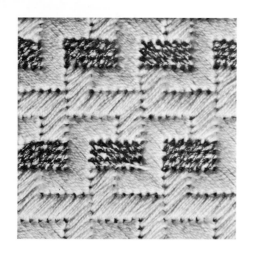

STITCH: FLAT *(Flat)*. FILLER: CHAIN *(Chain)* worked diagonally.

DESIGN:† From a 14th-century Persian miniature painting, brick wall detail. The white forms are upright or sideway Z's.

STITCH: SQUARE MOSAIC *(Flat)*

DESIGN:† From Timirud medieval tile column, Khargid. This Islamic ground (rescaled) is used as the pavement mosaic for the Cavalier playing card, Color Plate 12.

STITCH: FLAT *(Flat)* CROSSED CORNERS *(Cross)*.
SMALL UPRIGHT CROSS CENTERS (over CROSSED
CORNERS), BACK *(Flat)*

DESIGN:[†] From Persian painting, Khamsa of Nizami,
1524, interlaced brick wall pattern, Metropolitan
Museum of Art. One of the many fascinating wall
designs to appear in Persian manuscript painting.

STITCH: BYZANTINE VARIATION *(Flat)*

DESIGN:[*] Floating Tops. *See* Diagram 246.

STITCH: STRAIGHT GOBELIN *(Flat)*

DESIGN:[*] SMALL STEPPED CROSS. *See* Diagram 261.

STITCH: Square Mosaic *(Flat)*

DESIGN: * Interlaced Blocks. *See* Diagram 69.

STITCH: Flat Cushioned *(Couched, Laid and Tied)*

DESIGN: Typical 19th-century geometric sampler design. This one is shaded in clusters of 4. *See* Diagram 220 which is shaded in diagonal rows.

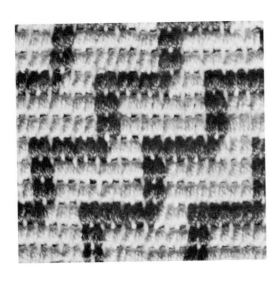

STITCH: Gobelin *(Flat)*

DESIGN: † From an East African basket, Museum für Völkerkunde, Berlin. *See* Diagram 261.

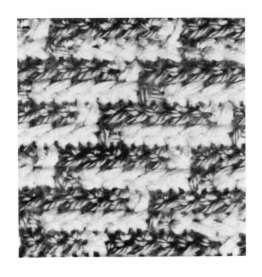

STITCH: LONG-ARMED CROSS *(Cross)*
Two threads vertical, four horizontal. May be rescaled to three, six, etc.

DESIGN:[†] The pattern was adapted from a Malayan basket. *See* Diagram 55.

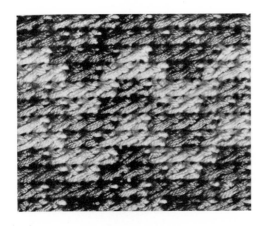

STITCH: * LONG-ARMED CROSS *(Cross)*
Stitched over two vertical and four horizontal threads. One of the many patterns possible in this stitch.

STITCH: DIAMOND RAY *(Flat)*. FILLER: DIAGONAL CHAIN *(Loop, Tied)*

DESIGN: * Quilting. The use of thicker yarn for the Ray Stitch and thinner for the Chain will give a pronounced quilting effect. This is a useful and effective ground and many tonal variations are possible. *See* Playing Card hanging, Cavalier of Hearts' skirt, Color Plate 12. *See also* Diagram 268.

STITCH: FLAT *(Flat)*

DESIGN:[†] Diagonal borders from an early 20th-century Japanese sampler, Cooper-Hewitt Museum, New York.

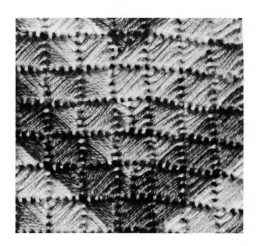

STITCH: FLAT *(Flat)*

DESIGN: There are many examples of this "broken-square" patterning (achieved by the arrangement of tonal elements) in Mexican samplers. They use a technique related to surface darning, but this square is worked in the conventional Flat Stitch way.

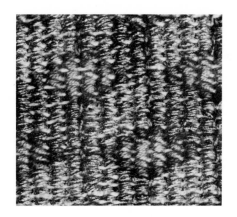

STITCH: STRAIGHT GOBELIN *(Flat)*

DESIGN:[†] Hexagonal Boxes from an 1864 Austrian sampler, Cooper-Hewitt Museum, New York. Gold and silver were used alternately for the sides of the Boxes, but this does not show adequately in the photograph. Four shades required, the lightest for the center and the darkest to outline the center.

478

STITCH: FLAT *(Flat)*

DESIGN: An especially popular Victorian design, can be seen in many 19th-century samplers of Germany, England and Austria.

STITCH: FLAT *(Flat)*

DESIGN:[†] This pattern is common to almost all Victorian samplers that explore small-scale geometric themes.
Start in center and form increasingly larger squares. The overstitching, covering the diagonal perforation marks, should be worked at the very end in Back Stitch, V-fashion.

STITCH: FLAT *(Flat)*

DESIGN:[†] From a mid-19th-century English sampler, Victoria and Albert Museum, London.

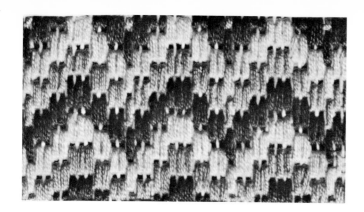

STITCH: FLAT *(Flat)*

DESIGN: Typical 19th-century sampler patterning.

STITCH: FLAT BLOCKS *(Flat)* with DIAGONAL WHIPPING

DESIGN: Typical 19th-century geometric sampler pattern. This one, an Austrian example, 1859, is from the Lerman-Foy Collection, New York.

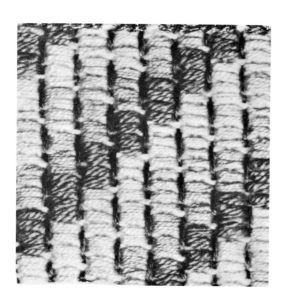

STITCH: FLAT, BACK *(Flat)*

DESIGN:[†] From a 19th-century German sampler, Metropolitan Museum of Art, New York, typical of the period in tone and structure.

STITCH: FLAT *(Flat)*

Work the dark Triangles first. Three tones were used.

DESIGN: Another Triangle pattern from a 19th-century sampler, this one an Austrian example, Lerman-Foy Collection, New York. Similar to patchwork quilt Wild Goose Chase pattern.

STITCH: FLAT *(Flat)*

DESIGN: Austrian sampler, 1859, Lerman-Foy Collection, New York. Shaded tone gradation or color contrast may be used in this pattern.

STITCH: CROSS *(Cross)*. FILLER: GOBELIN *(Flat)*

DESIGN: Victorian Meander pattern, Cooper-Hewitt Museum, New York, Austrian sampler, 1864. Copied from a photograph. It might be preferable to use a Cross filler (conventional, Oblong, or Long-Armed) rather than the Flat Stitch used in the sampler. Use contrasting colors or tones.

STITCH: FLAT *(Flat)*

DESIGN:[†] Typical and attractive Victorian Interlace, English sampler, Philadelphia Museum of Art.

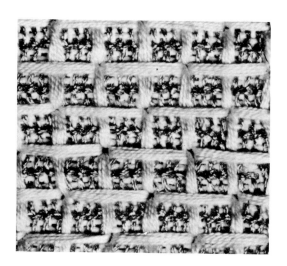

STITCH: UPRIGHT CROSS *(Cross)*. FILLER: BUTTONHOLE *(Loop, Tied)*
Make filler groups first.
The filler is in Buttonhole Stitch, but any small stitch may be used. Leave one vertical and horizontal row unstitched for Cross which is filled in as last step. *See* Diagram 115.

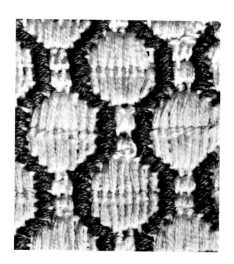

STITCH: GOBELIN *(Flat)*, TO-AND-FRO BUTTONHOLE *(Loop, Tied)*

The dark stitches are in Gobelin (*see* Diagram 258), and the light are worked in To-and-Fro Buttonhole in the Rococo method (*see* Diagram 199). The centers of each large pale group must have a double stitch, entering the same hole above and below and using three holes for the two ties.
DESIGN: A particularly striking mosaic floor design from 1st-century Pompeii.

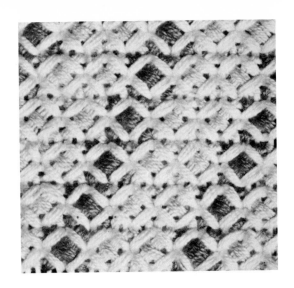

STITCH: CROSSED CORNERS *(Cross)*
This may be used for many geometric patterns by varying the shading. Its texture is excellent when worked in monotone. The tie lines may be thought of as lead stripping in stained glass, and color arrangement provides many geometric pattern possibilities. *See* Diagram 27.

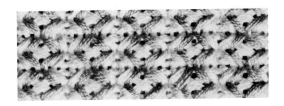

STITCH: * CROSSED CORNERS, VARIATION 1 *(Cross)*
Color change in Tie Stitches. *See* Diagram 27.

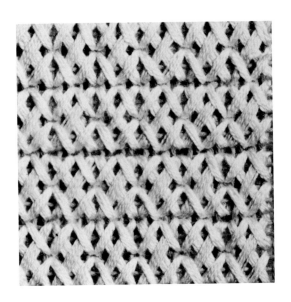

STITCH: * CROSSED CORNERS, VARIATION 2 *(Cross)* over six horizontal and four vertical canvas threads
The foundation Cross may be worked in a color that contrasts with the Tie-Down Stitches. Thicker yarn required for coverage. *See* Diagram 27.

STITCH: INTERLACED CROSS *(Cross)*
Variation of Diagram 132, over four canvas threads
instead of six.

STITCH: * RIBBON CROSS, ENCROACHED *(Cross)*
The same as Diagram 141 with color change. In this
square, metallic yarn is used to emphasize the ribbon
effect.

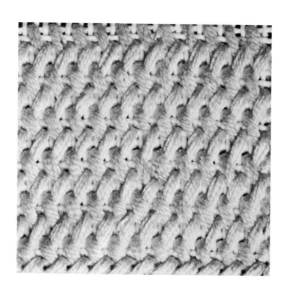

STITCH: PLAITED GOBELIN *(Plaited-Interlaced)*
One scale only. Thicker yarn essential for coverage.
See Diagram 153.

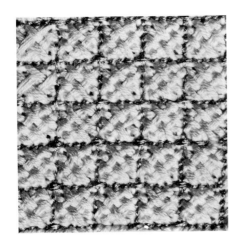

STITCH: * STRAP *(Plaited-Interlaced)*. FILLER: SMALL UPRIGHT CROSS *(Cross)*
The Back Stitch around the strap is worked in gold metallic yarn; the ground is very effective this way. *See* Diagram 172.

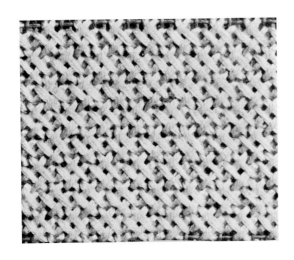

STITCH: * SMALL DIAGONAL STRAP GROUND *(Plaited-Interlaced)*
May be worked horizontally or diagonally. *See* Diagram 172

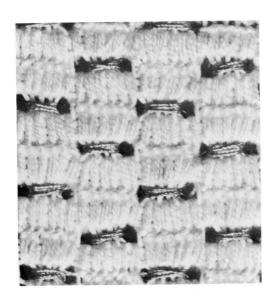

STITCH: * TO AND FRO BUTTONHOLE *(Loop, Tied)*, BACK *(Flat)*
The top and bottom of the stitches do not enter the same hole as they do in Rococo Stitch. The method of construction is the same *(see* Diagram 199).

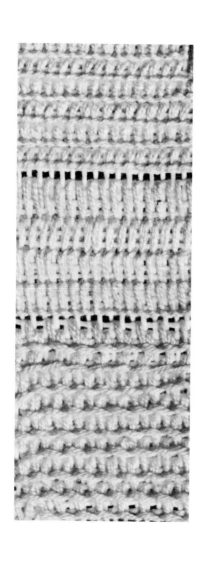

STITCH: BUTTONHOLE *(Loop, Tied)*
See Diagram 190

A.   Leaving link *free.*

B.   Worked *over* link.

C.* Worked from the *bottom* up. This results in a meshlike surface. *See* Playing Card hanging, the Knave of Clubs, sleeve detail, Color Plate 12.

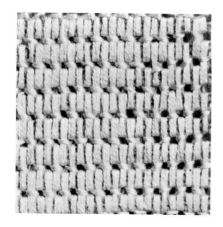

STITCH: FRENCH DOUBLE TIE *(Loop, Tied)* over four
See Diagram 204.

STITCH: Cable Chain over Laid Ground *(Chain)*
Cable Chain is worked in vertical rows, in this case with the Chains of all the rows touching and parallel, and the Cables parallel to one another. The ground is laid horizontally, one line over every four rows. *See* Diagram 206.

STITCH: Flat *(Flat)*

DESIGN:[†] Medieval mosaic pattern, the Baptistery, Florence. It is clearly related to the Jockey Cap motifs but the square blocks are cut only on the outer corners.

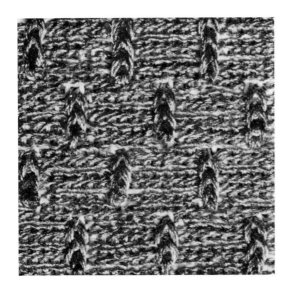

STITCH:* Chain Ground *(Chain)*
The ground is arranged in a bricking pattern. The horizontal rows are made with thinner yarn. The finished surface resembles a familiar knitting surface. This pattern was stitched in silver metallic yarn. *See* Diagram 205, top.

STITCH: WOVEN *(Couched and Laid, Woven)* and FLAT *(Flat)*

DESIGN:[†] From an English sampler, 1841, Philadelphia Museum of Art. Weaving techniques may be combined with other stitches. In this square, the yarn in the woven columns is laid horizontally and the interweaving is worked vertically. These columns are bordered by Flat Stitches. *See* Diagram 217.

STITCH:* SMALL WHEELS *(Couched and Laid, Woven)* around LARGE CROSSES *(Cross)*
The sub-ground is formed by Flat-Stitched Triangles. Crosses (Large X) are worked over the perforations formed by the triangles. The Wheels are woven at the meeting points of the Crosses. *See* Diagram 225.

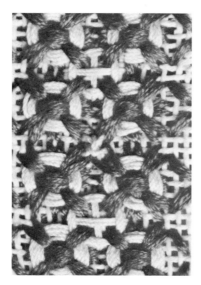

STITCH:* LACE WHEELS, REVERSED *(Couched and Laid, Woven)*. FILLER: CROSS *(Cross)*
Stitched in contrasting shades. The Cross foundation was worked in a contrasting color to that of the woven Circle. *See* Diagram 229.

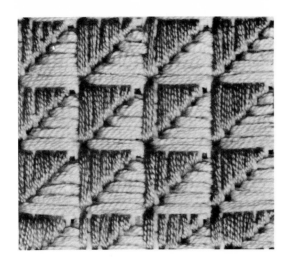

STITCH: FLAT *(Flat)*

DESIGN: Color variation; *see* Diagram 7.

STITCH: SCOTTISH *(Flat)*
A composite stitch traditionally called Scotch or Scottish. *See* Diagram 243.

STITCH: FLAT *(Flat)*
Simple color variation. *See* Diagram 244

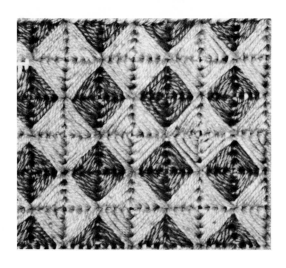

STITCH: FLAT *(Flat)*
Simple color variation.

DESIGN: Frequent motif for medieval mosaic pavements or walls. *See* Diagram 244.

STITCH: SMALL-SCALE LEAF *(Flat)*
See Diagram 264.

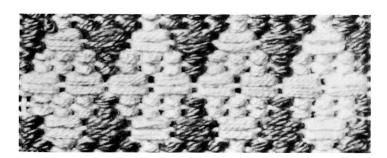

STITCH: DOUBLE HUNGARIAN *(Flat)*
Hungarian Stitch and Double Hungarian Stitch are especially useful for geometric patterning. This is a simple example of toned Double Hungarian Stitch, worked horizontally instead of vertically.
See Diagram 274.

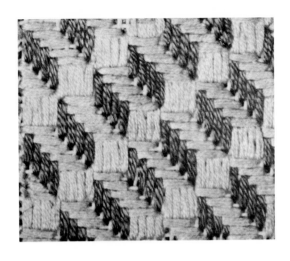

STITCH: * DAMASK with SQUARES *(Flat)*
See Diagram 281.

STITCH: * BASKETRY *(Flat)*
As in many other basketry patterns, it is best to work the center stitches first; in this case three vertical and three horizontal, leaving the outline stitches until last. *See* Diagram 283.

DESIGN:[†] In American patchwork quilting this design is sometimes called Roman Squares or Roman Stripes.

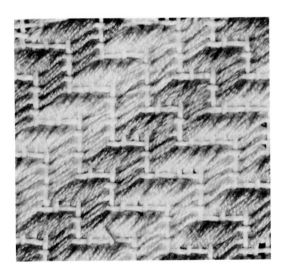

STITCH: * DARNING PATTERNING *(Flat)*
Darning is usually worked in monotone. Example of a two-tone arrangement. *See* Diagram 285.

491

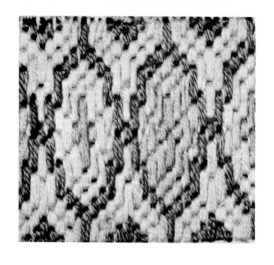

STITCH: HUNGARIAN POINT *(Flat)*

DESIGN: * This illustrates Hungarian Point used for lozenge structure. *See* Diagram 290.

STITCH: DIAMOND EYE *(Pulled Yarn).* FILLER: FLAT *(Flat)*

This illustrates the effect of thicker yarn in Pulled Yarn work. In this case, the perforation is minimal because of heavier yarn; the architectural structure of the Diamond is the same as Diagram 292.

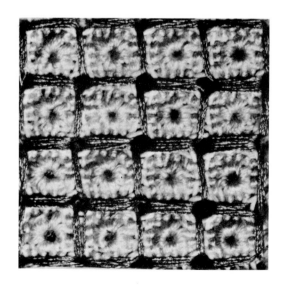

STITCH: EYE and FOUR-SIDED GROUND *(Pulled Yarn)*

This ground was composed to make these Pulled Stitches useful for normal canvas coverage. The center is a Small Circle Eye *(see* Diagram 297). The Four-Sided Stitch is worked in gold metallic yarn. All the Eyes were worked first, then the Back Stitch and finally, the Four-Sided Stitch *(see* Diagram 305) was worked around each unit.

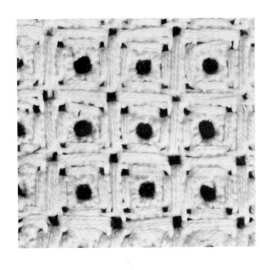

STITCH:[†] Eye Ground *(Pulled Yarn)* and Four-Sided *(Pulled Yarn)*

DESIGN: This is adapted from an Italian 17th-century lace sampler, Cooper-Hewitt Museum, New York. It is a variation of the preceding square. The center is a square Eye (*see* Diagram 304), the frames are Four-Sided Stitch (*see* Diagram 305).

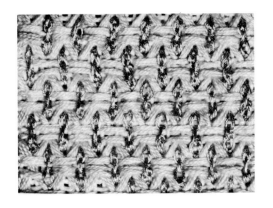

STITCH:[*] Medieval Smock *(Pulled Yarn)*. FILLER: Small Cable Chain *(Chain)*
To avoid showing the canvas a filler may be used. Vertical Cable Chain was used here to cover canvas threads. *See* Diagram 341.

STITCH: French Damask Pattern *(Pulled Yarn)*
The photograph shows how to convert this Pulled Yarn pattern to conventional canvas work by covering the center square with diagonal Flat Stitches and Four-Sided Stitches instead of a Cross. *See* Diagram 343, and Diagram 305 for Four-Sided Stitch.

STITCH: Mosaic Filling *(Pulled Yarn)*. FILLER: Buttonhole *(Loop, Tied)*, X Cross *(Cross)*
This sampler square shows how this Pulled Yarn pattern may be adapted for conventional canvas use, by relaxing tension and filling in unworked areas. *See* Diagram 346.

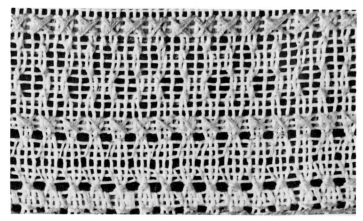

HORIZONTAL

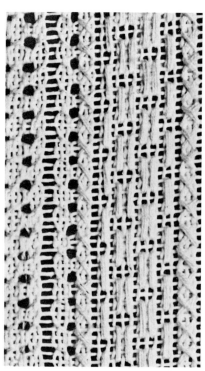

VERTICAL

BORDER: The Pulled Yarn sampler shown in the photograph on page 407 is outlined by conventional Cable Chain Stitch. Then it is worked in Four-Sided Stitch over three, Diagonal Ground Stitch over three, Cross Stitch over three, Small Window Filling Stitch over two and five (for the horizontal borders).
In the vertical border the Small Window Filling Stitch was used in reverse. In other words, the pattern ordinarily found on the underside is on the surface, and vice versa.

See index for "learning" diagrams.

494

SUPPLIES

The shops I list are all known to me personally. There may be many others, equally reliable, but this book is based on my own explorations and I feel the names I offer below should follow the same pattern. My judgment is impartial; I have no professional association with the world of needlepoint and its suppliers.

C. R. MEISSNER CO., INC., 22 EAST 29TH ST., NEW YORK
   An unusually broad range of quality materials. A good source for Paternayan Persian yarn, needles, French canvas in an especially wide selection of widths and gauges, French silk, either in stock or will order from color chart, gold and silver yarn, French Médicis wool, usually a large supply in stock. Will import special orders. Mail orders filled throughout U.S.

BOUTIQUE MARGOT, 29 WEST 54TH ST., NEW YORK
   Small skeins Appleton Crewel. Will order if desired shades are not in stock.

ALICE MAYNARD, 558 MADISON AVENUE, NEW YORK
   Paternayan Persian yarn, DMC embroidery cotton, French canvas, needles. Mail orders filled.

FREDERICK J. FAWCETT INC., 129 SOUTH ST., BOSTON, MASS. 02111
   Linen yarn available in small skeins for needlepoint canvas. Mail orders filled promptly. Literature available with color samples.

HANDWORK TAPESTRIES, 240 LAMBERT LANE, COPIAGUE, LONG ISLAND, NEW YORK
   Distributor of Laine Colbert Tapestry, Colbert 6 Persian yarns, Médicis yarns, French canvas. Will supply information with regard to local sources for these materials.

JOAN TOGGITT, LTD., 1170 BROADWAY, NEW YORK
   Distributor of Appleton Crewel, Appleton Tapestry yarns, canvas. Will supply information with regard to local sources for these materials.

NANTUCKET NEEDLEWORKS, 11 SOUTH WATER ST., NANTUCKET, MASS.
Exceptional quality, four-ply worsted woolen for needlepoint canvas.
The colors are clear, clean and strong. The geometric patterns in the
book, whatever their age, will look beautiful and instantly modern if
worked in this yarn. The strands separate with ease, which makes this
wool particularly useful for sampler work. Mail orders filled.

AMERICAN CREWEL AND CANVAS STUDIO, P.O. BOX 1756, POINT PLEAS-
ANT BEACH, NEW JERSEY
Abundant stock of Appleton Crewel yarn in many shades. Mail and
phone orders are dealt with speedily.

THE NEEDLEWOMAN, 146 REGENT ST., LONDON W1
Appleton crewel in skeins or hanks. American orders are customary
and filled with courtesy.

JUDY'S ORIGINALS, 182 MT. BETHEL ROAD, WARREN, NEW JERSEY
Appleton Crewel, Appleton Tapestry, Colbert 6 Persian yarns, canvas,
needles. Will fill all mail and phone orders. The shop will supply small
skeins of the Appleton yarns or large hanks that can be ordered by
the pound.

EXTENDED CAPTIONS FOR THE
COLOR PLATES

PLATE 1. *(facing page 14)*
The *Master Sampler*, worked for this book. This large piece is the repository of much of my research into historic geometric diaper pattern and textures, and contains adaptations from very varied media.
SIZE: 44" x 28".   CANVAS: 14 mono.   STITCHES: Hundreds.
YARN: Silk, gold metallic, white and ecru crochet cotton, all French.
Designed and worked by S. Lantz.

PLATE 2. *(facing page 15)*
Enlargements of two sections of the *Master Sampler*.

PLATE 3. *(facing page 78)*
Victorian geometric motif "strip" sampler rescued from a Viennese street garbage-disposal can by its fortunate owners.
DATE: 1859.
Collection Lerman-Foy, New York.

Pillow based on antique needleworked upholstery textile. Collection Mrs. Edward Kingsley. It is an example of Single Leviathan Stitch used throughout a heraldic field. The small and large square patterns are all outlined in beige silk.
CANVAS: 14 mono.   STITCHES: Single Leviathan and Back Stitch.
YARN: Appleton tapestry wool and English knitting silk.
Designed and worked by S. Lantz.

PLATE 4. *(facing page 79)*
Pastel stitch-and-pattern sampler.
CANVAS: 14 mono.   STITCHES: Varied (many).
YARN: French silk, French gold and silver metallic yarn.
Designed and worked by S. Lantz.

Patchwork pillow using various motifs including those of my own porcelain,

towels and textiles; historic patterns of particular interest to me; parts of previously worked pillows, etc. A personal, needleworked "collage." The white borders are composed of patchwork squares in 34 different stitches.
CANVAS: 12 mono.   STITCHES: Very varied.
YARN: Paternayan wool, French tapestry wool, French silk.
Designed and worked by S. Lantz.

PLATE 5. *(facing page 110)*
Norman-Moorish mosaic pavement, 12th century, La Capella di San Pietro, Palermo, Sicily. An especially fine example of Islamic geometric design and of the generosity of confinement (variety within limitation).
Courtesy New York Society Library.

PLATE 6. *(facing page 111)*
St. George and the Dragon pillow from a 14th-century Russian icon, Leningrad Museum. An example of Tent Stitch work. Because I prefer knife-edged pillows to boxed, I usually add one or more stitched borders to prevent the central designs from curving beyond visibility.
CANVAS: 14 mono.   STITCH: Tent.   YARN: Paternayan wool.
Designed and worked by S. Lantz.

Sampler study of medieval interlacement patterns with a few mosaic designs from earlier eras and three later carpet borders. The patterns come from Pompeii, Ravenna, Venice, Anatolia-Turkey, England, Morocco, the Caucasus, etc.
CANVAS: 14 mono.   STITCHES: Varied (many).   YARN: English wools, French silk, French gold and silver metallic yarn, Médicis wool.
Designed and worked by S. Lantz.

PLATE 7. *(facing page 174)*
Carpet (in work) composed of Islamic-Turkish designs from the 15th to 17th centuries. The central field pattern is based in part on the carpet on page 55 and both are closely related to the fabric design on page 55.
SIZE: 80″ x 52″ (projected).   CANVAS: 7 Penelope.   STITCH: Tent.
YARN: Paternayan wool dyed to my specifications and Appleton crewel yarn.
Designed and worked by S. Lantz.

PLATE 8. *(facing page 175)*
Sampler hanging. A study of Turkish carpet borders from European paintings of the 14th, 15th and 16th centuries (the carpets themselves were probably older) in Germany, Italy, and Flanders: van Eyck, Memling, the Sienese Masters, Ghirlandaio, Crivelli, Holbein, etc. The great artists painted these Middle Eastern knotted marvels under the feet of Madonnas Enthroned, on the library

498

tables of the aristocracy, hanging bannerlike from the windows of Venice, or adorning her gondolas, with meticulous care; the brushwork forms a unique and valuable history of Islamic carpets and geometric pattern. Most of the interlacement is based on the Arabic alphabet (Kufic) enfoliated into ornamental design. These "interwoven" patterns require intense concentration, and under and over enlacement was used far less frequently after the 16th century. Although I have tried to be faithful to the colors of the period, within the irksome limitations imposed by chemical dyes, I have not necessarily adhered to the original shades in the paintings.

Note: Where designs require dark outlines, I think it well to avoid black because its effect is too harsh. The darkest, least red, brown you can find is preferable.

SIZE: 68½″ x 18″.   CANVAS: 10 mono.   STITCH: Tent.
YARN: English, French, and American wool.
Designed and worked by S. Lantz.

Moroccan motif sampler pillow worked as an exploratory, initial step in preparation for a carpet. The motifs are taken from a book (Folio edition) published by the French Government in 1923 that sought to reestablish the authentic patterns and vegetable dyes of previous centuries. Despite the harsh penalties imposed on carpet manufacturers who ignored the strict guidelines, the effort was largely unsuccessful; the densely patterned, beautifully toned Rabat carpets, so beguiling to Matisse, belong to the past.

CANVAS: 10 mono.   STITCH: Tent.   YARN: Various wools, French silk.
Designed and worked by S. Lantz.

PLATE 9. (*facing page 206*)

Antique Moroccan carpet, adaptation. Motifs in Rabat carpets are mainly Turkish, but the positioning of color beside color without an intervening dark outline (and a slight but noticeable African influence in the handling of geometric patterns) gives them their own distinct and indigenous character. They are usually coarsely knotted, 5 to 7 knots to the inch, which gauge may serve as guide for canvas selection. Only four colors were used, plus brown and white, but the effect suggests a much broader palette.

SIZE: 73″ x 41½″.   CANVAS: 10 mono.   STITCH: Tent.
YARN: Paternayan wool.
Designed and worked by S. Lantz.

PLATE 10. (*facing page 207*)

Hungarian Point wall hanging.

SIZE: 51″ x 31½″.   CANVAS: 12 mono.   STITCH: Hungarian Point.
YARN: Paternayan wool.
Designed and worked by S. Lantz.

Hungarian Point pillow. Both linear pattern and tonal structure are taken from the celebrated Hungarian Point bed hangings at Parham Park, England. I found the technique, colors and yarns displayed in these 18th-century needle-worked panels exceptionally beautiful. My pillow was worked as a preliminary to a large wall hanging.

CANVAS: 12 mono.   STITCH: Hungarian Point.

YARN: Appleton tapestry wool (light, medium, dark shades), French silk (white and pastel shades).

Designed and worked by S. Lantz.

PLATE 11. *(facing page 270)*

Playing Card hanging (in work). A study of an early woodcut (Collection Fontenay) and an example of how diverse patterns may be used legitimately to enrich design. The hundreds of stitches and patterns (all from my samplers) are meant to be prominent so I selected neutral tones of whites, parchments, copper and bronze—thus avoiding a jarring warfare between color and texture. The dark brown outlines presented a difficulty because I wished them to retain their primary, woodcut power. Enlarging the figures made it necessary to double and triple these lines to reinforce their visual strength. Controlling the thickened outlines, around the curves or irregular contours, can be problematical in canvas work, especially when the contour line is not meant to fade into neighboring colors. The cards, though discovered recently, were printed between 1499 and 1515 and appear to represent an actual pageant—perhaps in connection with the wedding of King Louis XII and Anne de Bretagne. Their heraldic insignia are to be seen on the garments and shields. I have supplied each card with its own geometric pavement and background, and its own exploratory stitch theme. The field on which they lie will be worked in yarn matching the canvas, and will use the canvas thread as part of the design, an arrangement visible in the background and patterns of the center card, the *Valet de Trèfle*, (the Knave of Clubs).

SIZE: 100″ x 30″ (projected).   CANVAS: 14 mono.

STITCHES: Very varied.

YARN: Médicis wool (wall backgrounds), French silk and metallic yarns.

Designed and worked by S. Lantz.

PLATE 12. *(facing page 271)*

Enlargements of two sections of the *Playing Card* hanging.

Mrs. Lane's large Oriental hangings present a restrained and elegant use of textures. The stitches she selected make an important though subtle contribution to her works. In these she never allows the stitch patterns to intrude on her

500

compositions—rather she has used them to enhance the various elements within her designs.

PLATE 13. *(facing page 334)*
Ladies Playing Double Sixes from an 8th-century Chinese painting attributed to Chou Fang. Freer Gallery, Washington, D. C.
SIZE: 30″ x 30″.   CANVAS: 14 mono.   STITCHES: Basketweave and Brick.
YARN: Silk.
Designed and worked by Maggie Lane.

Swan and Cygnets from an early 20th-century porcelain plate designed by William de Morgan.
SIZE: 28″ x 28″.   CANVAS: 14 mono.   STITCHES: Various.
YARN: Nantucket needlework wool.
Designed and worked by Maggie Lane.

PLATE 14. *(facing page 335)*
Snow at Dusk from a 19th-century Chinese painting.
SIZE: 20″ x 64″.   CANVAS: 14 mono.
STITCHES: Basketweave, Brick, and Satin.
YARN: Silk.
Designed and worked by Maggie Lane.

PLATE 15. *(facing page 398)*
A Warrior's Farewell from a 19th-century Japanese snuff bottle carved of ivory and inlaid with *tête de nègre* lacquer (in work).
SIZE: 108″ x 31″.   CANVAS: 14 mono.   STITCHES: Various.
YARN: Pattern worked in silk, background in Médicis wool.
Designed and worked by Maggie Lane.

PLATE 16. *(facing page 399)*
The Scholar's Table from an 18th-century Korean painting by an unknown artist. Fogg Museum, Harvard, Cambridge, Mass.
SIZE: 62½″ x 21″.   CANVAS: 14 mono.   STITCHES: Various.
YARN: DMC cotton.
Designed and worked by Maggie Lane.

A Flower Basket from a Sung Dynasty album-leaf painting by Li Sung.
SIZE: 63″ x 23″.   CANVAS: 14 mono.
STITCHES: Basketweave, Brick, and Satin.
YARN: Silk.
Designed and worked by Maggie Lane.

BIBLIOGRAPHY

It was impossible to list the many volumes I have looked at over the years pertaining to mosaics, architecture, painting, illuminated manuscripts and geometric ornaments. They have contributed immeasurably to this book and I can only refer you to your libraries where they may be found in their respective categories. The Embroiderers' Guild in New York has a broad selection of additional needlecraft books for members and, I dare say, your local chapters will be useful too. The titles below all deal with varying aspects of needlework and are the ones I found most useful.

SAMPLERS

These books are particularly rich in motif design. After you have understood the formation of some of the stitches in this book, you may extract patterns from them with ease. You may have to use a magnifying glass for analysis but you will find the search entertaining.

Ashton, Leigh. *Samplers, Selected and Described*. London: The Medici Society, 1926.

Colby, Averil. *Samplers, Today and Yesterday*. London: B. T. Batsford, 1964.

Huish, Marcus Bourne. *Samplers and Tapestry Embroideries*. London: Fine Arts Society, 1900.

King, Donald. *Samplers*, in Victoria and Albert Museum, South Kensington, *Large Picture Books No. 14*. London: His Majesty's Stationery Office, 1960.

Philadelphia Museum of Art. *Samplers*. Philadelphia, 1972.

PRACTICAL

Casini. *Antico Lavoro Fiorentino*. Florence: Ortolani and Comp, 1925.

Christie, Grace [Mrs. Archibald Christie]. *Samplers and Stitches: A Handbook of the Embroiderer's Art*. 4th rev. ed. London: B. T. Batsford, Ltd., 1948.

Dillmont, Thérèse de. *Encyclopedia of Needlework*. Rev. ed. France: Mulhouse, 1890.

Enthoven, Jacqueline. *The Stitches of Creative Embroidery*. New York: Van Nostrand Reinhold Co., 1964.

Fangel, Esther. *Haandarbejdets Femmes Haandbøger*. Vols. I and II. København: I Kommision hos Høst, 1956.

Gibbon, M. A. *Canvas Work, A Practical Guide*. London: G. Bell and Sons, 1968.

Jacobsen, Astrid og Fangel, Esther. *Haandarbejder*. København: Med Billeder og Vejledning, Forlagskompagniet.

Karasz, Mariska. *Adventures in Stitches, A New Art of Embroidery*. New York: Funk and Wagnalls Co., 1949.

Snook, Barbara. *Florentine Embroidery*. New York: Charles Scribner's Sons, 1967.

Snook, Barbara. *Needlework Stitches*. New York: Crown Publishers, Inc., 1963.

Springall, Diana. *Canvas Embroidery*. Newton Center, Mass.: Chas. T. Branford Company, 1969.

Thomas, Mary (Hedger). *Mary Thomas's Dictionary of Embroidery Stitches*. London: Hodder and Stoughton, Ltd., 1935.

HISTORICAL

Alford, Marianne Margaret (Compton). *Needlework As Art*. London: S. Low, Marston, Searle, and Rivington, 1886.

Bolton, Ethel (Stanwood) and Eva Johnston Coe. *American Samplers*. Boston: The Massachusetts Society of the Colonial Dames of America, 1921.

Caulfield, S. F. A. *The Dictionary of Needlework*. 2 vols. 2d ed. London, 1887.

Crompton, Rebecca. *Modern Design in Embroidery*. Edited by Davide C. Minter. London: B. T. Batsford, Ltd., 1936.

Dreger, Moriz. *Künstlerische Entwicklung der Weberei und Stickerei*. Vienna: Museum für Kunst und Industrie, 1904.

Farcy, Louis de. *La Broderie du XIe siècle jusqu'à nos jours d'après des spécimens authentiques et les anciens inventaires*. Paris: E. Leroux, 1890.

Grönwoldt, Ruth. "Webereien und Stickereien des Mittelalters," in Hanover-Kestner-Museum Textilien, *Bildkataloge* 7. Hanover, Germany: Hanover-Kestner-Museum, 1964.

Harbeson, Georgiana (Brown). *American Needlework: The History of Decorative Stitchery and Embroidery from the Late 16th to the 20th Century*. New York: Coward-McCann, Inc., 1938.

BIBLIOGRAPHY

Holme, Geoffrey (Ed.). *A Book of Old Embroidery*. London: The Studio, Ltd., 1921.

Pulszky, Carl V. and Friedrich Fischbach. *Ornamente der Hausindustrie Ungarn's*. Budapest: Magyar Nemzeti Museum, 1878.

Remington, Preston. *English Domestic Needlework of the XVI, XVII, and XVIII Centuries*. New York: Metropolitan Museum of Art, 1945.

Schuette, Marie and Sigrid Müller-Christensen. *A Pictorial History of Embroidery*. New York: Praeger Publishers, Inc., 1963.

Sibmacher, Johann. *Schön Neues Modelbuch*. Nürnberg, Germany, 1604, Facsimile (partial), Wasmuthe, Berlin, 1884.

Sima, Josef. *Studien über nationale Stickereien aus Böhmen, Mähren in der Ungarischen Slovakei*. Brünn, 1909.

Symonds. *Needlework Through the Ages*. London, 1928.

Thesiger, Ernest Frederic Graham. *Adventures in Embroidery*. Edited by C. G. Holme. New York: The Studio, 1942.

Untermyer, Irwin. *English and Other Needlework, Tapestries and Textiles*. Cambridge: Harvard University Press, 1960.

Varjú-Ember, Maria. *Alte Ungarische Stickerei*. Budapest: Corvina Verlag, 1963.

Victoria and Albert Museum, South Kensington. *Elizabethan Embroidery*. London: Ministry of Education, 1948.

Victoria and Albert Museum, South Kensington. *Guide to the English Embroidery*. London: Her Majesty's Stationery Office, 1970.

INDEX

Many stitches appear more than once, in various designs and patterns. The pages listed below are meant as a referral to those diagrams and sampler squares best suited for learning the structures.

INDEX

507